1495/21M

SELECTED ESSAYS
ON EMPLOYMENT AND
GROWTH

SELECTED ESSAYS ON EMPLOYMENT AND GROWTH

RICHARD KAHN

Professor of Economics in the University of Cambridge,
Fellow of King's College

CAMBRIDGE

At the University Press

1972

Published by the Syndics of the Cambridge University Press
Bentley House, 200 Euston Road, London NW1 2DB
American Branch: 32 East 57th Street, New York, N.Y. 10022

© Cambridge University Press 1972

Library of Congress Catalogue Card Number: 78–187079

ISBN: 0 521 084938

Printed in Great Britain
at the University Printing House, Cambridge
(Brooke Crutchley, University Printer)

CONTENTS

PREFACE

The essays in this collection are a selection from my writings of the past forty years on the subjects of employment and growth. Some of the papers selected may be of interest in connection with contemporary debates on economic principles and problems and some, perhaps, may be of interest to students of the evolution of modern economics. Except for the final essay, the essays are reprinted in their original form. Thus considerable changes in viewpoint over time are evident.

Three papers in this collection deserve brief notes as to their origins. The first essay, which is often cited but apparently little read, was originally conceived in the late summer of 1930. As joint secretary, I circulated a very early version to the members of the Committee of Economists of the Economic Advisory Council in September 1930. This version was revised and considerably expanded as a result of discussions with Colin Clark of the Economic Advisory Council, who provided the necessary statistical material, and with James Meade and others in Cambridge, where I read it to Keynes' Political Economy Club in the autumn of 1930. The ninth essay appeared in a preliminary form in *Économie Appliquée* in 1958 before being revised into its present form for publication in English. The final essay has led an active life in draft since 1964 and has entered the literature in several places. I print it here for the first time in a slightly amended version prepared in the spring of 1971, but I have not attempted to bring it down from the stratosphere.

I should like to express my warm thanks to John Eatwell and Donald Moggridge for taking the selection of these essays in hand, preparing the manuscript and seeing it through the press, and to Susan Howson for preparing the index.

King's College,   RICHARD KAHN
Cambridge
July 1971

1

THE RELATION OF HOME INVESTMENT
TO UNEMPLOYMENT*

I

The case for 'public works' has often been discussed, and there is a final plea that the advocate almost invariably appends to his argument. It is important, we are told, not to overlook the beneficial repercussions that will result from the expenditure of the newly-employed men's wages. But little is done to evaluate these repercussions in concrete terms. The main purpose, though not the only purpose, of this article is to outline the means by which this gap could be filled, and incidentally to suggest that the case for 'public works' may be stronger than is always recognised.

The argument will apply to the effects of any net increase in the rate of home investment. The increased employment that is required in connection actually with the increased investment will be described as the 'primary' employment. It includes the 'direct' employment, and also, of course, the 'indirect' employment that is set up in the production and transport of the raw materials required for making the new investment. To meet the increased expenditure of wages and profits that is associated with the primary employment, the production of consumption-goods is increased. Here again wages and profits are increased, and the effect will be passed on, though with diminished intensity. And so on *ad infinitum*. The total employment that is set up in this way in the production of consumption-goods will be termed the 'secondary' employment. The ratio of secondary to primary employment is a measure of these 'beneficial repercussions' that are so often referred to.

It will simplify the process of exposition if *expenditure by the Government on roads* is taken as a convenient instance of an increase in home investment. But this simplification must not be taken to imply either that there is anything in the argument that confines its

* *Economic Journal*, June 1931.

application to investment taking place directly under the auspices of the Government, or that the building of more *roads* is a particularly desirable form of investment.

II

It is necessary, in the first place, to clear out of the way the objection that any reduction of unemployment that is effected by Government action will be at the expense of an equal increase of unemployment in some other quarter. If the Government were to raise the funds required to pay for the roads by means of taxation, it is obvious that unfavourable reactions would be probable. Of these the most important would be the 'secondary unemployment' that would result if increased taxation were to reduce the taxpayers' expenditure on consumption-goods. The amount of this 'secondary unemployment' would depend on the extent to which increased taxes are paid at the expense of consumption rather than of saving. But that is a matter for separate study; and throughout this article it will be supposed that the necessary funds are raised by means of borrowing.

It is sometimes claimed that if the Government borrows money for the purpose of building roads, this necessitates an equal reduction in the funds available for investment from other sources.[1] But it is clear that even if this claim has any force at all, it cannot have a universal application. For it is always within the power of the banking system to advance to the Government the cost of the roads without in any way affecting the flow of investment along the normal channels. If it assists the processes of thought, it may be imagined that the Government obtains its funds in this kind of way. But it will become clear in the sequel that no such hypothesis is really necessary. For it will be demonstrated later on[2] that, *pari passu* with the building of roads,

[1] How important is the influence that has been exerted upon British policy by this claim is forcibly demonstrated by the following information supplied in 1927 by the British Government to the International Labour Office: 'While it is not possible to give any specific indications that competition arose with other enterprises owing to the raising by the State of moneys for the various State-assisted employment projects, the decision taken by the Government at the end of 1925 to restrict grants for relief schemes was based mainly on the view that, the supply of capital in the country being limited, it was undesirable to divert any appreciable proportion of this supply from normal trade channels.' (*Unemployment and Public Works*, The International Labour Office, 1931, p. 30.)

[2] See p. 18

funds are released from various sources at precisely the rate that is required to pay the cost of the roads.

It is, however, important to realise that the intelligent co-operation of the banking system is being taken for granted. It is supposed that the object of the central bank is to achieve the maximum of employment that is consistent with remaining on the gold standard. If the increased circulation of notes and the increased demand for working capital that may result from increased employment are made the occasion for a restriction of credit, then any attempt to increase employment – whether it is by way of road-building or by any other means, or, indeed, by awaiting the return of world prosperity – may be rendered nugatory.

III

It will be assumed throughout the greater part of this article that money-wages are not raised as a consequence of the reduction in unemployment or of any rise in prices with which the reduction in unemployment may be associated. Even if this assumption is not entirely reasonable, it is clear that it is essential if the analysis is to proceed at all. (But it *is* suggested, though with some hesitation, that over a limited, and not so very limited, range the assumption is not appreciably wide of reality.) To take into account the effects of a possible rise in wages would necessitate, not only an estimate of the amount of the rise, but, far more serious, an analysis of the effect of a rise in wages on the level of employment; and such an investigation must be ruled outside the scope of this article.

An attempt will, however, be made[1] to demonstrate that there is *some* increase in employment, even though real-wages are maintained at their former level – or, in other words, if money-wages are raised so as to compensate for the rise in prices. But to the extent, on the other hand, that it is to the reduction in unemployment rather than to the rise in prices that wages respond, there is clearly no method whatever of increasing the volume of employment.

IV

Finally, no account will be taken, in assessing the effects on employment, of any increase in productive efficiency that may result from the

---

[1] In a subsequent number of the *Economic Journal*. [No note or article on this subject was written.]

Government's expenditure. That, perhaps, is why roads are a good illustration to adopt as an object of such expenditure.

For this reason, too, the argument of this article could, with suitable modifications, be applied to a discussion of the desirability of reducing the Sinking Fund or of the undesirability of reducing the dole.

V

Considerable use will be made in these pages of the expression 'saving on the dole'. It must be clearly understood that these words are not intended to imply any moral judgment on the system of unemployment insurance. The word 'dole' is used, purely as a matter of convenience, to cover the whole of the expenditure of an unemployed man on consumption, whether it is derived from the Unemployment Insurance Fund, from local authorities, from charity, from borrowing, from his friends and relations or from his own accumulated savings.

For the purpose of developing the argument it will be assumed that when a man obtains work, the 'saving on the dole' that results does not have the effect of increasing the consumption of other members of the community. Above all, this assumption presupposes that any change that occurs in the expenditure of the Unemployment Insurance Fund falls entirely on the rate at which the fund is increasing or diminishing its debt and on the amount of the budgetary Sinking Fund. Manifestly this assumption is a somewhat unreal one. Even if contributions to the Fund are not affected, a reduction in the cost of transitional benefit will almost certainly lead to some reduction of national taxation, and a reduction of the rate at which the Fund is getting into debt will lead to some scaling down of the Chancellor of the Exchequer's standards of respectability in regard to Sinking Funds – and so again to a reduction of taxation.

But, in relation to the amount of the saving on the dole, any reduction of taxation that occurs is likely to be small – this will be obvious if consideration is paid to the present level of the real Sinking Fund – and the consequent increase in expenditure on consumption will be still smaller. In so far, however, as it occurs, it adds an *a fortiori* force to the argument of the following pages. The secondary employment is increased if road-building results in less taxation and consequently in greater expenditure by taxpayers on consumption-goods.[1]

---

[1] If this increase in expenditure were exactly equal to the saving on the dole, and if it were divided between home- and foreign-produced goods in the

VI

I turn now to the often debated question of the effect of Government investment on the general level of prices. This question has been debated from various points of view. It has been debated with an eye on the expansion of bank credit that may accompany the building of roads. Somewhat more adapted, perhaps, to the end in view have been the discussions that have centred on the various alleviations that partially set off the increase in purchasing power caused by increased investment. Of these the most important are the saving on the dole and the increased imports of consumption-goods and of raw materials that take place when employment is increased.

But it is, I think, quite clear that a very important, though nevertheless extremely obvious, consideration is usually omitted in these discussions. It is, perhaps, its very obviousness that accounts for its being so persistently overlooked. For the line of approach that will now be taken up is the one that would be followed under the impulse of crude common-sense – there is no room here for analytical subtleties. No claims of originality are advanced for adopting it, but that does not mean that it is not very important.

The price-level and output of home-produced consumption-goods, just like the price and output of any single commodity, are determined by the conditions of supply and demand. If the conditions of supply can be regarded as fixed, both the price-level and the output are determined by the demand; and there is a unique correlation between price-level and output. For a given output of consumption-goods there corresponds a certain price-level of consumption-goods; and this is their price-level quite independently of the causes that are responsible for maintaining the given output. If there is a certain increase in employment on the production of consumption-goods, the change in their price-level is the same whether the increased employment is fostered by large advances from the central bank to the Government or whether it is the symptom of the return of prosperity

same proportions as the dole is divided, then the same consequences would ensue as would ensue on my assumption – that there is no such increase in expenditure – if the dole were zero, i.e. if the unemployed lived on air. If a greater amount were spent on home-produced goods than would have been spent on home-produced goods if the money had been spent by the unemployed, then the results can be gauged by supposing, on the basis of my assumption, that the dole is negative.

5

by a more natural route. If this is to be true, it is only necessary that the change shall be actuated by a change in the conditions of demand and not by a change in the conditions of supply. Then the volume of employment engaged in producing consumption-goods and the price-level of home-produced consumption-goods are uniquely correlated. For a given increase in the output of consumption-goods the change in their price-level depends only on the supply curve of consumption-goods in general, the curve being drawn from the point of view of the particular period of time that is under consideration – long, short, or otherwise. If the supply curve rises steeply, there is a large rise in prices; if conditions of constant supply price prevail, there is no rise in prices; and if the supply curve were falling, there would be a fall in prices.

VII

The relief of unemployment by means of national development is often objected to on the grounds that it will cause a rise in the cost of living. The extraordinary fatuity of this objection is, of course, quite apparent. There is nothing unnatural about the rise in prices caused by the building of roads. It will occur equally if employment in the production of consumption-goods is stimulated to an equal extent by more natural means (other than a reduction of costs). Indeed, if it is an improvement in world economic conditions that is the cause of increased employment, the cost of living will rise by considerably *more* than if the cause is the building of roads. And this for two reasons. In the first place, not only the whole of the secondary employment but also part of the primary employment will in this case be engaged in producing consumption-goods. For part of the primary employment will be engaged in the production of commodities that are to be exported or that were previously imported, and some of these commodities will be identical with commodities that enter into consumption at home. It follows that, for a given volume of primary and secondary employment, the output of home-produced consumption-goods is greater, and therefore the cost of living is higher, if the cause of the change is an improvement in the conditions of world demand than if it is the building of such things as roads, whose production can be carried on without appreciably affecting the condition of supply of consumption-goods. But it is the second reason that is likely to be more important quantitatively. An increase in

6

employment that is part of a general revival in world trade will be accompanied by a rise in the prices of imported consumption-goods (including the supremely important category of food) and of imported raw materials, while the rise in prices that is caused by a purely local policy of road-building will be almost entirely confined to that part of the national consumption that is produced at home. The effect on the cost of living is, therefore, far more serious in the former case than in the latter case.

Even more fantastic is it to argue at the same time that road-building causes a rise in prices and yet that it is not responsible for any *net* addition to the volume of employment. The rise in prices, if it occurs at all, is a natural concomitant of increased output, to a degree indicated by the slope of the supply curve. It is impossible to maintain at the same time that prices will rise and that there will be no increase in output. If the result, owing to the operation of some mysterious cause, of the construction of roads by the Government is an equal reduction of investment in other channels, there is no secondary employment and no rise in prices. But if it is a fall in the output of *consumption*-goods that compensates for the employment provided on the roads (as might *conceivably* be the case if the Government raises the necessary funds by taxation rather than by borrowing), then the effect of road-building is to cause a *fall* in prices (on the assumption that production takes place under conditions of increasing supply price).

VIII

It should now be clear why it is hopeless to discuss the possibility of a rise in prices in terms merely of the saving on the dole and the increase in imports that result from increased employment. These indeed are two factors, as we shall see later, that determine the amount of the secondary employment. But before it is possible to deduce the magnitude of the change in prices, it is necessary to introduce the slope of the supply curve. Nor is it as simple as that. For the amount of secondary employment itself depends, as will be shown later, on the extent of the rise in prices by which it is accompanied. The two are uniquely correlated, but the amount of secondary employment is effect as well as cause. The amount of secondary employment must be such that, together with the primary employment, it gives rise to just so much alleviation to the original investment (in the

7

shape of saving on the dole, increased imports, and so on) as will account for the rise in prices that is appropriate to that amount of secondary employment. If the supply of commodities in general is perfectly elastic, there can be no rise in prices and the secondary employment must be such as to make it so. If the supply of commodities is perfectly inelastic, there can be no secondary employment and the rise in prices must be so great that the net secondary employment is zero.

In general it can be said that, for a given supply curve, the secondary employment is smaller the greater are the saving on the dole, the increase in imports, and the other alleviations that accompany a unit increase in employment. It follows that it is perfectly true to state that the greater the extent of these alleviations, the smaller is the rise in prices that results from a given amount of road-building. But from such a view-point the problem is liable to assume a peculiarly distorted aspect. It is not merely that there would be a failure to recognise the predominant importance of the supply curve – the fact, for instance, that if supply is perfectly elastic, there *can* be no rise in prices. It might also appear that the claims of road-building as a national policy are stronger if the alleviations (saving on the dole, increase in imports, etc.) are great than if the alleviations are small, because it is when the alleviations are great that the rise in prices is small. But in fact it may just be if the alleviations are great that road-building is least justifiable, for it is then that the *secondary employment* is small – and the 'beneficial repercussions' are weak. It is possible to imagine a case – it is very far removed from reality – where unemployed men who are set to work on making roads devote the whole of the net increase in their incomes to goods that have to be imported. There would then be no rise in prices – the alleviations are equivalent to the whole of the original investment. But road-making would be a far weaker economic proposition than it is in fact, for there would be no secondary employment.

IX

Perhaps it is not altogether inappropriate to pause at this point to consider the appearance of our line of approach in the light of Mr Keynes' new equations. The building of roads represents an increase in investment. But before it is possible to assess the net effect on the difference between savings and investment, it is necessary to bring

8

into the account those alleviations which have already been several times referred to. Payment of the dole represents negative saving, and the saving on the dole represents, therefore, an addition to total savings. An increase of imports, whether of consumption-goods or of raw materials, represents a diminution of the foreign balance and therefore of total investment. If entrepreneurs continue to spend the same amount of money on consumption-goods as before although output has increased, their savings, in Mr Keynes' sense, have increased. On the other hand, to the extent that non-wage-earners (and wage-earners who were previously in employment) increase their expenditure on consumption-goods irrespective of any increase in total output – whether as a result of the fact that they have more to spend, because of increased profits, or of the fact that prices of consumption-goods have gone up – savings diminish: this is an *aggravation*. The new value of the difference between savings and investment, appropriate to Mr Keynes' equations, can only be deduced by subtracting the alleviations corresponding to the total new employment from the cost of the roads, and adding the aggravation.

If the supply of consumption-goods is perfectly inelastic, there is no secondary employment and the problem is considerably simplified. It is only necessary now to consider the alleviations associated with a *known* volume of primary employment – and to subtract the aggravation. Prices rise by an amount corresponding to the difference between the cost of the roads and the amount of these alleviations. If the aggravation can be neglected, the rise in the price-level of home-produced consumption-goods is equal to the increase in expenditure directed towards them by the road-makers divided by their volume. This is the case when all productive resources available for the production of consumption-goods are already being utilised and, over a certain range of output and over a sufficiently short period of time, it is not possible to increase their output appreciably and there is no incentive for an appreciable reduction of output.

But simplest of all is the case where it is not the supply of consumption-goods that is completely inelastic but *total* employment that is fixed, so that if investment increases, the production of consumption-goods must diminish by an equal amount. Then there is no alleviation, since there is no change in employment, and if in addition the aggravation is negligible, the rise in the price-level of consumption-goods is simply equal to the cost of the new investment divided by their volume. This is the case to which Mr Keynes' equations apply in their full simplicity. It occurs when the whole of the factors of production are employed, and continue to be employed, in producing either for consumption or for investment.

At the other end of the scale is the case, very much closer to the actual conditions that prevail today, where the supply of consumption-goods is perfectly elastic. The price-level of consumption-goods is then constant, and, however great may be the cost of the investment that is taking place in road-building, the secondary employment will be such that the total alleviation (*minus* the aggravation) keeps the difference between total savings and total investment at a constant amount (or, more accurately, at an amount that varies in direct proportion with the output of consumption-goods).

But this conclusion – that under certain circumstances employment can be increased without any significant alteration in the difference between savings and investment – does not in the slightest degree invalidate the causal force of Mr Keynes' argument. The motive force that increases employment is an increase in investment or a reduction in savings. As a concomitant of this increase in employment occur other changes in savings and investment which, partially or wholly, neutralise the effect on the difference between savings and investment of the change that is the cause of the increased employment.

X

It should now be clear that the whole question ultimately turns on the nature of the supply curve of consumption-goods. At normal times, when productive resources are fully employed, the supply of consumption-goods in the short period is highly inelastic. The building of roads carries with it little secondary employment and causes a large rise in prices. But at times of intense depression, when nearly all industries have at their disposal a large surplus of unused plant and labour, the supply curve is likely to be very elastic. The amount of secondary employment is then large and the rise in prices is small.

If there is in existence a large stock of surplus resources that are not very inferior to the worst of those that are actually being employed,[1] the elasticity of supply is likely to be very large indeed up to the

---

[1] As is, *par excellence*, the case when the 'short-time' method of working plant is in operation over a wide field.

level of output at which this surplus would be becoming inappreciable. Provided that output is not carried above this level, an expansion of employment bears with it only a very small rise of prices. The greater the depth of the depression, the greater is the expansion of employment that is associated with a given rise in prices. And the greater the expansion of employment that has already been secured by a policy of road-building, the greater is the rise in prices that accompanies a given further expansion of employment; for the short-period supply curve is concave upwards. It is clear, then, that if there is ever any justification for expenditure on 'public works' as a means of reducing unemployment, the justification is greatest when depression is most severe; and the scale on which it is desirable that such a policy should be carried on is also then most extensive.

XI

I turn now to a calculation of the ratio of secondary to primary employment, and I begin by assuming that the supply of consumption-goods is perfectly elastic over the range that is in question. (The adoption at this point of such a sweeping assumption is to be regarded purely as a means of simplifying the treatment – it would be quite possible, on lines that will be indicated later, to begin with a perfectly general case.) An attempt will be made below[1] to assess the extent to which the results require modification in the light of the conditions that prevail in this country at the moment, and it will be suggested that the modification is not very large.

Let each man who is placed in employment receive a wage W, and let the increase in profits that is associated with the employment of each additional man be P. Let the value of the increase in imports of raw materials and unfinished goods that accompanies the employment of each additional man be R. For the sake of simplicity it will be assumed that W and P are the same for both primary and secondary employment.

Let the employment of each additional man involve a *net increase* in the rate of expenditure on home-produced consumption-goods of mW out of his wages and of nP out of the addition to profits with which his employment is associated. Then the total increase in the rate of expenditure on home-produced consumption-goods is

$$mW + nP.$$

[1] See p. 15.

The direct result is a further addition to the volume of employment[1] of amount

$$\frac{mW+nP}{W+P+R} \text{ men}$$

$$= m\frac{W}{W+P+R}+n\frac{P}{W+P+R} = k \text{ (say) men.} \tag{1}$$

It follows that for each man placed in primary employment, the number who receive secondary employment is

$$k+k^2+k^3+\ldots$$

$$= \frac{k}{1-k}.$$

And the ratio of secondary employment to primary employment is

$$\frac{k}{1-k}. \tag{2}$$

Let the expenditure of an unemployed man (the 'dole') be U, and let a proportion m' of the increase that takes place in his income when he becomes employed be devoted to home-produced consumption-goods. Then

$$m'(W-U) = mW;$$

or $$m = m'\left(1-\frac{U}{W}\right). \tag{3}$$

It can be seen that, for every man put to work on the roads, the volume of secondary employment is great to the extent that the dole forms only a small proportion of a full wage, to the extent that a man who becomes employed devotes a large proportion of the increase in his income to home-produced goods, to the extent that a large proportion of any addition to profits that accompanies increased output is spent on home-produced consumption-goods, and to the extent that increased production necessitates the import of only a small proportion of raw materials. The more a country approximates to a closed system

---

[1] I am here considering the position in the final position of equilibrium when everything has settled down. But some time will, of course, elapse between the point when the primary employment begins and the point when the secondary employment reaches its full dimensions, because wages and profits are not spent quite as soon as they are earned. I do not enter into the question of this time-lag.

and the smaller the dole in relation to a full wage, the greater is the ratio of secondary to primary employment. Now the United States constitute a better approximation to a closed system than do most countries and the ratio of the income of an unemployed American to that of an employed American is notoriously small. It may be expected, therefore, that the ratio of secondary to primary employment is a good deal larger in the United States that in most other countries.[1] A perfectly closed system, to go one step further, is the world as a whole. It follows, as is indeed quite obvious, that an international policy of 'public works' would be far more efficacious from the point of view of each separate country than a purely local policy. Finally, as a limiting case, it may be instructive to contemplate a closed system in which there is no dole,[2] and in which any increase in profits that accompanies an increase of output is either negligible in amount or devoted entirely to consumption. One man put to work on the roads would then place all the remainder of the unemployed into secondary employment.[3]

It is a matter of considerable difficulty to make exact, or even at all approximate, estimates of the various quantities contained in the above equations. But it is hoped that, until more precise investigation can be undertaken, the following figures[4] will help to convey some idea of the orders of magnitude that are concerned for the case of this country at the present time.

I shall assume in the first place that the cost of imported raw materials and unfinished goods entering into the *addition* to output that is associated with increased employment constitutes $\frac{1}{10}$ of the *retail* price of the extra product. In other words, $R/(W+P+R)$ is

---

[1] The argument can, of course, be reversed to deal with the secondary unemployment that accompanies primary unemployment due to a *decrease* in the rate of investment. A slump in the rate of investment spread evenly all over the world would fall more heavily in those regions, like the United States, where the dole is relatively low than in those regions, like this country, where the dole is relatively high.

[2] Or in which any saving on the dole results in an equal increase of expenditure on consumption on the part of taxpayers, etc. (see p. 4).

[3] For a general statement of this possibility, to cover the case when supply is not perfectly elastic, see p. 18 below.

[4] They are based, for the most part, on statistical material that has been placed at my disposal by Mr Colin G. Clark, to whom I should like to express my great gratitude. But the responsibility for the statistical conclusions that I have attempted to derive from this material rests entirely with me.

supposed to be $\frac{1}{10}$. I shall then assume that $W/(W+P+R)$ (the ratio of marginal wages cost to the price of the product) is $\frac{7}{10}$ and that $P(W+P+R)$ is $\frac{1}{5}$.

It also seems reasonable to suppose that when a man becomes employed, $\frac{1}{6}$ of the *increase* in his income is devoted to imported *finished* goods (excluding the costs of transport and distribution, payment for which is to be regarded as expenditure on *home-produce* goods). In other words, I put m' equal to $\frac{5}{6}$.

The estimate of the ratio of the 'dole' to a full wage involves some consideration of the type of man who will be drawn into employment by a policy of the kind that is under consideration. It seems probable that a moderate addition to the ranks of the employed would be recruited mainly from the younger of the unemployed, whose families are of less than the average size. It may perhaps be concluded that U/W is rather *less* than $\frac{1}{2}$.

There remains only the quantity n, but here assessment is largely a matter of guess-work. The best that I can do is to suggest that it would be extremely unreasonable to suppose that as small a proportion as $\frac{1}{3}$ of any increase that took place in the rate of business men's earnings would be devoted to home-produced consumption-goods.[1]

The following table is intended to indicate how the value of the ratio of secondary to primary employment, given in the last column, depends on the values that are adopted for U/W and n.

$$\frac{W}{W+P+R} = \frac{7}{10}, \quad \frac{P}{W+P+R} = \frac{1}{5}, \quad m' = \frac{5}{6}.$$

$\dfrac{U}{W}$	n	$m = m'\left(1 - \dfrac{U}{W}\right)$	k (by equation (1))	$\dfrac{k}{1-k}$
$\frac{3}{7}$	$\frac{3}{4}$	$\frac{10}{21}$	$\frac{29}{60}$	$\frac{29}{31} = 0.94$
$\frac{3}{7}$	$\frac{2}{3}$	$\frac{10}{21}$	$\frac{7}{15}$	$\frac{7}{8} = 0.88$
$\frac{1}{2}$	$\frac{1}{2}$	$\frac{5}{12}$	$\frac{47}{120}$	$\frac{47}{73} = 0.64$
$\frac{1}{2}$	$\frac{1}{3}$	$\frac{5}{12}$	$\frac{43}{120}$	$\frac{43}{77} = 0.56$

The first row of figures is possibly on the liberal side, as supplying an estimate of the ratio of secondary to primary employment, but it

[1] The part played by the earnings of small shopkeepers, poor shareholders, etc. is not to be overlooked.

seems very much more certain that the last row is on the conservative side. If we were to suppose that in actual fact the ratio is ¾, we might, it may perhaps be suggested, be erring in the direction of under-statement.

XII

The next step is to make an allowance for the fact that supply is not perfectly elastic. Under the conditions that prevail at the moment it seems reasonable to suppose that the short-period elasticity of supply is not less than 4, i.e. that a 4 per cent increase in the domestic output of consumption-goods would be accompanied by a rise in prices to the *ultimate consumer* of less than 1 per cent. It is now necessary to make an estimate of the elasticity of demand for these goods. If people's expenditure on consumption-goods does not alter when their price-level is raised, the elasticity of demand for them is unity. But actually it seems probable that people would spend rather more on consumption, and save less, if prices were to rise. To the extent that they would do so, the elasticity of demand is less than unity. On the other hand, many classes of consumption-goods meet with foreign competition, either abroad, in the case of exports, or in the domestic market itself, and for them the demand may easily be elastic rather than inelastic.[1] Setting one consideration against the other and assessing each so far as it is possible to do so, I suggest that the demand for home-produced consumption-goods is likely to be in-elastic rather than elastic, provided that small changes are under consideration. Let us suppose that the elasticity is unity. A 1 per cent rise in prices would then, taken by itself, be responsible for a 1 per cent contraction of consumption, and consequently of output. But we are supposing that a 1 per cent rise in prices would be accompanied by an increase in output of at least 4 per cent. It would appear then that when the output of consumption-goods expands by 4 per cent, the extra expansion that *would* have taken place if there had been no rise in prices would have been less than 1 per cent – and the total expansion would then have been less than 5 per cent. It may be concluded, on the basis of the assumptions that have been made, that the fact that

---

[1] But the tendency of foreign competition to increase the aggregate elasticity of demand for our goods is offset to some small extent by the rise that takes place in the foreigners' demand curve as a result of the expansion in our imports.

15

supply is not perfectly elastic necessitates a reduction of the estimate of secondary employment of the last section by less than $\frac{1}{5}$. Such a small alteration is, of course, negligible.

But even this conclusion is unduly conservative.[1] It completely overlooks the fact that a rise in prices is the cause of an increase in profits and that part of these increased profits is likely to be spent on home-produced consumption-goods. It can easily be seen that if the whole of the increase in profits that is the direct result of higher prices were spent on home-produced consumption-goods, then, on the basis of an elasticity of demand of unity, output would be precisely the same as though there were no rise in prices at all. And if the demand for consumption-goods has an elasticity less than unity, then the same assumption leads to the conclusion that the rise in prices actually causes the output to be greater than it would be if there were no rise in prices. The less elastic the supply, the *greater* would be the secondary employment! This last result is mentioned here mainly as a *curiosum* – it is unlikely in practice that a sufficient proportion of the increase in profits that results from a higher level of prices would be devoted to home-produced consumption-goods – but the theoretical possibility of its occurring is worth emphasising.

XIII

Let us return for a moment to the case, worked out in section XI, in which supply is supposed to be perfectly elastic. If N men are placed in primary employment, the total increase in employment is, by equation (2),

$$N\left(1+\frac{k}{1-k}\right) = \frac{N}{1-k}.$$

For each man placed in employment the saving on the dole is U, the increase in imports of raw materials and unfinished goods is R in value, the increased imports of finished goods that result from the newly-employed man's expenditure are $(1-m')(W-U)$ in value, and the sum of the increase in unspent profits and of the increase in

---

[1] This section, and a considerable portion of the rest of the article, is largely the result of the co-operation that I have received from Mr J. E. Meade of Hertford College, Oxford. I must content myself with a general acknowledgment, but it will, I hope, be clear that my treatment is fundamentally based on work of Mr Meade's that is as yet unpublished.

imports of finished goods to which the newly-accruing profits are
devoted is $(1-n)P$. The total sum of these items is

$$U+R+(1-m')(W-U)+(1-n)P$$
$$= W+P+R-(mW+nP), \text{ by equation (3)}$$
$$= (W+P+R)(1-k), \text{ by equation (1)}.$$

But we have seen that if N men are placed in primary employment,
the total increase in employment is $N/1-k$. It follows that the sum of
these items is $N(W+P+R)$, which is precisely the value of the
product of the primary employment, i.e. the cost to the State of the
roads.

We have then the following relation:

Cost of investment = saving on dole + increase in imports +
increase in unspent profits.

The last head comprises that part of the increase in profits that is
devoted neither to home-produced consumption-goods nor to
imported goods.

Now this relation, far from being the logical consequence of
summing an infinite geometrical progression, is in reality self-evident
in nature and is merely a particular case of a general relation, due to
Mr J. E. Meade, that covers the case when supply is not perfectly
elastic, so that prices rise when employment increases. This general
relation is a derivative form of Mr Keynes' formula for profits.[1] In its
most general form Mr Meade's relation runs as follows:

Cost of investment = saving on dole + increase in excess of
imports over exports + increase in unspent profits − diminution
in rate of saving due to rise in prices.

In this equation the second term on the right-hand side includes both
the effect of increased employment in causing an increase in the
volume of imports of consumption-goods and of raw materials and
the effect of higher prices in causing an increase of imports and a

[1] It is to be noted that the word profits is here being employed in the ordinary
sense of the difference between business men's receipts and their outgoings,
and not in the sense in which Mr Keynes employs the word. But it is clear
that Mr Meade's relation is merely a special statement of Mr Keynes'
general proposition that 'profits' are equal to the difference between investment and savings. [For a formulation of this point in more modern terms, see
'The Financing of Public Works: A Note', *Economic Journal*, September
1932, p. 494.]

reduction of exports. The third term comprises the unspent portion (i.e. spent neither on home-produced consumption-goods nor on imported goods) of the profits that emerge as a result both of greater output and of higher prices. And the fourth term allows for the increase in people's expenditure that may result when prices go up.

The relation can be deduced in an *a priori* kind of way by considering that money paid out by the Government to the builders of roads continues to be passed on from hand to hand until it reaches one of the *culs-de-sac* indicated by the various terms on the right-hand side of the equation. By utilising it as a basis, it should be possible to deduce a formula for the ratio of secondary to primary employment that is applicable whatever may be the elasticity of supply of consumption-goods.

This relation should bring immediate relief and consolation to those who are worried about the monetary sources that are available to meet the cost of the roads. The increase in the excess of imports over exports is equal, if gold is not flowing at an appreciable rate, to the reduction in foreign lending. So that if one is looking for sources *outside* the banking system, they are available to precisely the right extent. The cost of the roads is equal to the saving on the dole *plus* the reduction in foreign lending *plus* the increase in unspent profits *minus* the reduction in the rate of saving.[1]

In a closed system, such as the world as a whole, the second term of Mr Meade's relation is *ex hypothesi* zero. If, in such a closed system, there were no dole (i.e. the unemployed lived on air) and the newly-accruing profits were devoted in their entirety to consumption,[2] the ratio of secondary to primary employment would be infinite. No matter how small the elasticity of supply of consumption-goods, 'one man put to work on the roads would then place all the remainder of

---

[1] There are some who maintain that if a tariff causes an increase of foreign lending, lending at home must necessarily be contracted in an equal degree. Without entering at all into the question of the general validity of their point of view, it would appear possible to defeat them *on their own ground* by using an argument precisely analogous to the argument of the text. For if a tariff is successful in causing an increase in foreign investment, funds will be released, and will – if one likes to think of it in that kind of way – be available for foreign lending, to an extent exactly equal to the increase in foreign investment – just as the building of roads (home investment) releases funds exactly equal to their cost.

[2] Or, more accurately, if the newly-accruing profits remained unspent at a rate equal to or less than the rate at which savings are diminished as a result of the rise in prices.

18

the unemployed into secondary employment'. Such a system would, of course, be unstable. A small decrease in the rate of investment would result in everybody becoming unemployed.[1]

XIV

I turn now to the question of the quantitative importance of the saving on the dole. Mr Meade's relation tells us that it falls short of the total cost of the roads by an amount equal to the increase in the excess of imports over exports *plus* the increase in unspent profits

---

[1] It may, finally, be of interest to notice how Mr Meade's methods can be applied to deal with the controversy that is at present raging as to the effect on a country's exports of a reduction in its imports. If there is no change in the rate of home investment, either in this country or in the rest of the world, the effect of a tariff on this country's imports can be represented as follows. (For the sake of simplicity the effect of an alteration in prices on the rate of saving is omitted. It can easily be brought in if its presence is desired.) For this country:

Decrease in excess of imports over exports = saving on dole + increase in unspent profits.

For the rest of the world (considered as a single country):

Decrease in excess of exports over imports = loss on dole + diminution in unspent profits.

If it were supposed that in the rest of the world there is no 'dole' (i.e. the unemployed live on air) and that business men reduce their expenditure on consumption to the full amount of any reduction in their profits, then it would be quite true that our tariff would cause such a large reduction in the foreigner's volume of output and employment that his purchases from us would fall by an amount precisely equal to the reduction of our imports. Exports then *would* pay for imports, even under those short-period conditions that underlie the argument. But this conclusion depends essentially on assumptions of an extraordinary degree of absurdity; and an examination of the actual conditions that prevail would, it may be supposed, lead to a result of an entirely different order of magnitude. Moreover, if we *are* to make absurd assumptions, it is hard to see why this country should not be allowed to participate. Let us therefore suppose that, in this country also, there is no dole and that business men devote to consumption the whole of any increase in their profits. Then it would follow from the above equation that the imposition of a tariff would cause such a large increase in the volume of our output and employment that (leaving on one side, as irrelevant to the present argument, the effect on our exports of a *rise in their price*, as opposed to that of a fall in the foreigner's demand curve) our imports would not contract at all in the aggregate. We might import less manufactured goods, but we should import more food and raw materials. Exports would pay for imports – yes, but a tariff would cause no net reduction in our imports.

minus the diminution in the rate of saving that may be brought about by the rise in prices. In a closed system there can be no change in exports or imports, and if only the increase in unspent profits were less than the diminution in the rate of saving, the saving on the dole would more than cover the cost of the roads. Now the world is a closed system. It follows that an international policy of digging holes and filling them up again would result in a net gain to the united treasuries of the world, provided only that business men could be persuaded to be sufficiently spendthrift with the additions to their profits which such a policy would secure for them. Such a hope is almost certainly a vain one. But no account has been taken of the increase in the yield of taxation that would accompany an expansion of output and of employment. If the treasuries of the world were to gain as increased revenue an amount equal to the excess of the increase in unspent profits over the diminution in savings, the promotion, on an international scale, of perfectly useless 'public works' would still be profitable, even from a narrow budgetary point of view. We are probably still a little way off reality – but can it be so very far?

To consider international action of this kind is perhaps a little premature. More interesting is the question of the cost that this country would be involved in if it were to act alone. Part of the benefit without any of the cost would then accrue to other countries. To the internationally minded this should not be an objection – indeed this is one of the main respects in which the stimulation of home investment is superior to the stimulation of foreign investment. Moreover, the adoption of a policy of this kind by this country would, by the force of example, induce other countries to adopt similar policies, in whose benefits we should then take a share. But I am content to consider the case where this country acts alone and where the benefits received by the rest of the world are left out of account. It follows from Mr Meade's relation that under conditions in which in a closed system the building of roads would *just* be a sound proposition (from the narrow budgetary point of view), the national debt, if a single country acts alone, will be raised by the value of the increase in imports (and reduction in exports) which the building of roads will bring about.

XV

But let us consider the saving on the dole in the case of this country in concrete terms. Let it be supposed that expenditure on road-building and other forms of home investment increases by £50 million per annum. The primary employment can then be supposed to amount to 250,000 and, on the basis of a ratio of ¾, the secondary employment will be 187,500 – to make quite certain let us call it 150,000,[1] so that the total employment will be 400,000. If the dole amounts on the average only to 25s. a week, the saving to the Unemployment Insurance Fund will be £25 million per annum, which is just half the total cost. This £25 million the Exchequer can then afford to contribute out of its own resources – that is to say, out of the Sinking Fund in so far as the saving on the dole diminishes the rate at which the Insurance Fund is getting into debt, and out of the ordinary budget to the extent that the saving is in respect to the cost of transitional benefit.

We still have to allow for the increase in the yield of taxation. For each man who is put into employment the money-income of the community increases by considerably more than £120 per annum (say in the form of profits £30 *plus* such increase in the value of output as a whole that takes place as the result of the rise in prices, and £90 as the difference between the wage and the dole). It seems reasonable to suppose that of this amount at least £15 will be paid to the Exchequer in the form of taxation. It follows that if employment is increased by 400,000, the revenue will expand by £6 million – and clearly this is an extremely conservative estimate.

At any rate it would appear safe to conclude that the Exchequer would actually reap a net gain if it were to subsidise capital investment to the extent of *one-half* the capital sum involved. A necessary condition is, of course, that the work would not be undertaken if no subsidy were forthcoming. This condition severely restricts the field over which subsidies to investment are applicable. But even if the Treasury were to confine itself to railway companies and local authorities, it might reasonably be expected that the payment of subsidies of one-half of the capital cost would induce a very substantial increase in the rate of investment.

[1] This is what the secondary employment would be if the ratio of secondary to primary employment were only ⅗.

Let us now take the case where the whole cost is borne by the State. Let us suppose that the Government, national and local, spends the £50 million per annum for three years, at the end of which time conditions may be imagined to have improved. Then if a saving of only one-half is allowed for, the addition to the national debt (including the debt of local authorities) will be £75 million, which, at an average rate of interest of $3\frac{1}{2}$ per cent, amounts to an annual charge in perpetuity of a little over £$2\frac{1}{2}$ million, or about $\frac{1}{15}$ per cent of the present national income and $\frac{1}{4}$ per cent of the revenue raised by taxation. For this, 400,000 men are put into employment for three years and £150 million, equal in money-value to about $\frac{3}{4}$ per cent of the national capital, are spent on capital works. To suppose that the consequent increase in efficiency could lead to an automatic expansion in the yield of taxation equal to the whole of this interest charge of £$2\frac{1}{2}$ million would be quite unjustifiable – particularly when account is taken of the reduction in foreign investment that is associated with this increase in home investment – but the increase of efficiency should certainly be taken into account if one wants to consider how a policy of public works at the present time would affect the budgetary problems of the future.

I turn now from the budgetary to the national standpoint. At first sight the natural line of approach might appear to be to regard the increase of £$2\frac{1}{2}$ million in the interest payable on the national debt as a burden on posterity and to measure against it the increase in their national income that would result from £150 million having been spent in the past on schemes of a greater or less degree of permanent utility and from 400,000 men having been given work to do for three years instead of having lived in idleness. If this view were correct, it would be sufficient to show that the national income of posterity would be increased by at least £$2\frac{1}{2}$ million as a result of this expenditure of £150 million, and then the policy would be fully justified without taking into account any of the benefits that it would confer on the present generation.

XVI

But this view is, of course, fallacious. The payment of interest on the internal debt is not a burden in the real sense of the term – it is a case of transfer expenditure. It is only if the policy results in a reduction of posterity's income that it can be said to inflict a real burden. The only respect in which such a burden can be inflicted is as a result of the reduction in foreign investment that results from the policy. The expenditure of £50 million per annum for three years might reduce our annual balance of trade by, say, £20 million per annum, resulting in a total diminution of our foreign investment of £60 million. The loss of interest from abroad on this £60 million represents, taken by itself, a real burden on posterity. But against it has to be set the benefits that will be permanently derived by increasing the national equipment at a cost of £150 million and by rescuing 400,000 men for three years from the deteriorating influences of involuntary idleness. It can scarcely be doubted that posterity would inherit an asset rather than a liability as a result of such a policy as we are considering.

But even if there *were* a net real burden on posterity, it would still remain to set against its discounted value the benefit that would be derived by the present generation. Here the problem is a simple one, at any rate so long as the community is regarded as a single entity. The aggregate consumption of the community is necessarily increased as a result of a policy of 'road-building', for both the production and the importing of consumption-goods are stimulated. This increase in consumption is a measure of the benefit received by the present generation.

And so long as the building of roads does not involve any diversion of resources away from the production of consumption-goods, it will continue to add to the rate of aggregate consumption of the community. Provided then that it does not result in an actual decrease in the rate of accumulation of capital, material and immaterial, i.e. provided that the benefit conferred at home is greater than the loss in respect to foreign investment, as it almost certainly would be – there would appear to be no limit to the period of time during which it would be desirable to continue this policy of public works, except the very important one imposed by the condition that the factors of production employed in building the roads would, if the roads were not being built, remain unemployed.

But this conclusion reaches too far. The progressive increase in the rate of taxation that is necessitated when the national debt increases faster than the national income only fails to involve any real burden on the community as a whole if its 'announcement' aspects can be neglected. As the rate of taxation becomes higher and higher, the 'announcement' effects become more and more serious – and it is on these lines that one would have to assess the undesirability of progressively increasing the national debt or of permanently retarding its liquidation.

So far we have considered the community as a whole. It remains to say a word about the effect of road-building, while the roads are being built, on the real incomes of the various constituent classes of the community. There are two classes whose real incomes are certainly increased – the newly employed and the business class – and, to the extent that prices rise, there are two classes whose real incomes are diminished – those who were already *fully* employed and the *rentier* class. It has already been said that the real income of the community as a whole is increased. But of more interest is the effect on the real income of wage-earners as a whole, taking employed and unemployed together.

This involves the question of the rise in prices that would accompany an increase in employment. Under the conditions that rule at present it seems certain that if 400,000 were put into employment, primary and secondary, the real value of the aggregate income (wages *plus* dole) of the wage-earning class would increase. But under conditions in which the supply of consumption-goods were considerably less elastic than it is likely to be to-day it is quite possible that an increase of employment, brought about in this kind of way, would entail a reduction of the real value of wage-earners' aggregate income. But even then it would not necessarily follow that it would be contrary to the interests of wage-earners as a class for a policy of national investment to be adopted. It is too often forgotten that the main purpose of schemes of this kind is to *reduce unemployment,* and that unemployment does not fail to be an evil when its persistence involves a higher real income to the wage-earning class than would otherwise be obtainable. If this were not so, it might often be in the interests of wage-earners to advocate steps that would still further increase unemployment. But unemployment is an evil in itself, it is an evil on account of the *maldistribution* of the wage-earners' aggregate income that it usually causes, and it is an evil, together with the depression of the industrial system with which it is generally associated, on account of its effect in retarding the rate of economic progress.

XVII

It is necessary, finally, to turn to the effect on the foreign exchanges of an increase in the rate of home investment. Increased employment means increased imports of raw materials and finished goods and, to the extent that prices rise, there is a further increase of imports and a decrease of exports.

The result is that the net amount lent abroad by this country has to be reduced. It has been suggested above that the employment of 400,000 men might mean a reduction in the balance available for foreign lending of £20 million per annum. Unless other factors are brought into operation, this reduction in lending has to be effected by a rise in the various rates of interest. If others things remain equal, there ensues some decrease in the home investment that flows along normal channels, and this partially offsets the increase in investment that takes the form of road-building. It is important to assess the magnitude of this counteracting effect. Two factors are involved: (*a*) the sensitivity of foreign lending to the rate of interest, and (*b*) the sensitivity of home investment to the rate of interest. It seems reasonable to suppose that, provided that the change that is under consideration is a fairly small one, the sensitivity of foreign lending to a rise in the rate of interest is considerably larger than the sensitivity of home investment. Moreover, under the conditions that prevail in this country at the present time, an increase in home investment, in the form of road-building, provided it is not undertaken on too large a scale, will result in a considerably smaller diminution in the amount available for lending abroad. It may therefore be concluded that it is not necessary to make any substantial deduction in respect to the effect of the rise in the rate of interest.

But if an attempt is made to increase home investment by a very considerable amount, the reduction in foreign lending is likely to be relatively greater – because a less elastic portion of the supply curve for consumption-goods will now come into operation and because the demand for goods that meet with foreign competition is likely to become more elastic as their price is raised.[1] It also seems likely that

---

[1] On the other hand, the ratio of secondary to primary employment is likely to be less and, therefore, the ratio of the increase in employment (to which a portion of the increase in imports is directly proportional) to the cost of the roads is likely to be less. If follows that the reduction in foreign lending *may* be relatively less when many roads are being built than when only a few roads are being built.

the sensitivity of home investment to a rise in the rate of interest becomes greater as the extent of the rise in the rate of interest is increased. It may, therefore, be concluded that the case of an extremely bold policy of road-building might necessitate more serious consideration of the effects of the rise in the rate of interest on home investment. But even then it must not be forgotten that the whole point of a policy of public works is that it enables an increase in the rate of home investment to take place without that *fall* in the rate of interest that would be necessary if we were relying on private enterprise. The fact that it necessitates some rise in the rate of interest is not in itself a valid objection.

But there are available, of course, methods for curtailing, partially or completely, the necessity for this rise in the rate of interest. In the first place, there are the various devices that could be employed with the object of restricting the freedom of foreign lending. Secondly, there is the possibility of combining a vigorous policy of home development with the imposition of a tariff. By combining the two measures in suitable proportions, it would be possible to maintain the value of imports at its present level. In this way each would be freed of one of the main objections that can be raised against it. The strain inflicted by road-building on the foreign exchanges would very largely disappear and the tariff would fail to impoverish our customers.

So far it has been supposed that a policy of national investment has no influence on the schedules of people's desire and ability to carry on investment at home and to lend abroad. This is a manifestly unwarranted supposition, but two opposing forces have to be reckoned with, and it is not at all clear where the issue lies.

An increase of output, and of the margin of profit that goes with it, cannot, taken by themselves, fail both to increase the attractiveness and to facilitate the process of investment at home. It is quite obvious that this effect is of great quantitative importance. If there were no opposing forces in operation, it might easily happen that, in spite of the rise in the rate of interest, the ordinary processes of home investment would be promoted rather than retarded by a policy of public works.

This supposes that the state of general confidence is not affected. There is strong justification for concluding on *a priori* grounds that the inauguration of an active economic policy would promote confidence rather than upset it. But this is not a valid reason for disbelieving the warning, so frequently put forward at the present time, that an extensive policy of public works would promote a feeling of distrust. For the state of confidence is a function of what people are thinking, even though their thinking may be completely irrational, and therefore only those who are in touch with the minds of the people are competent to pass judgment on this question.

A lowering of confidence may operate in two ways. It may, in the first place, reduce people's willingness or ability to carry on real investment at home. But also of great importance is its effect in increasing people's desire to hold their money abroad rather than at home. To the extent of the increased pressure to lend abroad, to which the phrase 'flight from the pound' is often employed to give exaggerated prominence, the rise in the rate of interest that is necessary to protect the exchanges becomes greater, and its depressing influence on the rate of home investment also becomes greater.

But it is very difficult to believe that the dangers are as great as is often suggested. There can be no doubt that close contact with men of affairs must lead further towards a realisation of these dangers than can *a priori* reasoning. The only question is whether it may not lead too far. When a practical man declares that a policy of national development would result in a 'flight from the pound,' his judgment is really valuable only if he means that he himself would fly from the pound – and if he really would undertake the flight when the occasion arose. But too often the economic theory held by the business man bears little relation to his own practices – it is only if the practices of himself and of others like him were different from what they are that their theories could be correct. When a business man's theory involves a hypothesis about men's behaviour to which his own individual conduct fails to conform, he cannot be regarded as a very much sounder judge than the theoretical economist.

APPENDIX: PUBLIC WORKS AND INFLATION*

The main object, I take it, of economic policy at a time like the present is to raise the level of output and of employment. Judged by this criterion success can be attained only by raising the demand for output as a whole. Now all methods of raising the demand for output can be classified under two heads: those that involve an increase of investment, increased output of non-consumable goods, and those that involve a reduction of saving, increased consumption of consumable goods. So far as concerns a reduction of saving by private individuals, much might be said, but little can be hoped. If we turn to the promotion of private investment we find a heart-breaking task, to which bankers are beginning to address themselves by forcing down the rates of interest and expanding the basis of the credit structure. But it is clear that things have come to such a pass that, while it is all the more necessary to give every possible encouragement to private investment in order to prevent further deterioration, if we are thinking in terms of recovery there is little to be hoped. The normal channels of private investment, like those of private spending, are hopelessly choked, and such stimulus as can be devised meets with but a sluggish response.

We turn, therefore, to the state, and here again we must look either to a diminution of saving or to an increase in investment. The one involves an increase in the budgetary deficit, the other can be illustrated by a programme of public works financed by borrowing.

But the advocacy of budget deficits must be regarded as a hopeless cause. The problem for the world today is how to repair the ravages that are resulting from the attempts of one country after another to follow the dictates of orthodox finance. It began with England, where the balancing of the budget has done much to obscure the benefits of the fall in our exchange which the balancing of the budget was powerless to prevent. I shall therefore talk of public works, leaving it to be understood that the difference between the effects of public works and of a budgetary deficit is mainly one of degree.

The point is, of course, that the money is raised by borrowing. If

* *Journal of the American Statistical Association*, Supplement, March 1933.

public works are financed by taxation the benefit is of an entirely different order of magnitude, for, in evaluating the effect on employment, we have to subtract the effect of the diminution in taxpayers' consumption. That case I shall not consider.

The object of the policy is to promote output and employment by raising the demand for goods. Accompanying the increase in output is likely to be a rise in prices, the extent of which is dependent on the technical conditions of supply. At a time of severe depression like the present – when there is a considerable surplus of unused plant and labour – supply is highly elastic, and a substantial increase in output would involve only a small rise in prices. What I should like to emphasise is that it is quite beside the point to regard a rise in the level of prices as the *objective* of economic policy. What one is trying to do is to increase output by raising consumers' demand. It is quite true that output can only be increased at the *expense* of higher prices: the supply curve of output as a whole slopes upwards. But that is quite a different thing from saying that the *object* is to raise prices. Indeed, it is just at a time like the present when, supply being highly elastic, a given increase in output would be accompanied by a comparatively trivial rise in prices, that the case for securing such an increase of output is strongest. The rise in prices is not an end in itself, and it is not even a means to an end. It is merely a by-product, and in many respects an undesirable though a necessary by-product, of a rise in output. 'Reflation of output' should be the cry rather than 'reflation of prices'.

And that brings me to a related point. It is often said that one measure is less desirable than another because it is more 'inflationary'. Such a manner of speaking seems to me to have no meaning. Any measure that raises output can be said to be inflationary – apart from such measures as involve a reduction of costs – for any increase in output is necessarily accompanied by a rise in prices. And all such measures are inflationary to an equal degree, for a given increase in output is always accompanied by the same rise in prices no matter how it is brought about. The rise in prices is determined by the supply curve and by nothing else. It is impossible to differentiate between so-called 'natural' remedies and 'unnatural' remedies on the ground that the one class is more inflationary than the other. If one policy is more potent than another in raising prices, this can only be because it is also more potent in raising output, and it is not an objection but a recommendation. If it appears too potent, then all that is required is to apply it in a lesser degree. There is no need to discard it altogether.

To sum up, there is a unique correlation between output and prices, given by the supply curve of output as a whole, which depends only on the technical conditions of production. In the same way, to turn now to a different matter, there is a unique correlation between output and the quantity of money in circulation. A given output is associated with a given level of incomes and of prices, and at that level of incomes and of prices there is a certain quantity of money that people will want to carry about in their pockets and to hold in their banking accounts. This quantity of money is an effect, not a cause. If output is raised, say by pursuing a policy of public works, the quantity of money that people want to hold is increased, both because incomes are higher and because prices are higher. But the quantity of money has gone up *because* output has expanded, and this expansion of output is necessarily accompanied by the same increase in the quantity of money whatever the cause to which it is due. To condemn a particular policy because it seems to be based on an expansion in the currency is therefore quite impossible. If it is to be successful at all in increasing output it must involve an increase in the quantity of money held by the individuals who comprise society – no more, and no less, than any other policy.

The fallacy that I have in mind is, of course, quite insufficiently disguised when it takes the form of some reference to the printing press, coupled perhaps with a reminder of what happened to Germany in 1923. But in more insidious shapes it has, I believe, stood in the way of an enormous amount of useful action. The question of the source of the funds to be expended on public works – or on a budget deficit – is always a worrying one. If the money can be raised by borrowing from the public, then according to the usual view all is well. Now it is easy to imagine a situation where a national or local authority would have difficulty in floating a loan. The alternative is to borrow from the banking system, from the private banks if they are able and willing to lend, and failing that from the central bank, subject, of course, to any necessary changes in the law. But as soon as recourse to the banking system is alluded to, the cry of 'inflation' is raised and fears are expressed as to the 'safety of the currency'; and the policy is probably doomed. But in the light of common sense it can be seen that it does not make the slightest difference where the money comes from (so long as it can be obtained without diverting consumption or investment from other bodies or individuals). If public works were financed by loans from the Federal Reserve Banks or if in some way they entailed an expansion in the amount of backing to the currency, the rises in output, in prices, and in the quantity of money would be just the same as they would be if the money were obtained by borrowing from the public.

I turn now to the effect on employment. The *primary employment*, as I term it, is provided in the actual construction of the public works themselves and in the provision of materials. But associated with this primary employment is *secondary employment* arising as a result of the increased expenditure on consumption: newly employed men spend their wages and the contractors spend their profits. The output of consumption goods is increased in response to this increased demand, more men are employed, more profits are earned, and the effect is passed on once again. And so on, *ad infinitum*. But at each stage there is, so to speak, a certain amount of leakage and the effect is passed on with diminished intensity. This leakage takes three forms. In the first place, not the whole of the wages of the newly employed represents a *net* addition to spending power. They were previously in receipt of a 'dole', a word which I use for convenience, and without any malice, to represent the income of an unemployed worker, whether it is derived from the state, from organized charity, from friends and relations, or from personal possessions. Part of this dole is obtained at the expense of the consumption of other individuals: this part represents a mere redistribution of consumption. But not the whole of the contributions toward unemployment relief is made at the expense of consumption. Part is made at the expense of saving or is borrowed, and this part may be called the *non-transfer portion of the dole*. It then follows that the net addition to expenditure when an additional man enters into employment is equal to the excess of the wage that he earns over the non-transfer portion of the dole that he was previously receiving. In the second place, not the whole of the extra profits that accrue when an extra man is drawn into employment is spent on commodities. Part of these profits is saved. Finally, it has to be remembered that not the whole of the fresh expenditure, out of wages and out of profits, is directed to home-produced goods. Part is devoted to imports.

31

The leakage of which I have spoken is thus made up of the non-transfer portion of the dole, of savings out of profits, and of imports. The secondary employment, provided in the production of consumption goods, is represented by an infinite but converging geometrical progression, whose common ratio depends on these three crucial quantities. The smaller the dole in relation to the wage and the smaller the extent to which the dole is financed out of savings and borrowings, the larger is the ratio of secondary to primary employment; the more spendthrift the entrepreneurs, the larger is the ratio of secondary to primary employment; and the more self-contained the system, the larger is the ratio of secondary to primary employment.

Now if we compare the United States with my own country, it is clear that the dole is here a smaller proportion of the wage; and still more the ratio of the non-transfer portion of the dole to the wage is smaller in the United States than in England. Furthermore, the United States is a far more self-contained country than is England. There is a doubly good reason, therefore, for expecting the ratio of secondary to primary employment to be considerably larger in the United States than it is in England. A policy for combating unemployment will be more effective in the United States than in England; and the argument can also be reversed to show that any decline in investment or increase in saving will be proportionately more disastrous in a country like the United States than in a country like England. In other words, the American system is more sensitive to changes, whether they are for the better or for the worse, than is the English system.

But I am not really able to attempt even a rough guess as to the orders of magnitude of my fundamental ratios for the United States. In the case of England the system of unemployment insurance provides a securer basis for computation. The result of my calculations, based on summing an infinite geometrical progression, is to suggest that for every man put into primary employment in England probably over three-quarters of a man is drawn into secondary employment in the production of consumption goods.[1] But that is making no allowance for the effect of the reduction in taxation which, under the régime in force since September, 1931, would ensue from a reduction in the cost of unemployment relief. After sufficient time had elapsed

[1] See above p. 21

for the reduction in taxation to be effected and for this reduction to work its way through to increased consumption, the ratio of secondary to primary employment would be raised from three-quarters to one, and possibly more. That is for England. For the United States, as I say, the figure must be considerably greater. For every extra man employed, directly or indirectly on public works, well over one additional man would be drawn into the ordinary industries that cater for the nation's consumption.

This secondary employment, which, if I am right, is of an extraordinary magnitude, is usually completely ignored in discussions on the adequacy and the cost of various measures for dealing with unemployment. Its exclusion from the argument makes the cost of providing a given amount of employment appear to be double, or more than double, its true amount. The effect is even more remarkable if allowance is made for the saving on the cost of unemployment relief. Once again I may perhaps be excused for quoting figures that apply to my own country. The expenditure of one million pounds per annum on public works would, according to the most conservative estimates, provide primary employment for 4,000 men. But if allowance is made for the secondary employment and for the saving on the dole, a net expenditure of one million pounds per annum would on the same basis employ altogether, not 4,000 men, but over 12,000; in other words, 1,200,000 men could be employed at a *net* cost of 100 million pounds per annum.

There is another very important conclusion to be drawn. My figures suggest that the saving in respect to unemployment benefit amounts to about half the cost of the public works. That means that even from the narrowest budgetary point of view it would pay the British Government to subsidise schemes of this kind to the extent of one-half the capital cost. When I mention that this calculation excludes any allowance for the increased yield of taxation when profits increase and for the increased consumption of the taxpayer when taxes are reduced, it will be seen that it is a very conservative estimate.

But as, I suppose, is well-known, the trend of sentiment in my country is entirely in the opposite direction, and I hasten to say a word about the application of these figures to the United States. Here again I am held up in almost complete ignorance of the orders of magnitude. I have already shown that the ratio of secondary to primary employment is certainly considerably greater for the United

States than for England. But it would, of course, be wrong to deduce that a greater proportion of the cost of public works is covered by a reduction in the cost of unemployment relief. For the relatively low level of the dole in the United States as compared with England is itself part of the reason why the secondary employment is so great. It is not, however, the whole of the reason. There is also the fact that non-transfer payments form a less important element in the American dole than in the English dole, and, far more important, that a smaller proportion of any addition to expenditure is devoted to imports. I should, therefore, be inclined to guess that the saving in respect to unemployment relief out of Federal and State funds and out of the funds of organised charities, while it might not amount to as much as one-half of the capital cost of the public works, would not fall a great deal short of one-half. At any rate there can, I think, be little doubt that subsidies considerably in excess of the 20 per cent level that Colonel Rorty advocates[1] would pay for themselves without bringing into the account any allowance for the alleviation of distress, for the value of the completed works, or for the likelihood that it is only in this kind of way that the wheels of private investment and spending can be set revolving so that the system could be left to carry on once again under its own momentum.

[1] M. C. Rorty, 'How may Business Revival be Forced?', *Harvard Business Review*, April 1932, Supplement, p. 391.

2

THE DOLLAR SHORTAGE
AND DEVALUATION*

I

The primary purpose of this article is to enquire whether the recent re-adjustment of rates of exchange has curtailed or eliminated the 'shortage of dollars', and whether the persistence of such a 'shortage' would mean that further re-adjustment of rates of exchange is called for. But such an enquiry would be fruitless if it did not include an attempt to determine the meaning and significance of the phrase 'shortage of dollars', and in fact it is to such an attempt that a large part of the article will have to be devoted. Distinguishing between purely temporary disequilibrium in the balance of payments and chronic 'dollar shortage', Professor Samuelson has said: 'Precise descriptions of what is meant by this concept are hard to find. Indeed if one interprets the classical theory of comparative advantage in a narrow sense, such a chronic unbalance will appear to be an impossibility.'[1] There in a nutshell is the main difficulty.

II

An important subsidiary difficulty has been underlined by Professor Haberler: 'It is quite wrong to look at the problem as a contest between the dollar as against the rest of the world. What is going on in reality is a *bellum omnium contra omnes.*'[2] This raises an important issue which I defer until later in this article and for the present I will abstract from it by assuming that there are only two countries in the world – let us call them the United States and the Dis-united States (U.S. and Dis-U.S. for short) – and let us call their currencies the dollar and the libra.

* *Economia Internazionale*, February 1950.
[1] P. A. Samuelson, 'Disparity in Post-war Exchange Rates', *Foreign Economic Policy of the United States*, ed. Seymour Harris (1948), p. 406.
[2] G. Haberler, 'Dollar Shortage?', *ibid.*, p. 442.

3-2

I then define a situation in which there is a 'shortage of dollars' as follows. Dollars are short to the Dis-U.S. if it is necessary for the Dis-U.S. to restrict her imports or to suffer unemployment in order to avoid either a continuing loss of monetary reserves to the U.S. or borrowing from the U.S. of the kind which can be described as 'distress' borrowing, being onerous and objectionable on account of the capital charges involved, or of a threat to the country's liquidity, or on political grounds, or because it is precarious.[1]

Defined in this way, shortage of dollars is expressed by the degree of deviation on the part of the Dis-U.S. from the position in which she would be in balance of payments equilibrium while admitting imports freely under free-trade conditions and while enjoying reasonably full employment.

By balance of payments equilibrium I mean a situation in which any adverse balance of payment on income account is matched by overseas borrowing of the kind which is perfectly 'acceptable' in the sense that the Dis-U.S. would be able and willing to go on with such borrowing over a considerable period of time and would not be trying to take steps to avoid the necessity of incurring it. In one sense there is no equilibrium so long as any borrowing is taking place, because a stream of lending cannot last indefinitely, and because the mere fact of borrowing alters the situation by piling up liabilities. But from a commonsense point of view it is possible to distinguish lending which is normal, in the sense that it can be expected to continue for a considerable time and that it is matched by investment in the borrowing country which, directly or indirectly, provides for interest payments. The other kind of lending or borrowing, which is inconsistent with balance of payments equilibrium (in the same sense as is actual loss of monetary reserves), is 'distress' lending or borrowing, which the borrowing country (and possible the lending country) is anxious to terminate in as short a time as possible, or on the continuance of which it cannot rely. And by a balance of payments deficit I shall mean that part of the international account which has to be paid for by loss of monetary reserves, and 'distress' borrowing. (The distinction between 'acceptable' and 'distress' borrowing is closely related to the distinction which Professor Dennis

---

[1] Cf. F. Machlup, 'Three Concepts of the Balance of Payments and the so-called Dollar Shortage', *Economic Journal*, March 1950, p. 47 (Professor Machlup's article was published after this one had been set up).

Robertson once drew between ̄ ¦ 'common-or-garden' and 'hot-house' borrowing.)

Shortage of dollars prevails then to the extent to which the Dis-U.S. is enabled to meet her commitments through the operation of one or more of the following factors:

(*a*) import restrictions;

(*b*) the prevalence of unemployment, which reduces the demand for imports and increases the supply of exports from what they would otherwise have been;

(*c*) loss of reserves and 'distress' borrowing.

A good deal has been written about unemployment as the factor on which a country has to rely for achieving balance of payments equilibrium. For Great Britain at the present time unemployment is not, however, a factor which needs seriously to be taken into account and I intend to abstract from it in this article and to assume throughout that whatever means the country does employ – e.g. import restrictions or exchange depreciation, supported by appropriate fiscal and monetary measures – it aims at, and succeeds in maintaining, a tolerably stable level of employment.

There is a tendency in the literature to associate shortage of dollars with balance of payment deficits.[1] But it would be absurd to argue that the Dis-U.S. had cured her shortage of dollars because, having exhausted all her dollar reserves, she was compelled to impose a severe curtailment of imports. A balance of payments deficit is an alternative to import restrictions as a means of dealing with a dollar

[1] Such association is indicated by Professor Seymour Harris' definition ('Dollar Scarcity', *Economic Journal*, June 1947, p. 165), which has been justifiably rejected by Professor Howard Ellis ('Dollar Shortage in Theory and Fact', *Canadian Journal of Economics*, August 1948, p. 358), who points out that 'a shortage of any currency is not basically a *capital* phenomenon' (*ibid.*, p. 359). Professor Harris' article was inspired by Lord Keynes' last article ('The Balance of Payments of the United States', *Economic Journal*, June 1946). Professor Harris follows Lord Keynes in interpreting the inter-war figures for balances of payments and gold and capital movements as indicating the degree of dollar shortage, without any examination of the extent to which import restrictions were in fact militating against the development of a large favourable trade balance by the United States of America – a point which is conceded by Professor Haberler, without much display of enthusiasm, and is emphasised with vigour in the same volume by Dr Balogh ('Dollar Shortage?' p. 432; The United States and International Economic Equilibrium', *Foreign Economic Policy of the United States*, pp. 462, 463).

shortage – an alternative which is open only so long as the deficit can be financed.

To the extent that a balance of payments deficit on *income account* is financed by 'acceptable' lending there is no dollar shortage, the shortage which would otherwise exist being relieved by the lending.

It sometimes appears to be argued that dollar shortage prevails only to the extent that consumption and investment exceed production, i.e. that a country is 'living beyond its means'.[1] According to the definition here proposed, the fact that a country's imports exceeded its exports would denote dollar shortage, except in so far as the deficit was financed by 'acceptable' lending, but dollar shortage can exist in the absence of such a divergence (import restrictions – or internal depression – operating to keep imports down to the level of exports).

III

So far I have not made any provision for assistance of the kind which we can conveniently describe by the general term Marshall Aid. The question is whether it can be included with 'acceptable' borrowing, which relieves dollar shortage, or whether it should be added in with 'distress' borrowing, which is a symptom of conditions of dollar shortage.

The answer to this question turns on the attitude of the Dis-U.S. (which will be affected, if not completely determined, by the attitude of the U.S.) towards the receipt of Marshall Aid. In considering various alternative methods of dealing with her economic situation, does the Dis-U.S. regard the availability of Marshall Aid as something which can be taken as given, and which can and should be taken advantage of whatever the situation, or is Marshall Aid to be regarded

---

[1] Professor Haberler refers to the school of thought which 'insists that the dollar shortage is merely a consequence of the fact that many countries are unwilling or unable for one reason or the other to live within their means' ('Dollar Shortage?', p. 435), and by way of example quotes from Mr Harrod, who says of the 'dollar famine' that it is 'one of the most absurd phrases ever coined'; 'this allegation of a world "dollar shortage" is surely one of the most brazen pieces of collective effrontery that has ever been uttered' (Roy Harrod, *Are These Hardships Necessary?* (1947), pp. 42, 43). But Mr Harrod was contemplating, when he wrote in 1947, a situation in which 'there is a market [in the United States] which could take many more goods than it is getting'. He admitted that 'the situation may arise in the future when the United States is not willing to take a sufficient supply of goods in return'.

as something which it should be the object of policy to avoid the need for, one method being positively preferable to another if it reduces the need for Marshall Aid even at the expense of a lower standard of consumption and investment. On the former interpretation it would (roughly speaking) be the object of policy to secure the highest possible standards of consumption and investment with the help of the Marshall Aid that was going;[1] on the latter interpretation it would be the object of policy to strike a compromise between the desirability of avoiding too low economic standards and the desirability of reducing to a minimum the need for Marshall Aid.

In so far as the former interpretation is correct, the Marshall Aid is a relief of dollar shortage and is not to be included in measuring the degree of dollar shortage. In so far as the latter interpretation is correct, the Marshall Aid is included in the shortage, the full impact of which on imports is avoided so long as the Aid continues. In practice, Marshall Aid is of course a mixture of the two – to some extent it is taken as given; to some extent efforts are made to avoid the need for it and these efforts are limited only by the desire to maintain tolerable standards of consumption and investment so long as may be possible.

The distinction depends partly on moral considerations. If the Dis-U.S. is reluctant to accept the Aid, and does so only because her economic position would be so desperate without it, she will frame her policy with the object of achieving freedom from the need for it. Such reluctance may be derived from reluctance on the part of the U.S. to grant the Aid, but it might exist despite positive willingness on the part of the U.S. to grant it.

But the more important question is one of time. Economic systems lack flexibility and in the determination of their shape regard has to be paid to the future as well as to the present. A definite amount of Marshal Aid may be a certainty for the next nine months but if considerable doubt exists as to what will happen after nine months, economic policy must to a considerable extent be determined by the doubts and not entirely by the certainty. So long as the Aid goes on it can be used to alleviate the effect of the dollar shortage, but the

---

[1] Of course, the amount of Marshall Aid is in a sense determined by the gap on the balance of payments. But I dismiss the unworthy suggestion that the Dis-U.S., being able to rely on an amount of Aid that covered the gap, would aim her policy at making the Aid as extensive as possible by having as wide a gap as possible.

shortage is there so far as the determination of policy is concerned, and any reduction, or complete withdrawal, of the Aid will necessitate a restriction on imports to the full extent of the shortage.

But for two opposite reasons the amount of the Aid is not a correct measure of the amount of dollar shortage. On the one hand, some degree of import restriction will usually be still necessary even when Aid is being given, and to that extent the amount of Aid understates the dollar shortage.

On the other hand, even if the whole of the Aid enters, in the above sense, into the balance of payments deficit, and even if it was so substantial as to render import restrictions unnecessary, it would be wrong to regard the amount of the Aid as a measure of the degree of dollar shortage. This can easily be seen by taking the case of a country which is in balance of payments equilibrium (with full employment) despite the absence of restrictions on imports. The fact that this is so does not necessarily mean that the country is not in some sense poor – poor in some fairly permanent sense or impoverished by some catastrophe like war. And by reason of its poverty it may be a very suitable object of Aid. It does not need the Aid because of any 'difficulty' in achieving a balance of payments; it needs the Aid purely and simply to raise its standards of consumption and investment[1] (which will be increased by the introduction of suitable fiscal and monetary changes, which will have such an effect on the system as to raise the demand for imports and reduce the supply of exports sufficiently to take advantage of the available Aid).[2]

[1] Professor Samuelson has exposed the error of thinking of Marshall Aid purely in terms of the relief which it affords to the balance of payments and overlooking the simple fact that if Aid worth, say, 5 billion dollars per annum is cut off 'the loss to Europe will necessarily be a loss of at least that much worth of goods and services. She will have at least that much less of output available for domestic consumption or capital formation' ('Disparity in Post-war Exchange Rates', p. 400). But it seems to me that Professor Samuelson is in some danger of falling into the opposite error that a country can be said to be short of dollars simply because it is in need of extra *resources*. This suggestion (which is rather implicit on p. 400 but becomes quite explicit on p. 411) appears also to be inherent in Professor Haberler's treatment in the same volume ('Dollar Shortage?', p. 433). Poverty (taking its origin in low productivity, famine, over-population or the ravages of war) provides a strong case for Aid, but to base this case on anything other than shortage of *goods* can only lead to confusion of thought. Cf. F. Machlup, 'Three Concepts of the Balance of Payments', p. 65.

[2] But the fact that, even without Aid, the country needs no import restrictions to achieve balance of payments equilibrium makes it more probable

If, even in the absence of Aid, no import restrictions would be necessary on the part of the Dis-U.S., the benefit of the Aid is measured by the amount of the Aid. But if import restrictions would be necessary in the absence of Aid, i.e. if the Dis-U.S. is experiencing dollar shortage, Marshall Aid confers a further benefit by enabling the Dis-U.S. to secure more of the benefits of international division of labour than she can enjoy without it, concentrating her additional imports (if she is allowed by the U.S. to do so) on those goods in the production of which she has a comparative disadvantage.

This further, or secondary, advantage may be greater in magnitude than the primary advantage,[1] though it cannot occur without it.[2] To what extent, at each stage of the history of E.R.P., Marshall Aid has been instigated by thought of the one advantage rather than the other is a nice question.

IV

I have so far taken the necessary restriction of imports as the criterion of the degree of dollar shortage. But this is correct only on the assumption that there is no other form of interference with the free play of market forces. Any action, involving a departure from the free operation of the pricing system, which is calculated to discourage imports or to increase exports, such as domestic and export subsidies of various kinds offered by the Dis-U.S. authorities – or indeed any discouragement on the part of the U.S. authorities to U.S. exports or encouragement of U.S. imports, designed to assist the Dis-U.S. – must be taken into account in assessing the degree of dollar shortage.

On the other hand, the mere fact that the Dis-U.S. maintains tariffs on imports means, even if in all other respects her economy is completely subject to the free operation of a pricing system, that she is *pro tanto* faced with a shortage of dollars.

There is one other point to be made clear. When I take balance of payments equilibrium with unrestricted imports as the datum position deviations from which are a measure of the dollar shortage of the

that exchange appreciation or a rise in wages will have to serve as a basis for the receipt of Aid.
[1] In the case of a Dis-U.S. whose sole interference with the free play of market forces takes the form of restrictions on imports, the secondary advantage is, on the usual assumptions of perfect competition, etc., a matter of the difference between the internal and c.i.f. prices of imported goods.
[2] As Professor Samuelson emphasises.

Dis-U.S., I am thinking of a free-trade Dis-U.S. and not necessarily of a free-trade world. The U.S. tariff is to be accepted as part of the data, though of course any change in its height will affect the degree of dollar shortage of the Dis-U.S.

V

Shortage of dollars, and the extent to which it prevails, is not determined by the fundamental physical factors of the world situation; or at any rate not completely so. It is partly a matter of historical accident – in that it depends on the relative levels of wages and currencies that happen to have got established. But it is only in a partial sense that it is a matter of history – and often in a very slight sense. For the fundamental physical, social and institutional factors of the world situation will roughly determine the real characteristics of the position which the Dis-U.S. would have to assume if she were to be in free-trade equilibrium with the U.S. And these real characteristics will often play a large part in determining how close to the free-trade position of balance of payments equilibrium the Dis-U.S. gets. If such a position involves an excessively low real income, either to the community at large or to certain sections of it, she is the less likely to get close to it and her dollar shortage is the more likely to be large.

It would, however, be misleading to suggest that it is likely that the Dis-U.S. would move deliberately from a position of lesser to a position of greater dollar shortage in order to secure an improvement in her economic position at the expense of the U.S. What usually happens is that, something or other having worsened the economic position of the Dis-U.S., she feels that, since at best her position is bad enough, there is no reason why she should make it even worse than it need be. Serious dollar shortage is usually generated by some change the impact effect of which is to create a balance of payments deficit for the Dis-U.S., the elimination of which by free-trade methods would involve a further heavy decline in the standard of living or otherwise impose a heavy strain. In considering examples of such changes, we should bear in mind that there can be no question of asking what a particular dollar shortage is due to, but only of explaining how it happened to arise. The most frequent example is, of course, sheer impoverishment, brought about, for example, by war. Then there is the common example of a slump in the U.S. A boom in the Dis-U.S. is a parallel example.

VI

Those economists who claim that orthodox remedies are good enough for dollar shortage have, of course, in mind that the Dis-U.S. should always be able to find a dollar–libra rate of exchange which secures balance of payments equilibrium with freedom of imports into the Dis-U.S. (an appropriate fiscal and monetary policy also being assumed).[1] If such a rate of exchange can be found and is established, there is then no shortage of dollars, as above defined, no matter how onerous the situation. But as long as the value of the libra in terms of dollars differs from the rate which makes free trade possible for the Dis-U.S., or so long as free trade is thus rendered possible only at the expense of a balance of payments deficit, dollar shortage prevails.

Two questions then present themselves. The first is whether such a rate of exchange exists at all. The second is – if it does exist, what stands in the way of its being established?

VII

It is often argued, in effect, that there is no rate of exchange at which the Dis-U.S. could both avoid a balance of payments deficit and forgo import restrictions, and other kinds of interference designed to discourage imports ('save dollars') and encourage exports. (I am assuming throughout that the preservation of something like full employment is accepted as a basic condition of equilibrium.) The argument is that the relevant elasticities may be so small that, in any given situation, a fall in the exchange value of the libra would increase the balance of payments deficit. To this argument there are three replies:

(a) As a matter of statistical assessment, there is a danger of taking as a measure rather short-period elasticities, which will almost always be pretty small, whereas it is moderately long-period elasticities, which will usually be a good deal bigger which are relevant.[2] There are, however, some factors worth mentioning (no complete catalogue

[1] An even better example than Professor Haberler ('Dollar Shortage?" p. 427) is Professor Frank Graham, 'Cause and Cure of Dollar Shortage', *Essays in International Finance, no. 10* (Princeton University, Jan. 1949), though he would dislike the suggestion of exchange *management* involved by the words 'the Dis-U.S. should always be able to *find* a rate of exchange'.

[2] Professor Howard Ellis ('Dollar Shortage in Theory and Fact', p. 361) emphasises this point.

is here possible) which tend towards low elasticities. The size of the Dis-U.S. compared (in economic terms) with that of the U.S. is, as a matter of practical importance, highly relevant in this connection.[1] And a Dis-U.S. the economy of which has been disrupted by war will give rise to low elasticities. Furthermore, allowance has to be made for the internal reactions of the U.S. to a deterioration in her balance of payments, and to the unemployment which is likely to accompany such deterioration. If these reactions are calculated to preserve the U.S. favourable balance of payments, the fall in the exchange value of the libra will be frustrated.[2]

(b) If the exchange is sufficiently depreciated (and Dis-U.S. money wages do not rise correspondingly) there will come a point at which some of the relevant elasticities begin to increase.[3]

(c) If exchange depreciation does harm this does not mean that exchange adjustment is no good, but that we are on the wrong tack. What is wanted is a *rise* in the exchange value of the Dis-U.S. currency. In this case the cure for so-called overvalued currencies is more overvaluation.[4] The objections to devaluation, to which we shall

---

[1] If the world is divided artibrarily into two parts, A and B, the elasticities are likely to be high when A is small and B large, they are likely to reach a minimum when A and B are equal, and to become high again when A is large and B small. This is presumably what Professor James Meade had in mind when he wrote: 'Thus there is no reason to believe that a simultaneous depreciation by a large group of countries will be any the less effective in putting the group into equilibrium than a depreciation by a single country in putting that country into equilibrium. Nor is there any reason to believe that the effect on the terms of trade of the group as a whole with the rest of the world will be any more adverse than the effect on the terms of trade of a single country with the rest of the world' (*Planning and the Price Mechanism* (1948), p. 99).

But, on the basis of random frontiers and probability considerations, this is only true if the group is so large as to comprise the whole world except for one 'single country', a point overlooked by Professor Meade.

[2] The position is eased if the internal reactions of the United States include the active promotion of foreign lending (of the 'acceptable' rather than the 'distress' variety).

[3] Joan Robinson, 'The Pure Theory of International Trade', *Review of Economic Studies* no. 36, 1946–7, p. 102.

[4] P. A. Samuelson, ('Disparity in Post-war Exchange Rates', p. 401). The same point is made by Professor Howard Ellis ('Dollar Shortage in Theory and Fact', p. 360). We need not be unduly perturbed by Professor Samuelson's statement that such a position of equilibrium will be unstable. Stability is determined by shorter-period elasticities than those which are relevant to the determination of the position of equilibrium and in this sense equilibrium will usually be unstable; the idea of a 'free' exchange

come in the next Section, are (in reverse) positive recommendations for revaluation, and if in fact devaluation would increase the balance of payments deficit, the case for revaluation is overwhelming (on the assumption, which we are making, that the deficit is calculated after taking full credit for loans and gifts which are of the 'acceptable' type) although there is no guarantee that it will be possible by this means alone to reach balance of payments equilibrium, for the elasticities concerned may increase in magnitude before an equilibrium point is reached.[1]

VIII

The argument against devaluation, when it was still fashionable to argue against devaluation, was usually put forward in terms of the preceding Section. It was claimed that, at the time in question, the relevant elasticities were so low that devaluation would only make matters worse. It was seldom realised that if that was really so, appreciation of currencies was desirable. But the argument was almost certainly unsound, although, as it happened, the conclusion drawn from it could, up to a certain point of time, be justified by quite a different line of thought.

Before I explain what it is there is one possible source of confusion that should be removed. These discussions are usually conducted in terms of reducing the balance of payments deficit – of 'bridging the dollar gap'.

There is first the question whether it really is desired to forgo the additional resources which an excess of imports represents. That can be dealt with, as is suggested above, by taking credit for any 'acceptable' borrowing or gifts before the deficit is calculated, so that the deficit measures only what is necessary by way of 'distress' provision.

The second question is whether it is not the *total* of exports and imports which is a much more significant factor than the *difference* between them. Looked at in this way, devaluation is a means, not of improving the balance of payments by increasing exports and diminishing imports, but of increasing exports and *consequently* of enabling

rate, in the absence of stabilising speculative forces acting through short-term capital movements, is completely untenable – any slight movement in either direction would usually become cumulative.

[1] Professor Samuelson in a similar connection draws attention to the important distinction between 'point' and 'arc' elasticity ('Disparity in Post-war Exchange Rates', p. 409).

45

the country to enjoy more imports, the restrictions against which can now be relaxed. In other words, devaluation is a means of getting closer to the free-trade position. But according as devaluation would, if the degree of import restriction were left constant, improve or deteriorate the balance of payments, it would, if the balance of payments were to be left constant, necessitate a relaxation or tightening of import restrictions. So it does not really matter whether we think in terms of an improvement in the balance of trade or of an improvement in the total of trade.

The correct reason why devaluation would not, until recently, have been wise is, it seems to me, because the resulting improvement on international trade (which I believe would, after a little time had been allowed for adjustment, have occurred) would have been too small to compensate for the factors operating in the other direction. These factors are:

(i) The effect on the terms of trade;

(ii) The effect on the distribution of income internally, and, more generally, on prices and wages expressed in money.

IX

It will be convenient to deal first with the second set of factors. They can be expressed in terms of 'difficulty' rather than 'burden'. Their importance has not perhaps been adequately recognised.[1] In addition to the elasticities which determine the efficacy of devaluation in real terms (the elasticity of demand for exports is an example) there are the elasticities which determine how *big* a depreciation is necessary to produce a given real effect. The elasticity of supply of the country's exports is a leading example. If the elasticity of supply of the exports of the Dis-U.S. is small this does not mean that devaluation does no good, but that, no matter how great the elasticity of demand for her exports may be, a given amount of devaluation will, in terms of foreign trade, have relatively little effect. If it were not for the effect on the terms of trade this would logically be an argument for a *large* devaluation rather than for not devaluing at all. In practice it was until recently the decisive argument for postponing devaluation until,

---

[1] Except in the obverse case of devaluation as a remedy for the troubles of a country in which the producers of primary products are suffering from depressed world prices.

46

with the growth of flexibility in the system, enough benefit would result from a given devaluation to justify the internal strains involved.

These strains take the form, in essence, apart from the effect of more adverse terms of trade (which is a burden on the country *taken as a whole* and is discussed in the next Section), of an internal re-distribution of real income from the rest of the community to those engaged in export trade, who benefit from the higher prices paid for their products.[1] For a given improvement in international trade, this redistribution will be larger the less elastic the supply of exports. And if the improvement is small in relation to the redistribution, the game is not worth the candle. It is true that the redistribution of income in favour of those engaged in export trade is the means by which exports are encouraged. But the means may be too expensive measured in relation to the end.

This conclusion holds good even if the general level of money wages is fairly stable. The effect of devaluation on the movement of money wages in general is a further consideration.[2] It would be frivolous to

---

[1] Let us start with a Dis-U.S. in a balance of payments equilibrium which it owes to a uniform tariff. Let us now imagine that the tariff is lowered and that simultaneously the currency is devalued to such an extent as to pre-serve balance of payments equilibrium, and let us ignore both the change in the terms of trade and the advantages of more international division of labour. Let us assume that the general level of domestic wages remains constant (apart from wages in export industries), or alternatively that prices are measured in terms of it. Then prices of exported goods will have risen. Prices of imported goods will have fallen, because the lowering of the tariff will be greater than the degree of devaluation (measured relatively to the general level of wages), a greater part of the onus of balance of pay-ments equilibrium now being carried by exports. But the taxpayer (who benefits from the revenue from the tariff) will have lost more than the consumer of imported goods has gained, and the two taken together will have suffered a net loss equal to the gain of those engaged in export trade.

This brings out a point which is perhaps overlooked by Sir Hubert Henderson in the course of his slashing and successful attack on those who discuss the virtues of flexible exchange rates on the assumption of constant money wages ('The Function of Exchange Rates', *Oxford Economic Papers*, January 1949). In discussing the effect on money wages of a rise in domestic prices brought about by exchange depreciation (as opposed to the effect on money wages of a rise in the level of demand, which could be countered by credit restriction or similar means), Sir Hubert Henderson fails to compare it with the similar effect of import restrictions designed to have the same influence on the balance of payments.

[2] In the terms of the preceding footnote, we may assume that the revenue derived from the tariff is used to subsidise the wage-earner (or, better still, that it is used to subsidise the prices of the goods that wage-earners buy).

suggest that this points merely to the need for a bigger devaluation than would otherwise be necessary, or for an unending series of devaluations or a continuous process of exchange depreciation. For 'the extent of an inflationary movement, once it has been set going, cannot be forecast. The process is apt to be self-perpetuating, and indeed to gather momentum, unless and until it is checked by some obstacle or counter-force, for which there is no provision in the technique of exchange depreciation'.[1] Certainly it was not justifiable in the case of the United Kingdom to imperil the Government's wages policy until such substantial dividends could be expected to result from devaluation as to justify the risks involved.[2]

X

What has been said in the preceding Section would apply to the case of a Dis-U.S. which was so small compared with the United States and so unidiosyncratic that the terms of trade between her and the U.S. could be regarded as a constant – independent of her policy and actions. The explanation thus presented of the phenomenon of dollar shortage is connected mainly with the idea that change involves difficulty and dislocation and it points largely to the need for a historical explanation of the situation.

The main essence of dollar shortage lies, however, in the relationship between the terms of trade and the volume of trade.[3] The

The taxpayer is then, in the relevant sense, identical with the wage-earner, who may try to protect his declining standard of living by demanding higher wages.

The case in which the import restrictions take the form of quantitative import control, which can be relaxed as a result of devaluation, has more practical importance. If the importer is free to sell at unregulated prices, the loss is borne entirely by him, and the wage-earner actually gains. But if prices are controlled so as to allow of a fixed rate of profit, the loss is borne entirely by the wage-earner, as it is also to the extent that the Government is unwilling to increase the subsidies on Government-imported goods consumed by wage-earners, or to sacrifice revenue from the tariffs on them, or to the extent that the restrictions on imports discriminate in favour of goods consumed mainly by wage-earners.

[1] H. D. Henderson, 'The Function of Exchange Rates', p. 8.

[2] It is neither here nor there that these dividends may partly take the negative form of an avoidance of deterioration in the position and not entirely of positive improvement.

[3] This is what Professor Haberler describes as 'the milder version of the dollar shortage doctrine which is at least theoretically defensible', though

argument is in no way incompatible with the classical theory of free trade – indeed it is the direct descendant of the Bickerdike–Edgeworth discovery that restrictions on imports, provided that they are not too drastic and provided that they do not cause other countries to do likewise, are bound, on account of the favourable effect on the terms of trade, to benefit a country.[1] If the Dis-U.S. is going to take advantage of that discovery, dollar shortage is the inevitable result.

The form in which the phenomenon presents itself is not that of a Dis-U.S. greedily moving away from free-trade policy and securing a gain on the terms of trade (at the expense of a larger loss to the U.S.). It is rather that of a Dis-U.S. which, for historical reasons, has got itself involved with import restrictions, and other forms of 'dollar-earning' and 'dollar-saving' Government interference, and finds that devaluation, taken beyond a certain point, even though it will render such restrictions and interference less necessary, will reduce the average standard of living because the adverse movement of the terms of trade will outweigh the benefit of a greater resort to international division of labour. That, it seems to me, is the essence of the present

in his opinion 'it is based on untenable factual judgments and assumptions' ('Dollar Shortage?', p. 441). Professor Haberler goes on: 'It is difficult or even impossible to find a clearly reasoned statement of this milder, theoretically tenable dollar shortage theory'. While regretting that, after presenting a succinct statement of this so-called 'theory', Professor Haberler finds it 'impossible within the short space of an article to deal adequately with the issues involved in this view', one has some sympathy with him in his difficulty in finding a clear statement of it. But the fact is that its practical significance is intuitionally so deeply imbedded in most writings on the subject (Professor Frank Graham, 'Cause and Cure of Dollar Shortage', perhaps provides an exception) that the necessity for an explicit statement is seldom realised. Actually the literature is full of references to the effect of devaluation on the terms of trade (or to the concomitant effect on the general standard of living). A pioneer in this field is Dr Thomas Balogh, whose 'The Concept of a Dollar Shortage' is merely the last (so far) of a long series of heroic broadsides (*The Dollar Crisis*, (1949), and *Manchester School*, May 1949). Professor Samuelson is clear and emphatic: 'If the exchange rate variation is even to begin to work as envisaged by classical theory, it will succeed in turning the terms of trade substantially against Europe – for if it does not work in this direction, the classical remedy is licked to begin with' ('Disparity in Post-war Exchange Rates', p. 401).

[1] For references to some of the earlier literature, see my 'Tariffs and the Terms of Trade', *Review of Economic Studies*, 1947–8, no. 37, in which I attempted to evaluate, by means of an algebraical formula, the quantitative significance of this factor and arrive at the conclusion that in any ordinary case the optimum degree of restriction of imports is surprisingly large.

situation. And it lies at the bottom of a great deal of what is to-day thought and said about international trade policy.

In basing the phenomenon of dollar shortage on the Bickerdike–Edgeworth discovery, one is not exposed to the customary objections to using that discovery as a basis for policy. Rightly or wrongly, it is often claimed that abandonment of free trade will result in other countries abandoning it too, so that everybody will be worse off.[1] But few would claim that devaluation on the part of the Dis-U.S., with consequent relaxations of import restrictions, would induce an important lowering of the U.S. tariff – in fact, quite the contrary.[2] We therefore, in reverse, get the Bickerdike–Edgeworth motivation in its purest form.

The optimum degree of import restriction depends on the extent to which the relevant elasticities fall short of infinity. Under (a) of Section VII above, I mentioned some of the factors which tend towards low elasticities. All these, and many others besides, are relevant here and explain why dollar shortage has been especially acute in recent years.

But that is not all. It is not only a question of the extent of the gap between the optimum position and the free-trade position. It is also a question of the nature of the free-trade position itself. The greater the sacrifice involved in assuming it, the less likely is it that the

[1] Professor de Scitovszky has pointed out in an article, which has done so much to illuminate the whole subject, that the question of abandonment of a *regime* of international free trade could arise only if the *regime* came into existence in the first place ['A Reconsideration of the Theory of Tariffs', *Review of Economic Studies*, vol. IX, no. 2, reprinted in *Readings in the Theory of International Trade* (American Economic Association, 1949)].

[2] I do not say that it might not have happened as the result of tariff bargaining. But unfortunately the I.T.O. negotiations have not covered import restrictions other than tariffs. It occurs to me that Professor A. M. Henderson, in his article (very relevant to this whole field of discussion) on 'The Restriction of Foreign Trade' (*Manchester School*, Jan. 1949), is rather too apt to take it for granted that a *general* lowering of obstacles to imports which was linked to concomitant changes in exchange rates is in fact a relevant alternative, so far as present international arrangements go. It sounds as though some integration of I.T.O. and I.M.F. may sooner or later be desirable. It is only fair to add that at the end of his article Professor Henderson admits that 'the results of recent international conferences are hardly encouraging' and, speaking for the United Kingdom (in January 1949), states that 'we should almost certainly worsen our position to-day if we were to abolish exchange control, tariffs and quotas and to devalue the pound. This is true because other countries would not be inclined to follow our example'.

Bickerdike–Edgeworth improvement will be forgone. It is partly a matter of degree. International sentiment in favour of free trade will carry countries fairly far away from the optimum position and fairly close to free trade provided that they find it tolerable. But the more burdensome the free-trade position, the more they will be driven in the direction of the optimum. Also, the fact that the Dis-U.S. can on these grounds claim justification for maintaining import restrictions makes it even less likely that the height of the U.S. tariff can to any important extent be ascribed to the import restrictions maintained by the Dis-U.S. as a means of avoiding an intolerable situation – the gap between the free-trade position and the optimum being thus further widened. Furthermore, it must here be borne in mind that the constitution of the Dis-U.S. as a single economic unit cannot be taken for granted. It is, as we shall see, a matter almost of *force majeure*, and it is the more likely to take place the more intolerable is the situation which would exist in its absence. 'The larger the group of countries, the more likely is it to be advantageous to it to use discriminatory import controls against the rest of the world rather than exchange depreciation as the method of restoring equilibrium.'[1]

The obstacle to moving in the direction of the free-trade position lies in the reduction in economic welfare which would result. This obstacle may take the particular form of a refusal on the part of wage-earners to accept the burden involved without attempting to avoid it by pushing up money wages, which, unless unemployment is resorted to, may rise as fast as the exchange is depreciated, rendering the depreciation completely nugatory.[2] The wage-earners might have been perfectly content with the standard of living offered by the free-trade position had they not previously enjoyed a higher standard. But having in the past enjoyed a higher standard, which, despite deterioration in the country's economic position, the Bickerdike–Edgeworth effect of import restrictions enables them to maintain, they are unwilling to see it depressed.[3]

[1] J. E. Meade, *Planning and the Price Mechanism*, p. 99. On this occasion we are not called upon to quarrel with Professor Meade over the question of the implication of relative size. The point is that whereas exchange depreciation is essentially a reciprocal process – the change in the exchange rate of the libra being equal and opposite to that of the dollar – import restriction is a non-reciprocal process.

[2] Cf. A. M. Henderson, 'The Restriction of Foreign Trade', p. 23.

[3] Professor A. M. Henderson deals sympathetically with the case in which a 'sudden decline in the standard of living of a people may be intolerable

4-2

The economic losses caused by war are the most important factors which have had these consequences by causing deterioration in the economic position of the Dis-U.S. Any decline in economic activity in the U.S., such as occurred to a slight degree and for a short time early in 1949, would also have this effect.[1] The lowering of the U.S. tariff is an offsetting factor, but it is an offsetting factor which could have been a good deal more influential had it been carried further.

A few months ago the Dis-U.S. looked as though she was becoming committed to a policy of import restriction carried to a degree of autarchy which it required very violent assumptions about the behaviour of the terms of trade to justify. The advantages of division of labour with the U.S. were in danger of being overlooked. 'Dollar saving' was the battle-cry, and indeed it seemed obvious that very drastic restrictions on imports into the Dis-U.S. would be necessary if ever her international accounts were going to be balanced. Devaluation has now intervened to give international trade a fresh lease of life. But nobody would maintain that it has been so drastic as to make free trade possible for the Dis-U.S. (or even for the Dis-U.S. that degree of freedom of trade which is practised by the U.S.). Dollar shortage will still prevail, in the interests of maintaining terms of trade which will leave life reasonably tolerable for the Dis-U.S. Devaluation has ensured that the necessary import restrictions will not have to be overdone but it has not been carried so far that their beneficial influence when taken in moderation will cease to be enjoyed.

XI

A word should be said about a factor which has always been emphasised by Dr Balogh – the fact that economic progress in the U.S. is more rapid than in the Dis-U.S. and the responsibility of that fact for dollar shortage.[2] Professor Haberler is critical of Dr Balogh's

and lead to wild inflation or revolution' (*ibid.*, p. 23) but points out that this provides a case only for *temporary* retention of controls.

[1] A decline in activity in the U.S. is normally associated with more favourable terms of trade for the Dis-U.S. But this is because normally the Dis-U.S. has permitted such a decline to exercise a depressing influence on her own level of activity. If exchange depreciation were carried to the point required to maintain Dis-U.S. activity against a slump in the U.S., the terms of trade of the Dis-U.S. would probably have to become *less* favourable than they were before the slump occurred.

[2] For Dr Balogh's later treatment, see his *Dollar Crisis*, e.g. pp. 8, 9, 28, 90

THE DOLLAR SHORTAGE AND DEVALUATION

thesis.[1] While Professor Haberler admits that economic progress in the U.S. can have various effects on the economic position of the Dis-U.S., there is no reason why they should be in one direction rather than the other. Professor Haberler is concerned with the final position of classical equilibrium[2] and pays no attention to the behaviour of money wages and so of money costs in the U.S.; Dr Balogh is very largely concerned with the difficulty of getting to the position of classical equilibrium, particularly if the process involves a continuously falling level of money wages, presumably forced down by pressure of unemployment. Professor Haberler would probably prefer to conceive of adjustment brought about by a depreciation of the Dis-U.S. currency, to compensate for the reduction in U.S. costs.[3] And although unemployment no longer has then to be cited as an essential part of the mechanism of change, it is still likely to result from the adjustment failing to take place sufficiently fast. This is a danger which Dr Balogh rightly stresses.

To discuss it would be inconsistent with the assumption made throughout this article that full employment is preserved. But the

and the appendix on 'The Concept of a Dollar Shortage' (also in *Manchester School*, May 1949). Similarly Professor Seymour Harris: 'So long as the gains in the competitive position of the United States (e.g. reduced relative costs and prices, offer of new products) continue at a rate rapid enough to more than neutralise the corrective effects of gold or exchange movements, so long will the dollar remain scarce' ('Dollar Scarcity', p. 170).

[1] 'The United States and International Economic Equilibrium', pp. 437–40.
[2] In which there is no resort 'to crude protectionist policies which, even if they succeeded in alleviating transitional strains, would do so only at the cost of permanently impeding the international division of labour and preventing the optimum allocation of resources' ('Dollar Shortage?', p. 440).
[3] 'Exchange-rate variations have been assigned a high constructive role in the ultra-liberal philosophy' which not long ago was 'disposed to stress and even to exaggerate the advantage of fixed exchange-rates' (H. D. Henderson, 'The Function of Exchange Rates', pp. 1, 2). Professor Kindleberger shares Sir Hubert Henderson's scepticism as to the smooth operation of exchange-rate adjustments. If 'wage rates are tied to changes in the cost of living, the expansion in the total value of exports may not occur at all. Under these and other imaginable circumstances, exchange depreciation is a very clumsy device and may prove ineffective because of progressive inflation at home' (C. P. Kindleberger. 'Monetary Stabilization', *Postwar Economic Problems*, ed. Seymour Harris (1943), p. 388). By assuming in another passage 'no change in the exchange rate' (*ibid.*, p. 363), Professor Kindleberger has quite properly been criticised by Professor Howard Ellis ('Dollar Shortage in Theory and Fact' p. 381).

53

possibility of a lag gives rise to a further consideration. Let us assume that under fairly stable conditions the Dis-U.S. would gradually have been pushed by international sentiment fairly close to the free-trade position. Now we have to deal with a falling level of money costs in the U.S. By dint of mere slothfulness in allowing, or in causing, her rate of exchange to react to U.S. progress, the Dis-U.S. finds herself securing a favourable shift in the terms of trade (compared with those which would rule if adjustment was rapid and complete); and she may in this way succumb to the temptation of maximising her economic welfare. Here again it would be difficult to argue that greater promptness in depreciating her currency would lead to a lowering of the U.S. tariff. Nor should the attitude adopted in 1949 by the U.S. authorities on the subject of devaluation lead us to suppose that prompt and drastic currency depreciation will invariably be acceptable to the U.S.

XII

Before we abandon the artificial device of a single Dis-U.S. there is one further point which it is convenient to make at this stage. From the theoretical point of view the simplest method of deviating from the free-trade position is by imposing a uniform *ad valorem* tariff. And to each value of such a tariff there will correspond a certain volume of trade. But in practice it is a question not only of the optimum volume of trade, but also of the optimum composition of any given volume. By imposing non-uniform import restrictions, the Dis-U.S. can secure a greater benefit for any given volume of international trade than the same volume would confer if it took place under the influence of a uniform tariff. The natural course is clearly to take account of the various elasticities of demand and supply which are involved and of the varying extents to which different imported commodities enter into the consumption of the poorer classes of the community. In other words, it is a matter not only of the benefit to be secured by discriminating in favour of domestic *vis-à-vis* foreign production but also of the further benefit to be secured by exercising such discrimination on a discriminatory basis.

XIII

It is high time to consider Professor Haberler's plea that 'the fact that so many countries of entirely different economic structures, different policies, different economic development all suffer from a dollar shortage weakens the case for the criticised doctrine instead of strengthening it', and that 'it is mathematically inconceivable that restoration of a free market equilibrium should turn the terms of trade against all of them'.[1]

To deal first with the mathematics, it all depends of course from what it is that the free market equilibrium is restored. If it is from a position in which a number of countries have been maintaining drastic restrictions on imports from the U.S. while admitting one another's goods fairly freely, then restoration of a free market equilibrium is likely to turn the terms of trade against all of them.

And that is precisely the situation which exists at the present time. To say that is not, of course, to explain anything. The reasons for the present situation are the crux of the problem.

Before we attempt to indicate what they are it is worth noting that it will always pay a number of countries sufficiently large in the aggregate to exercise some influence on the terms on which the group as a whole trades with the outside world, to get together and discriminate against the rest of the world. The gain from doing so will be great if the group is not too small (so that it can exercise a substantial influence on its terms of trade) and not too large (so that there is a substantial volume of trade with the outside world in respect of which to secure improved terms), if the countries composing it are similar in some respects (so that they can exercise a substantial influence on the prices of the goods which they trade in with the outside world) and dissimilar in others (so that they provide a fruitful field for international division of labour between themselves), and so on.

It may be that the non-dollar world at the present time is not such a bad group examined by these criterions. But it would be absurd to argue that it had consciously constituted itself in a purposive kind of way. The reasons for its manifestation must be sought elsewhere.

XIV

Before we seek the reasons there is a point of definition to be cleared up. At a time like the present most currencies are scarce in greater or smaller measure. The point about the dollar is that it is scarcer than

[1] G. Haberler, 'Dollar Shortage?', p. 443.

55

the others. Are we to talk about *degrees* of scarcity? Or are we to say that the dollar, unlike other currencies, is scarce because it is so much scarcer than the others? The latter course seems the more convenient. But in addition to the dollar there are a few other currencies, like the Swiss franc and the Belga, as well as the Canadian dollar, which, though to a lesser degree, can conveniently be described as scarce. The essence of scarcity of a country's currency then is that balance of payments equilibrium between it and the rest of the world can be secured (at current exchange rates and on the basis of current wage levels) by discriminatory import restrictions on the part of a large number of other countries which are a good deal more drastic than any which have to be maintained among themselves.[1]

What we then have to explain is why it is that, by and large, it is the relationship of the values of most countries' currencies to the value of the dollar rather than to one another that is out of line with what would be necessary to secure balance of payments equilibrium without any import restrictions. And this can be explained by the manner in which rates of exchange became established as the war came to an end. The relevant elasticities were for a time very low and any attempt to adjust the economy to the changes caused by the war and to the post-war inflation by means of a depreciation of the exchange would have involved heavy burdens and dislocations, and would indeed have failed, quite apart from the fact that economic help, most of which had to come from the United States, was justified by the physical realities of the situation rather than any problem of currency. Many countries were, one way or another, in much the same kind of position, with the result that there was a general 'over-valuing', so to speak, of currencies in terms of the dollar (quite different from the position in the early twenties when the terms of trade went heavily against many European countries).

[1] Non-discrimination is not inconsistent with equilibrium under these conditions but is compatible only with a much lower volume of world trade. Cf. Professor Ragnar Frisch, 'Forecasting a Multiple Balance of Payments', *American Economic Review*, September 1947. Dr Balogh is a pioneer in this field too.

XV

That position having been attained strong forces have operated to sustain it.

Lack of convertibility of most currencies into dollars has served to concentrate the impact of import restrictions on to dollar goods. But it would be wrong to regard non-convertibility as a necessary concomitant of dollar shortage. It results from the fact that balance of payments equilibrium between the dollar and the non-dollar worlds has not yet been established rather than from dollar shortage as such. If and when the dollar shortage is represented entirely by restrictions on imports of dollar goods, and not still in part by balance of dollar payments deficits, it should be possible to introduce full convertibility on income account.

Another factor which has operated in the same direction is the nature of the payments arrangements governing trade between many non-dollar countries, so long as dollar convertibility does not operate. Whether these take the form of the ordinary payments agreement or of the machinery of a monetary area like the sterling area, there is a tendency for an increase of imports from the other party to lead to some quite appreciable increase of exports. In trade between any one non-dollar country and the dollar world that tendency is very small, with the result once again that a preference is given to imports of goods from non-dollar sources.

A factor that would, or at least should, remain powerful even after convertibility is introduced – if it weakens, convertibility itself will be imperilled – is the idea of mutual aid which has gradually attached itself to dollar earning and dollar saving. It takes precise shape in the operations of the O.E.E.C. and of the sterling and other monetary areas, but even more widely it is beginning to be dimly recognised that the non-dollar world stands and falls together and that its standard of living, as now established, depends on each country taking its fair share of the brunt of forgoing dollar goods.

The encouragement of trade between the non-dollar countries, by a positive relaxation of the restrictions on imports from one another as well as by discriminatory restrictions on dollar imports, is an important part of the process of self-preservation. It follows from Section XII above that even after the volume of imports into the non-dollar from the dollar world has been reduced to what its dollar

57

earnings (together with acceptable borrowing, etc.) will pay for, there may still be considerable further room for improvement by importing less of the commodities which the non-dollar countries can fairly easily provide for one another and correspondingly more of the others.

In the sort of situation envisaged here, which in its essence consists of a large number of countries banded together by ties of every kind varying from definite treaties to scarcely conscious ideas of international solidarity, there is always the strong possibility that the degree of monopoly influence will wane as members of the group succumb to the temptation of undercutting.[1] Here the existence of the International Monetary Fund has played a useful part. The knowledge that competitive exchange depreciation is out of keeping with modern ideas has helped to hold the ring.

So perhaps Professor Haberler is wrong after all when he depicts a *bellum omnium contra omnes.*

XVI

Some economists, notably Dr Balogh, have attempted to reconcile these protectionist leanings of the non-dollar world with an internationalist approach by appealing to the inequality of incomes per head, which prevail between the dollar and non-dollar worlds.[2] It is quite true that whereas the application of the economics of welfare to domestic problems is always qualified by considerations of distribution of income, in dealing with international trade it is usual to argue as though income per head was the same for all countries. It is also true that the average level of income per head is much higher in the dollar than in the non-dollar world, and that on that basis it is possible to construct a case for deviating from the free-trade position in such a way as to secure a gain for the non-dollar world which, in

---

[1] 'It is the dollar shortage which forces a decrease of U.S. exports and not "wickedness" of "planners". The *only* question which is open is *whose* purchases from the U.S. will be reduced. This question can be answered by planned distribution of available dollars... or by an internecine struggle for dollars through competitive deflation and devaluation', T. Balogh, *Dollar Crisis*, p. 86.

[2] E.g., *ibid.*, pp. xiii, 13, 14, 63, 228, but the idea is prominent in a good deal of Dr Balogh's writings. He does not seem quite so happy about it when it is Britain herself which, as a member of a European Customs Union, might, with other 'relatively rich countries', have her standard lowered (*ibid.*, p. 67). Professor A. M. Henderson uses the same concept ('The Restriction of Foreign Trade', pp. 15, 19 and 22), though with less specific reference to dollar shortage.

terms of welfare as opposed to goods, more than offsets the loss to the dollar world. And there is much sense in the idea that it is precisely because of this difference in wealth that these discriminatory practices are accepted as necessary and, therefore, are, on the one hand, tolerated and, on the other hand, carried out with some sense of loyalty.

But if we are going to talk about differences in income per head, the differences between the averages of the dollar and the non-dollar worlds pale into insignificance compared with those between Asia and Africa, on the one hand, and, on the other hand, the other three continents. If it really is the 'optimum' in Dr Balogh's sense which we are after, we should be advocating a very different disposition of resources from that accounted for by, and accounting for, dollar shortage as we know it to-day.

3

MONETARY POLICY AND THE
BALANCE OF PAYMENTS*

'One of the surest ways to make sterling stronger is to make it scarcer, and that is what we intend to do', said the Chancellor of the Exchequer in announcing, in the course of his Budget statement on 11 March, that Bank Rate was being raised to 4 per cent. It is not easy to disentangle the variety of means and ends which lies behind statements of this kind, introducing as they do the shibboleths which are the stock-in-trade of addicts to the *mystique* of the monetary mechanism. No one would deny that there is some truth in the view that dearer money and tighter credit will be helpful to the balance of payments. But there is considerable confusion as to the best method of making money dearer, as to the consequences of doing so and as to the lengths to which such consequences should be taken.

The confusion has its psychological origin. There is a venerable economic tradition about the mechanism by which balance of payments equilibrium can be maintained. The traditional doctrine belongs to the field of economic thought, associated in more modern times with the Quantity Theory of Money, which had become, more than any other, subject to mysticism in its exposition. The conflicts involved in the process of rationalisation are the more intense because the rationalisation brings to the surface matters of bitter controversy – to what extent, for example, unemployment is a necessary ingredient in the smooth working of an economy based on free enterprise and to what extent 'natural' processes are in themselves preferable to those requiring government decisions and government intervention.

A good example of traditional presentation is provided by John Stuart Mill in his *Principles of Political Economy* (1848). 'In international, as in ordinary domestic interchanges, money is to commerce only what oil is to machinery, or railways to locomotion, a contrivance to diminish friction.' Mill imagines England and Germany to be the

* *Political Quarterly*, July–September 1952.

only two trading countries, the one exporting less cloth to the other than will pay for the linen which she imports. The excess will be paid for by a movement of money. 'The efflux of money from England, and its influx into Germany, will raise money prices in the latter country and lower them in the former... As soon as the price of cloth is lower in England than in Germany', and so on; England's exports go up, her imports go down, and the process continues until equilibrium is restored.

In modern times it is usually recognised that a good deal more needs to be said as to the nature of the mechanism. And when it is said, it is found that the mechanism is painful and its operations are slow. Professor Lionel Robbins might be regarded as an upholder of the old tradition. At the outset of his Stamp Memorial Lecture (1951) on 'The Balance of Payments',[1] Professor Robbins takes an imaginary case, but it becomes clear subsequently that a good deal of the weight of his argument rests on this imaginary case. It is a case in which there are no banks, no credit system, and the only money is metallic coinage, freely exchangeable between different countries at a fixed rate determined by the metal content. Then, claims Professor Robbins, there would 'be no question of monetary difficulties of the kind that we are investigating'. Such difficulties arise from the existence of separate credit and fiscal systems in different countries.

Assume that the treasury in one country is borrowing at a rate which permits an increase of local expenditure more rapid than the increase of expenditure abroad...Or, alternatively, assume that, if demand for the product of one of the countries falls off, then, for reasons of internal policy, the treasury there compels the central bank to take steps to replace, by a new creation of credit, the means of payment which otherwise would disappear. At once, in either of these cases, you have all the essentials of a modern balance of payments crisis. The seamless robe of a unitary monetary system is divided. Excess payments out involve no automatic reduction of spending power within. There is no presumption of any equilibrating mechanism. Equilibrium, if it occurs, is a matter of pure fluke.

Hence it is that Professor Robbins arrives at his battle-cry: 'When in surplus expand, when in deficit contract', intended to simulate the mechanism of an automatic monetary system.

If it was as simple as Professor Robbins' treatment of the subject seems to make it, the extraordinary thing would indeed be that the

[1] University of London Athlone Press.

lesson he teaches had not long ago been learnt. But is it so simple? Even in the illustrative case from which the argument starts of currency systems based on convertible metal coinage, is it really just the waving of a magic wand? Suppose that in such a case a country lost ground in export industries to competitors. Its exports no longer would pay for its imports and coins would leave the country to pay the deficit. And this would go on until prices had fallen sufficiently to restore the balance of trade. But why should prices fall? This is the crucial question, on which Mill and the other 'classical' economists throw no light. Nor does Professor Robbins, although he entirely bases the development of his argument on this simple case. 'There is always a level of internal prices and incomes at which the balance of payments would tend to equilibrium.' But how is it established? It is at this point that the distasteful concept of trade depression and unemployment as the instrument on which the restoration of equilibrium depends has to be brought into the argument. Keynes was the economist who first brought this issue to the surface but there are still many who prefer to keep it out of sight and out of mind. Even in the simple case which we are discussing no sense can be made of the argument without bringing into it this sordid and inhuman Keynesian mechanism. The slump in the exporting industries itself means depression and unemployment, not only in those industries but, by the usual process of diffusion of a drop in purchasing power, in other industries too. The unemployed now carry less coins in their pockets and depressed businesses require to keep less coins in their coffers and tills. The coins thus released are available to go abroad. At the same time trade depression means lower prices. And unemployment means a downward pressure on wages. It is, however, unlikely that this by itself will do the trick in time to dispense with the need for a further release of coins to pay for the external deficit. At this stage we have to ask ourselves where any further release of coins can come from? The answer is that rates of interest will go up, and generally credit will be tightened, and that as a result some of those who hitherto have been holding coins, not as a matter of convenience to conduct their daily transactions, but in the form of 'hoards', will be induced to give up part of these hoards and to become lenders instead. And lending will be made more attractive than it was to whatever extent is needed to secure the necessary substitution of lending for hoarding of coins, which has to match the fall in saving caused by the reduction in incomes, resulting from the slump in exports, and to supply the coins required to pay foreigners for the external deficit. This rise in interest rates and tightening of credit, which will be cumulative through time, will now reinforce the forces of trade depression by reducing the willingness and ability of business men to go in for capital development. Unemployment will grow until under its pressure wages, and with wages prices, begin to fall, so as to restore the country's competitive position, and unemployment will then persist for a time and eventually begin to dwindle, until the restoration is complete, so that, with foreign trade once again in balance, the level of employment is recovered.

So Professor Robbins' simple case has indeed much to teach us and the importance of the lesson is reinforced by his later admission that 'the rigidity downwards of the contract system is notorious'. It is only fair to Professor Robbins to say that he is thinking mainly, to quote from his concluding words, of 'the urgent necessity, by some means or other, of arresting the tendency to inflation which frustrates all our efforts towards recovery... Stop the inflation, stop it at all costs: that is the paramount need of the moment in the economic sphere.' Here Professor Robbins is on much safer ground. Inflationary conditions obviously aggravate, and may indeed cause, balance of payments difficulties. There is no need necessarily to think in terms of large-scale unemployment mercilessly forcing the trade unions into accepting heavy cuts in wages. It is more comforting to think in terms of an alleviation of the shortage of labour, moderating the competition for labour between employers (an important cause of the upward movement of wages) and curbing the pressure of trade unions to secure a further round of wage increases. But if this more modest, and less ruthless, process is what is in mind, it cannot do more than prevent the country's competitive position from getting worse, rather than positively improve it – unless an inflationary process of rising wages is being allowed to persist in competing countries.

The curbing of inflationary pressure does help also in a more positive sense. The lightening of the competing pressure from the home market releases goods for export which would otherwise be consumed or used at home and releases labour for additional production of goods for export. Such diversions are partly the result of, and partly at the expense of, the creation of 'slack' in the labour market, but the amount of additional unemployment might be small although the transfer of labour between jobs and of commodities between destinations was substantial. This, rather than the traditional effect on incomes and prices, is what is in many people's minds at the present time. (Indeed, Mr Roy Harrod, the leading advocate of the need to curtail capital development at home, so far from desiring a reduction of costs, still maintains, with steadfast consistency, that our troubles are largely due to the fact that we are selling our exports too cheap.) But the trouble is that much of the benefit of disinflationary measures goes to the consumer, who gains from the fall in prices and the greater availability of goods. This point is too often overlooked by those who advocate such measures as a means of extracting more exports out of an over-stimulated economy. Of the resources released from capital development only part will find their way into production of additional exports because part will contribute to additional consumption. This is true only so long as prices are abnormally high and shortages prevail. When inflationary pressure has been removed a further curtailment of capital development will mean a reduction of incomes and of consumption and the emergence of real unemployment, but by the same token exports are no longer seriously hampered by the pressure of home demand, and a good deal of the sacrifice, in terms of improvements in efficiency, involved in curtailing capital development will be represented by unnecessary unemployment rather than by additional exports.

In recent years the curbing of inflationary pressure has been the big issue. This a comfort to those who advocate a more drastic monetary policy. But they should not talk, as many of them are apt to talk, as though it is only as a result of inflationary pressure that a country can be in balance of payments difficulties. It is becoming rather a habit to draw golden pictures of a past in which economic forces were allowed to operate without interference and the word 'crisis' was unknown! Lord Cherwell was thinking of the 'comfortable certainties of the nineteenth century', when currencies did not fluctuate and there were no import 'quotas', in saying recently in the House of Lords of this 'brave new world' that 'it is the people who have to live in it who have to be brave rather than the world'. It is clear that to anybody who has never been unemployed it is hard to explain what unemployment feels like. But at least it should be remembered that a combination of balance of payments difficulties and large-scale unemployment has been a common feature in the country's history, the unemployment being largely due, directly and indirectly, to the loss of export markets which lay behind the balance of payments difficulties. And it is a feature which is likely soon to recur. What has Professor Robbins to say about the use of the monetary mechanism in such a situation? He admits that it 'is formally correct' to argue against 'the import of deflation and mass unemployment', and that 'in certain circumstances the danger which it indicates might be a real one'. But he then rides away from the argument by complaining that 'it is characteristic of the poor thought of our day that it has had most influence at a time when it was supremely irrelevant'. May be, yes. But what of the future? Professor Robbins is non-committal, being clearly torn between, on the one hand, his faith in 'all the delicate mechanism of financial control which the experience of ages was gradually fashioning' and, on the other hand, his natural dislike of anything which would add to the volume of unemployment: possibly an adjustment of the exchange rate would be called for, but this 'does not enable us to avoid some upward movements in interest rates and some over-balancing the budget, if external conditions become adverse'.

Professor Robbins had already admitted that there may sometimes be a case, as after the war, for emergency measures. He has 'no desire to adopt a doctrinaire attitude to the quantitative control of imports'. But 'in the long run there is nothing desirable that they can do which cannot be done by less clumsy methods', though 'at the present time ...there is a strong case for direct action on imports, while financial policy gets into action'. One wonders whether Professor Robbins has asked himself what the volume of our imports would be if quantitative control of imports ceased. If abandonment of import control is his objective he is certainly asking a great deal of financial policy and one would like to be clearer what level of wages and prices he is aiming at, how much temporary unemployment would be needed to get down to it in a measurable period of time, and to what extent permanent unemployment would be necessary to keep down the demand for imports in the absence of import controls.

This is not intended to be a review of Professor Robbins' lecture. If it were there would be a good deal to be said about the wisdom interwoven in it and the felicity and wit of its presentation. But before we part company from it, appreciative attention should at least be drawn to Professor Robbins' legitimate weariness with the threadbare catalogue, drawn up on 'every schoolboy knows' lines, of the reasons why ever since the war we have been constantly getting into a mess and to his legitimate mockery over the fact that 'it is sometimes a little difficult to conceive any circumstances in which, in present moods, we could be expected to prosper. American prices fall a few points; and we are compelled to devalue thirty per cent. American prices rise and we are again in the utmost embarrassment'.

To turn now to practical men there is one banker who shares a beautiful faith in the magic of the monetary wand. Lord Balfour of Burleigh, the Chairman of Lloyds Bank, in his statement to their annual general meeting felt no need to go into the nature of the mechanism:

If people have...been spending too much, it is because they have had too much money, in relation to the goods available. And this in turn, means – since balances held on current account or deposit account with the banks are by far the most important form of spending power in a developed community – that bank deposits have been excessive...What we have needed has been an actual reduction in the volume of deposits...When costs and prices are rising fast it is impossible, with the best will in the world, to prevent an expansion in the money total of advances if legitimate trade is not to be hampered.

The view that the aims of monetary policy can be achieved without hampering legitimate trade is not, however, widely held. It is commonly recognised nowadays that somebody has got 'to get hurt' (to use the phrase of the *Economist* newspaper, which has been consistently arguing in favour of 'a progressive toughening of monetary policy'). But even among Lord Balfour's bank-chairman colleagues there is a marked diversity of view as to who it is who will, or should, get hurt. Mr Harold Bibby (at the annual meeting of Martins Bank) talked of 'some re-orientation of trade': 'the home consumption trades will suffer most and no doubt the hire purchase business...will be among these'. On the other hand, Sir Thomas Barlow (District Bank) said that if 'monetary measures and taxation...should imply an undue restriction of domestic consumption, there is less solid ground for believing such action would be beneficial either to the country or to essential industries'; for 'it is excessively difficult to maintain and develop an export trade in many types of goods – particularly those of high quality – unless there is an adequate home market to provide ample opportunity for research and an outlet for

experimental work'. Sir Thomas Barlow's hopes are centred, therefore, on 'the elimination of unnecessary spending by Government
departments and the curtailment of unproductive capital outlay not
only by the Government but by local authorities and the nationalised
industries'. The Earl of Selborne (National Provincial Bank) referred
favourably to control of bank credit and capital investment but went
on to complain about the effect of heavy taxation in preventing 'the
formation of capital and the replacement of machinery', which it is
usually agreed it is the main purpose of dear money to achieve – an
inconsistency of which many others are equally guilty. Lord Alden-
ham (Westminster Bank) was more cautious and in welcoming 'the
return to a flexible bank rate' said that 'there can be little doubt that
an important part of the influence of a change in the bank rate was
always psychological'.

Scepticism about the virtues of leaving the economic system to be
governed by blind economic forces is evidently not confined to the
Government's critics. The present Government themselves are not
by any means relying entirely on dear money but are continuing, and
in many respects tightening, the system of controls which they
inherited. Even the monetary weapon itself is being wielded with a
more elaborate display of interventionism than is congenial to the
natural supporters of a restrictive monetary policy: highly detailed
instructions are given to the Capital Issues Committee and are
recommended to the banks, who are asked in addition to pay special
attention to the needs of agriculture, to reduce by 10 per cent their
advances to hire-purchase concerns, etc., etc. But to the extent that
the Government do believe in the magic of the monetary wand their
attention to other methods of control and stimulus is bound to waver.

It would, however, be untrue and unjust to suggest that the
Chancellor of the Exchequer, so far as he himself is concerned, is an
advocate of the traditional monetary policy. In his mind unemployment, particularly in the consumer-goods industries, is something to
be feared and avoided rather than welcomed. In the course of the
debate on the Budget Mr Gaitskell, dealing with the purchase-tax on
textiles, enquired whether the Chancellor of the Exchequer thought
'that the level of unemployment in Lancashire and other areas is only
just what he wants to secure the turnover to defence'. The Chancellor's interjection that he considered this 'to be an insulting question'
led to his being criticised by the *Economist* on the grounds that 'he

certainly ought to have thought about it'. The *Economist* has been consistently taking the line that the credit screw should be 'allowed to press upon the industries that are, or will be, in a position to release labour for more essential work'. The monetary weapon 'will have to cut consumption as well'. 'This is the ultimate question in economic policy. But Mr Butler's concern about the industries now coming under fire does not suggest that monetary policy will be allowed to answer it.' A week earlier (on the Budget statement itself) the *Economist* commented: 'the diversion of manpower was not so much as mentioned'. A week later: disinflation 'is not a perfect policy, but the Conservatives have no other; to draw back from it at the first signs of unemployment would be to have no policy for solvency at all'. In the same article the *Economist* admitted that 'if the Government reduces home demand, the things people give up first are not – in general – the things that can be exported'. The *Economist* makes this admission in advocating a more drastic use of monetary policy, so that the reduction in capital development does more than offset the cuts imposed on imports, but results in a reduction in incomes, and to some extent employment, and in consumption. Mr Roy Harrod makes the same point as part of his argument why capital development should be restricted *rather than* consumption: a large part of the consumer's 'marginal consumption goes on services of various kinds, including those of distribution'.[1] From whichever angle one looks at it, this line of thought makes pretty good nonsense of the traditional reliance on the monetary mechanism. If we follow the lead of the *Economist* we are going to get patches of useless unemployment and to forgo unnecessarily production which could have contributed to consumption; if we follow Mr Harrod's lead we are going to place an undesirably large part of the burden of adjustment on industrial capital development, on which technical progress so much depends. The economic system is a sticky and patchy affair – very far from the ideal world of perfect mobility and foresight beloved of theoretical economists. If waste is to be avoided and efficiency defended, the operation of blind economic forces has to be tempered by intervention which is discriminatory in character, in the sense in which monetary policy is not, but a discriminatory purchase tax, allocations of output backed by steel allocation, and building licencing are, particularly if they are combined with a real readiness to influence the movement of

[1] *District Bank Review*, March 1952, p. 14.

labour from one job to another by making full use of the Notification of Vacancies Order (introduced by the present Government in the place of the old Control of Engagements Order, which was abandoned by the Labour Government). There is every justification for curtailing consumption. But there is no point in curtailing it needlessly. The object should be to release labour at points at which it can effectively be reabsorbed in useful production.

All this the Chancellor of the Exchequer would presumably admit (though he may at the moment welcome the threat of slightly more drastic consequences as an argument to support his belated appeal for restraint to the trade unions). He bases the use of the monetary weapon on the shortage of steel. He has, in view of conditions in world markets, abandoned Mr Gaitskell's idea of relying on the consumer-goods industries for the maintenance of our exports. Indeed, he has to face the prospect of a decline in exports of consumer goods. It is the products of the engineering industry for which the export outlook is still reasonably hopeful. In winding up the debate on the Budget the Chancellor said:

I am taking the steps I am taking, including the monetary steps, in order that we can push some of the products of engineering into exports. . . The consumer industries cannot export to outside countries as much as we would like them to do. No one wants to cut home investment if it can possibly be avoided. It would be much better to get more exports by increasing plant and machinery, but, having regard to the supplies of steel which are likely, we could not avoid the investment cuts.

A policy of dear money which is derived from a scarcity of steel is a very different thing from the dear money policy which is welcomed by admirers of the old order of things. The question is what will happen to the policy if, as seems likely, additional supplies of steel soon become available, partly from domestic and partly from overseas (particularly American) sources. Will the Government cease then to emphasise their faith in monetary policy and tackle seriously the job of manning up the engineering industry, taking full advantage of the unemployment already existing in the textile and clothing industries and aiming at further releases of labour from other industries and trades at the points best suited for securing a smooth transfer? Or will the Government by that time be deeply committed to the efficacy of monetary policy so that, forgetting the Chancellor's original line of thought, they ignore the possibilities of increasing the size of the engineering industry (and incidentally evade the difficulties involved in doing so), perhaps arguing that we cannot afford to spend foreign exchange on additional steel? If, as is possible, part of the balance of payments deficit proves to be stubborn, the Chancellor's critics will try to press home their contention that the fault lies in a namby-pamby use of the monetary mechanism, and in desperation the Government may give way. On the whole this seems unlikely. A failure on the part of the balance of payments deficit to disappear will probably be the result of a decline in exports, and this will almost certainly mean a further growth in unemployment, to which the Government will be most unwilling to contribute by a more drastic application of monetary policy.

It is also conceivable that the importance, from any long-run point of view, of promoting industrial efficiency by encouraging, rather than restricting, capital development will also by that time be fully apparent. The natural victim of dear money is house-building, other forms of building, and expansion of public utility services – all of them representing highly durable kinds of investment, and therefore fairly sensitive to changes in the rate of interest, and comprising a high proportion of the country's total investment. But the Government want house-building to expand rather than contract; building generally is looked after by a severe system of building licensing; and public utilities by *ad hoc* decisions. It is in the relatively small field of plant and machinery that the monetary mechanism is relied upon to operate. So far as it is a matter of rates of interest it will need a heavy increase to produce much effect – sufficiently heavy to add substantially to the interest charge on the national debt. But here is another bewildering aspect of this whole question of monetary policy? Is it supposed to operate through higher rates of interest? If so, why is the rate of interest on long-term Government securities not much higher than it was before the announcement, in the Budget statement, of the rise in Bank Rate from $2\frac{1}{2}$ to 4 per cent? Or was Mr Oliver Lyttelton right when he told the House of Commons that 'of course, it is true that in planning extensions to an industrial plant, or, indeed, in planning any new enterprise, the mere rise in interest rates from $2\frac{1}{2}$ per cent to 4 per cent will not by itself deter the industrialist from putting up new buildings or buying plant and machinery'. Should we take the view, as many do, that the effect of credit restriction is secured mainly through a limitation on the expansion, and perhaps later an actual contraction, of bank advances? And if so, is the main effect, as is sometimes stated, the purely temporary one of a liquidation of surplus stocks of finished goods? And what happens to the argument that credit restriction naturally prunes out the least urgent projects if everything then depends on whether the particular concern happens to have used up all its liquid resources and is too small to raise additional capital on the market? And that leads to the final question – is the effect of credit restriction secured largely by causing the state of congestion on the new issue market which prevails at the present time?

Different experts will give different answers to these various questions, and some – also no doubt expert – will dismiss them all and assert that it is almost entirely a matter of psychology. There is as wide a dispersion of view about the practical mechanism of monetary policy as there is about its theoretical basis and about its objectives. That alone is a sufficient reason for examining with caution some of the claims advanced for it.

4

SOME NOTES ON LIQUIDITY
PREFERENCE*

'To say that the rate of interest on perfectly safe securities is determined by nothing else but uncertainty of future interest rates seems
to leave interest hanging by its own bootstraps.'[1] In this famous
passage Professor Hicks expressed his dislike of bootstraps. He sought
to find a line of escape, based on explaining long-term rates of interest
'in terms of speculation on the future course of the short rate,'[2]
rather than of the long-term rate itself. The same line of escape has
been explored by Mr Kalecki,[3] Mr Kaldor,[4] and others. Mr Harrod is
'inclined to think that this account of interest hanging by its own
bootstraps is an exaggeration'.[5] In following Mr Harrod's lead against
the Hicks school, I find myself in well-assorted company, that of Sir
Dennis Robertson[6] and Mrs Robinson.[7] (Sir Dennis Robertson, while
rejecting this particular line of escape from the bootstraps view, does
feel that 'liquidity preference, if the phrase must be kept, needs
emancipation from the prison of the "speculative motive", where it
was set to work to grind out a "boot-strap" argument the objections
to which have never been met'.[8] The part of the speculative motive

* *Manchester School*, September 1954, Based on portions of two lectures I
delivered in the University of Manchester.
[1] J. R. Hicks, *Value and Capital* (1946), p. 164.   [2] *Ibid.*, p. 166.
[3] *Studies in Economic Dynamics* (1943), essay 2, and *Theory of Economic
Dynamics* (1954), Chapter 7.
[4] N. Kaldor, 'Speculation and Economic Stability', *Review of Economic
Studies*, vol. VII, no. 1, October 1939.
[5] R. F. Harrod, *Towards a Dynamic Economics* (1948), p. 66.
[6] D. H. Robertson, 'Some Notes on the Theory of Interest', *Money, Trade,
and Economic Growth* (published in honour of J. H. Williams) (1951),
pp. 206–8. [*Utility and All That* (1951), pp. 111–14.] Sir Dennis Robertson
concerns himself with Mr Kaldor's formulation rather than with that of
other members of the school.
[7] Joan Robinson, 'The Rate of Interest', *The Rate of Interest and Other
Essays* (1952), pp. 8n and 18n.
[8] 'A Revolutionist's Handbook', *Quarterly Journal of Economics*, February
1950 (*Utility and All That*, p. 79).

will be discussed later in these Notes. At the moment I am concerned, in harmony with Sir Dennis Robertson, with an examination of the line of escape sought by the Hicks school.

In dealing with it, it will be convenient to suppose that all securities are either irredeemable *bonds* or short-term *bills*. A *person*, who owns wealth and holds it in the form of securities or of money, is to be thought of as either an individual or an institution. The *public* consists of all persons but excludes the banking system. And while we are about it we might note that a *bull* is a person who expects the prices of securities to rise, i.e., the rate of interest to fall, while a *bear* expects the prices of securities to fall, i.e. the rate of interest to rise. A person will therefore be described as bullish about the rate of interest if he expects it to *fall*, bearish if he expects it to *rise*.

If a person is indifferent between bonds and bills, then, apart from considerations of risk, it must mean either that the two rates coincide and he expects the long-term rate to remain constant, or that the rate (measured as a proportional rate per annum) at which he expects the long-term rate of interest to be rising (i.e. the price of bonds to be falling) is equal to the excess of the long-term rate of interest (the rate on bonds, measured as a rate per annum) over the short-term rate of interest (the rate on bills, measured as a rate per annum) – or a similar proportion in terms of an expected fall in the long-term rate of interest if the short-term rate is higher than the long-term rate.

We can now proceed to what must be common ground, whether one is a member of the Hicks school of thought or not. If there is a unanimous view held with complete conviction by everybody as to how rates of interest are going to behave through time at all dates in the future, there must be a unique correlation between the expected time pattern of the long-term rate and that of the short-term rate, so that at every moment of time in the future the excess of the expected long-term rate over the expected short-term rate is equal to the expected rate of change of the long-term rate. In fact, complete unanimity, although a sufficient condition for this proposition, is not a necessary condition. What is required is not necessarily complete unanimity but the existence of a sufficient mass of like-minded persons, all holding the same views with complete conviction.[1] If this homogeneous mass of opinion is sufficiently large in terms of wealth, and if it is so placed in the hierarchy of varying views about the

[1] Cf. Hicks, *Value and Capital*, p. 170.

behaviour of rates of interest (in relation to the supply of bonds, on the one hand, and of bills, on the other hand, to be held by the public), that both some of the bonds and some of the bills must necessarily find a home within this homogeneous mass, then the proposition is correct. If, on the other hand, the position is such that this homogeneous mass hold *either* nothing but bills *or* nothing but bonds, *either* all the bonds *or* all the bills being held by members of the public who hold different views, then the proposition is not correct.

The important point is that it is no good if it is just one individual who thinks that he knows definitely what is going to happen. For if he also knows that others hold views different from his own and if he believes that they are certain to be proved wrong, he will expect to profit by their mistakes. He will therefore expect to be at some dates in the future in bonds and at other dates in bills, and only at rare moments to be indifferent between them. For such a person no relationship can be established between the prospective prices and changes in the prices of bonds and bills.

In any case, the relationship which holds good when there is unanimous conviction on the part of a large body of the public cannot be imbued with any causative significance. It is merely a statement of necessary consistency. But it would be wrong to argue that the members of the Hicks school go so far as to assume a unanimous state of completely confident belief. Different members of it present their views in different ways, and various complications are introduced to render the treatment more realistic. It seems to me, however, that the essence of the treatment is to examine the margin of indifference between bonds and bills. There is a particular person who happens at the moment to be indifferent whether he holds bonds or bills. The argument is that it therefore follows that his expectation of the time pattern of the short-term rate is actuarially equivalent to the actual long-term rate of interest.

The first point to notice is that the changes which have to be considered are calculated by their very nature to cause a shift in the identity of this marginal person who is indifferent between bonds and bills. What is at issue, for example, is the way in which banking policy influences the long-term rate of interest. If the banking system buys securities from the public it will almost certainly, except in a coincidental border-line case, affect the relationship between the quantity of bonds and the quantity of bills held by the public in such a way as to shift the margin between them. This is even more obviously the case if the banking system operates by altering the proportions in which it holds bonds and bills rather than the quantity of the two taken together. If the identity of the person who is marginal between bonds and bills alters, the relationship between the long-term and expected short-term rates depends on expectations different from those underlying the relationship in the original position. Nor, if risk is allowed for, is it a matter purely of expectations based on the best guess of the person concerned. Different individuals react to risk in different ways (widows and orphans prefer bonds, bankers prefer bills). Unless here again there is a very dense concentration on the margin, a shift in the margin will involve a change in the relevant expectations and a change in the nature of the relevant relationship between the expected behaviour prices of different securities as a result of the change in the character of the person on the margin.

So far I have been content to undermine the outer fortifications of the Hicks school. I now come to the major assault. It is most easily delivered by considering Mr Kalecki's formulation of the 'anti-bootstrap view': 'Imagine a person or enterprise considering how to invest its reserves. The security holder is likely to compare the results of holding various types of securities for a few years. Thus, in comparing the yields he takes into account the expected average discount rate over this period...and the present long-term rate of interest.'[1] But there is absolutely no reason why this person need take it for granted that if he decides at the moment on bills, he need renew the bills when they mature. He may have it in mind that when the bills mature he may decide to put the proceeds into bonds. All that he is concerned with is what will happen during the lifetime of the *bills*. He is therefore concerned with the probable behaviour of bond prices during the lifetime of the bills but not with anything beyond that span. The Hicks school seem to argue as though a decision to hold bills at the moment implied an indissoluble contract to remain in bills in perpetuity and as though a decision to hold bonds at the moment implied an indissoluble contract never to sell the bonds and switch into bills. If a person happens at the moment to be marginal between bonds and bills it does not mean that he would remain marginal if he was told that any decision in favour of one or the other would bind

[1] *Theory of Economic Dynamics*, p. 80.

75

him under such an indissoluble contract. Alternatively, it seems to be implicitly assumed under the Hicks theory that everybody who is to-day marginal between bonds and bills must, by the same token, expect to remain marginal for all time. Neither postulate has anything to recommend it. For example, it might happen that a particular individual, at a time when bonds yield a considerably higher rate of interest than bills, thinks that the price of bonds is going temporarily to fall even lower, and he will therefore be prepared for the moment to accept a low rate of interest on bills and to forgo the higher rate on bonds. It is perfectly true that if he believes that the bill rate is going permanently to remain low, it is extremely likely that he will believe that the bond rate will ultimately come down into line. (This will only not be so if he regards the greater part of the public as likely for all time to persist in taking the wrong view.) It does not, however, follow that he may not look forward to a period in the near future in which the discrepancy between the two rates of interest will actually become even wider. If I understand the Hicks view correctly it suggests that the only thing which could keep this person in bills is the prospect of the bill rate in the future rising above the present bond rate of interest, so as to secure that bills, despite the relatively low rate which they offer currently, will be as attractive as bonds.

It is reasonable to suppose, in a world in which different persons hold different views and none of them hold any views with complete conviction, that those who are to-day marginal between bonds and bills will expect that shortly somebody different will become marginal who at present entertains different expectations from their own. The point at issue is of great practical importance. It would seem to follow from the Hicks view that a change of monetary policy can affect the long-term rate of interest only by influencing the expectations of the public as to what the short-term rate is going to be at various dates in the future. It is true that normally a rise in short-term rates will cause the public to expect the persistence into the future of rather higher short-term rates than would otherwise have been the case. This will bring about – in a causative sense – an upward revision of expected long-term rates of interest, since the long-term rate of interest at every moment of time is known to be related to the short-term rate actually ruling at that time. This is not really a concession to Professor Hicks, as the causation is quite different from that envisaged by him, and it does not really amount to saying more than that the long-term rate of interest is influenced by expectations of banking policy. But even if we assume away all of such repercussions of expectations of the future behaviour of short-term rates of interest, we are still left with important – and indeed major – influences of current banking policy on the long-term rate of interest.

The simplest case to take is that in which the banking system simply buys bonds from the public. The result is a change in the position of the margin between bonds and bills – in the identity of the person who is indifferent between them. Since there is no change in the quantity of bills held by the public the position of the margin between bills and money is unchanged. (This is on the assumption that there is no appreciable margin between money and bonds: the removal of this assumption provides an interesting exercise but we leave it on one side.) There is no change therefore in the bill rate. The fall in the bond rate is such as to re-establish the relationship between the excess of the bond rate over the bill rate and the expectation on the margin of the rate of change in the bond rate. The fact that the person on the new margin is more bullish of bonds than was the person on the old margin means a fall in the bond rate so as to accord with this relationship. Allowance has to be made for the element of risk involved in predictions of the bond rate, differences between the two persons in the valuation of the risk, and differences in their attitudes towards risk. Of very great importance also is the effect of the change in the bond rate on expectations of what it is going to be – a factor which will be discussed below. The point here is that expectations about the bill rate come into the calculation only in so far as they influence expectations about the bond rate. If the bill rate does not itself fall there seems, in any case, no reason why the expected bill rate should be lower than it was, and this would mean that according to the Hicks point of view there is no reason why the bond rate itself should fall.

Or let us take a case in which the banking system adds to its portfolio exclusively in the form of bills. The bill rate is reduced and the bond rate falls too in accordance with the relationship between the difference between the two rates and the expected rate of change in the bond rate. (In this case there is no change in the position of the bond–bill margin if there is no appreciable margin between bonds and money.)

Or let us take the effect of a change in the composition rather than the size of the banking system's portfolio, bills being bought from the

77

public and bonds sold to them in their place. The result is a fall in the bill rate and a rise in the bond rate, and the determination of the magnitude of the changes can easily be worked out in terms of the various margins. If the Hicks school want in this case to explain a rise in the bond rate they must postulate that whilst the actual bill rate falls the expected bill rates rise. Their logical position is, however, that neither the bond rate nor the bill rate is altered. The fact that in the real world the two rates will be moved in opposite directions testifies that we live in a world of doubt and of disagreement and one in which different persons not only take different views and are influenced by different degrees of conviction, but are sensitive to risk in different ways. There is no factual basis for assuming that the relevant elasticity of substitution is infinite. Both blades of Marshall's pair of scissors must be allowed freedom of movement – a change in the position of the margin, and of the identity of the person situated on it, carries with it a significant change in' all the relevant expectations and dispositions.

As I have indicated, the whole point is that a decision to go long rather than short, or *vice versa*, is not indissoluble. When a bill is bought rather than a bond the only relevant expectation determining the decision is what the bond rate will be when the bill matures. That expectation is certainly related to the expectation of what the bill rate will itself be at that same date. Furthermore, the expectation of what the bond rate will be when the bill matures is related in its turn to expectations of what the bond rate will be at more distant dates, and these in their turn are related to expectations of what the bill rates will be at those same dates. All this is, however, a very different thing from saying that the bond rate *depends* on expectations about the future of the bill rate itself, rather than of banking and monetary policy generally. Professor Hicks tries to reconcile the two different views, but only by appealing to the necessity for consistency between the two different sets of expectations,[1] which brings us back to an imaginary world of expectations held with unanimous and complete conviction. Much the same comment applies to Mr Kaldor's statement that 'the expected long-term rate...depends on the average of (expected) short rates'.[2]

[1] Hicks, *Value and Capital*, p. 152.
[2] N. Kaldor, 'Speculation and Economic Stability', p. 13n.

II

One object of this preliminary disquisition is to clear the way for the simplification of the subsequent treatment. It is a great convenience if one can conduct the discussion in terms only of a long-term rate of interest – of assets and securities which are perpetual in character and of money on which no interest is paid. I propose therefore to assume away the existence of short-term securities, or, indeed, of any securities which are not irredeemable. This simplifying assumption involves a serious departure from reality, but if what has been said so far is justified nothing fundamental is lost. Of course the short-term rate of interest will still remain lurking in the picture in a certain sense, in the guise of expectations about the behaviour of the long-term rate itself, but these are subjective and personal to each individual concerned and are obscured by risk and uncertainty.

The banishment of bills need not carry with it a continued exclusion of all means of holding wealth other than bonds. Not only can we accept the existence of different kinds of bonds and of preference shares, involving in different degrees the risks of enterprise, but we can also accept ordinary shares, and indeed physical assets themselves in so far as they are held directly by the owners of wealth and not through the intervention of securities. This means however that it is necessary to think in terms of a complex of rates of interest, each associated with a particular kind of risk of enterprise, and when reference is made, as a matter of shorthand, to *the* rate of interest, it is the complex which is intended to be indicated.

The admission of ordinary shares into the analysis raises two questions which, though they are very important, would take up too much space to deal with here. The one question (which applies with even more force to physical assets themselves) is in what sense an ordinary share can and should be regarded as though it was an irredeemable security with an unlimited life. The second question is what is the rate of interest on an ordinary share: obviously it is in some sense the expected yield reckoned at the market price of the share; but whose expectation is to be taken as the basis (this question applies also to physical assets held directly), and is it the expectation of dividends or of earnings, or of something between the two?

Leaving these difficult questions on one side, we see that 'the rate of interest', in a given state of expectation of profits, is the inverse of

79

the price level of securities. Now the total wealth of the community (together with its National Debt) is represented by the total amount of securities in existence and by physical assets held directly. Part of the securities are held by the banks themselves; part of the securities held by the public is financed by the banks; and banks finance the holding of physical assets by businesses, thus reducing the supply of securities. The extent to which the banks hold securities, finance the holders of securities, and finance the holding of physical assets, is equal to the quantity of money. The quantity of money is the means by which the public hold that part of their wealth which is looked after by the banking system. The prices of securities are such as to secure a home for all of them with the public, apart from what the banking system looks after itself. That is the essence of the Keynes liquidity preference theory of the rate of interest, the supply and demand for money being the obverse of the supply of securities in the hands of the public and the demand for securities by the public.

It is not intended in these Notes to discuss the various ways in which 'the real forces of productivity and thrift' exercise an influence on the rate of interest, but an important point about the Keynes theory is that these forces exercise their influence through their effect on liquidity preference and on the quantity of money. When the quantity of money is increased the consequent effect on the rate of interest partly depends on how much activity is increased as a result of the fall in the rate of interest, and how much wages and prices are raised. These repercussions – which involve the demand for money as a means of exchange – depend on the operation of 'the real forces'. The fall in the rate of interest sets up a complicated time pattern of 'real' reactions over an indefinite future period. The repercussions are the more important the longer the period of time allowed for their operation, and they are relatively the more important the smaller the elasticity of substitution between money and securities. (In the limiting case in which this elasticity is zero, the liquidity preference theory is compatible with any level of the rate of interest, which is therefore indeterminate except in so far as the real forces operate.)

To isolate the problems at issue, the elasticity of the demand for money will be examined in these Notes as it would be if there were no such repercussions on output, wages and prices, and so on the demand for money. It is possible that economy in the operation of the transactions motive (the use of active balances as part of the processes of exchange) may be practised as a result of a rise in the rate of interest. If this possibility is ignored the investigation boils down to a study of the precautionary and speculative motives, and of the interest-responsiveness inherent in their operation. The precautionary and speculative motives for holding money are what, by their operation, provide a home for that part of the total stock of money which is in excess of what is required to satisfy the needs of the active circulation, as determined by the facts of physical activity, wages and prices.

III

One of the difficulties is to distinguish between the precautionary and speculative motives. In practice the distinction is very blurred. But in principle the precautionary motive can be said to operate in so far as some persons think that the rate of interest is likely to move; the speculative motive in so far as some persons think that on balance it is likely to move one way rather than the other.

For the purposes of exposition, a person's expectations will be conceived in the form of a probability distribution and his 'best guess' is defined as his weighted average expectation.[1] The words 'risk', and 'uncertainty', are used in the conventional manner as indicating the degree of dispersion of the probability distribution, and the reliability of the probability distribution. The extent of conviction of a person's best guess then becomes a measure of the degree of absence of risk, and therefore of uncertainty as well.

The risk of movements of the rate of interest operates on behaviour in various ways. The operation can be examined by distinguishing between two extremes, though normally every person will be subject to the feeling of risk in a manner intermediate between the two extremes. At the one extreme is the feeling of *income risk*, at the other extreme the feeling of *capital risk*.[2] It is more picturesque than accurate

---

[1] The considerations advanced by Professor Shackle in *Expectations, Investment and Income* (1938) are ignored in these Notes. Professor Shackle is mainly concerned with the risks of business investment, which is essentially a 'once-and-for-all' operation, and the concept of a probability distribution is perhaps less unhappily applied to expectations about the movements of the prices of securities. (See also G. L. S. Shackle, 'The Nature of Interest Rates', *Oxford Economic Papers*, January 1949.)

[2] See R. G. Hawtrey, *Capital and Employment* (1937), pp. 216–19, and Joan Robinson, 'The Rate of Interest', p. 9.

to associate income risk particularly with widows and orphans, and while the feeling of capital risk is experienced particularly by financial institutions, it in fact applies very widely. Income risk operates *par excellence* in a situation in which there is no prospect of capital having ever to be realised. The possibility of having to realise capital generates a feeling of capital risk, which then exists side by side with the feeling of income risk. For each person it is a question not of whether he is subject to the one kind of risk or the other, but which is the stronger, the feeling of income risk meaning, taken by itself, that it is income which matters, and that the fear of some loss of income is not balanced by an actuarially equal prospect of gain, while the feeling of capital risk, taken by itself, means that it is capital which matters, and that the prospect of some loss of capital is not balanced by an actuarially equal prospect of a gain of capital.

In deciding how to distribute his wealth between securities and money each person will have in mind his best guess as to the behaviour of the rate of interest. Let us, for the sake of simplicity, ignore the expenses of dealing in securities. Then if a person's best guess is that the rate of interest is rising at a rate (per annum) which is greater than itself (measured as a rate per annum),[1] this means that if his best guess turns out to be justified he will by momentarily holding his wealth in money be losing less by forgoing income than he gains on the fall in the prices of securities. The speculative motive then tells bearishly in the direction of holding money. If his best guess is that the rate of interest is falling, or at least rising less rapidly than itself, the speculative motive tells bullishly in favour of holding securities. In the border-line case in which the person's best guess happens to be that the rate of interest is rising at a rate equal to itself the speculative motive will leave him indifferent between securities and money.

How far this person gives way to the operation of the speculative motive depends on the extent of his feeling of risk and uncertainty about the behaviour of the rate of interest. The greater the conviction with which he entertains his best guess the greater is the weight with which the speculative motive operates. In the limiting case in which

[1] This simple formulation turns on abstracting from the effect of taxation of incomes, or alternatively on assuming that capital gains and losses (whether realised or not) are brought fully into account before taxes are assessed. The formulation also assumes the American system of quoting the prices of bonds at all times *ex* all accrued interest.

his expectation is held with complete conviction the speculative motive operates on his behaviour in a completely unspeculative way – that at least is how it appears to him but of course his conviction may turn out in the outcome to have been wrong. A person who simply 'hasn't a clue' as to how the rate of interest is going to move – who thinks it equally likely that it will go up or go down – will have a slight speculative motive for holding securities rather than money, because the one offers income and the other does not.

Now let us consider how the precautionary motive operates and let us begin with a person who feels income risk rather than capital risk. Then if his best guess is that the rate of interest is falling, or rising less rapidly than itself, he will *a fortiori* put everything into securities – the precautionary motive reinforces the speculative motive. But now he will continue to hold all his wealth in the form of securities even though his best guess about the behaviour of the rate of interest is a bearish one provided that it is not sufficiently bearish to start conflicting with the precautionary motive to hold securities, i.e. the fear of income loss more than offsets a mild chance of capital loss. If his best guess as to the rate at which the rate of interest is rising is sufficiently bearish to start conflicting with the precautionary motive, dominated by the feeling of income risk, he will hold part of his wealth in money, but despite his bearishness the precautionary motive will continue to keep him partly in securities. The principle of increasing risk applies and a point of balance is reached between the operation of the speculative and of the precautionary motive: with a given degree of risk and uncertainty, the effectiveness of a given disposition to feel income risk increases with a growing proportion of wealth held in the form of money. Eventually, however, with a sufficient degree of bearishness, the speculative motive will completely prevail and nothing but money will be held.

In the case of a person who feels capital rather than income risk it works the other way round. The precautionary motive now works in the same direction as bearish sentiment, in the direction of holding money, and even if the person feels bullish, on the basis of his best guess, he will be entirely in money provided that the degree of bullishness is not sufficiently great to start conflicting with the precautionary motive, i.e. the fear of capital loss more than offsets a mild chance of capital gain. With a higher degree of bullishness he will be partly in money and partly in securities, and if the bullishness is sufficiently

83

great completely to outweigh the feeling of capital risk nothing but securities will be held.

The intensity with which the precautionary motive operates depends partly on the lack of conviction with which the best guess about the behaviour of the rate of interest is entertained and partly on the strength of the disposition to feel the particular kind of risk – income risk or capital risk as the case may be.

According to this presentation of the theory, a person whose best guess it happens to be that the rate of interest is rising at a rate equal to itself, so that the speculative motive is inoperative, will be entirely in securities if he is subject to a feeling of income risk and entirely in money if he is subject to a feeling of capital risk. In practice, however, both kinds of feelings of risk will, as has been indicated, operate in conjunction. Unless the disposition to feel the one kind very heavily outweighs the disposition to feel the other kind, the two will balance in such a way that both securities and money are held. The greater the proportion of money the greater the effectiveness of a given disposition to feel income risk and the smaller the effectiveness of a given disposition to feel capital risk; and *vice versa*. This again results from the principle of increasing risk, which applies separately to each kind of risk. A thoroughgoing widow-and-orphan will not hold money at all, except for the purpose of transactions, unless she is sufficiently bearish for her feeling of income risk to be at least partly overcome. But a widow-and-orphan who has a lively fear of appendicitis and a deep horror of the National Health Service will keep part of her wealth in the form of money even though she is not bearish at all – provided that she is not too bullish.

The upshot is that over a certain range of best guesses about the behaviour of the rate of interest, covering both bullishness and bearishness, securities and money will both be held simultaneously, more of one or more of the other being held respectively according to the degree of bullishness or bearishness, as the case may be, and according to the relative strengths of the disposition to feel income risk and capital risk. Furthermore, the greater the lack of conviction with which the best guess about the rate of interest is entertained, the greater the amount of money that will be held if the best guess is bullish and the greater the amount of securities if the best guess is bearish; in the former case money, and in the latter case securities, are held under the influence of the precautionary motive, playing against the speculative motive, in the former case the operation of the precautionary motive being dominated by the feeling of capital risk and in the latter case by that of income risk.

If this treatment demonstrates anything it demonstrates how impossible it is to identify the quantity of money held on account of the speculative motive as something different from the quantity of money held on account of the precautionary motive. The two motives do not act additively: the demand for money is a complicated outcome of their interplay.

The importance of all this lies in its implications for the elasticity of the liquidity preference curve, and in particular the interest-responsiveness of the amount of money held on account of the operation of these two motives. The thesis which I want to advance is that it is to the speculative motive that we must look as the source of interest-responsiveness and not at all to the precautionary motive. To demonstrate this, it is necessary to take the case in which the precautionary motive operates in isolation. This is the case of a person whose best guess it happens to be that the rate of interest is rising at a rate equal to itself (our sophisticated substitute for the person who 'hasn't a clue'). Let us suppose that, as a result of the inter-play between the feelings of capital risk and of income risk, he holds some money as well as some securities. Now we have to suppose that the rate of interest is lowered and, in order to exclude the operation of the speculative motive, we have to imagine that with the lowering of the rate of interest goes a change in the person's expectations such that he now expects the rate of interest to rise at a rate equal to the new (lower) rate of interest. The question is what happens to the quantity of money held. On the one hand, the yield offered by securities, and forgone by holding money, is reduced. But, on the other hand, the rate of fall in security prices, expected on the basis of the best guess, is reduced equally. It follows that the position of the margin on which income risk and capital risk balance is left unaltered. The amount of money held is completely unresponsive to a change in the rate of interest so long as it is only the precautionary, and not the speculative, motive which operates. We eliminated the speculative motive by postulating in effect that when the *actual* rate of interest is lowered the *expected* rate of interest is lowered in an even greater proportion, so as to keep the expected rate of rise of the rate of interest equal to the rate itself. (If, as in fact is almost certain to happen, the expected rate of interest falls less than this – e.g., if it falls only in the same proportion as the actual rate, so that the expected rate of rise is left unaltered, and *a fortiori* if the expected rate falls even less than this, or not at all – the speculative motive comes into operation, and the amount of money held increases. This is discussed below.)

It is then to the speculative motive that we have to look if we believe in some degree of interest-responsiveness – if we believe that, even apart from the operation of the real forces, a small change in the quantity of bank credit does not cause violent changes in the rate of interest. This contention, if it is valid, goes even further than Professor Fellner's statement that 'if the liquidity provisions of the public and of the commercial banks are mainly of the contingency variety [as opposed to speculative], the elasticity of the L function is not likely to be high'.[1] It is in one sense in line with Keynes' contrast between the amount of cash 'held to satisfy the transactions and precautionary-motives', M_1, which 'mainly depends on the level of income', and 'the amount held to satisfy the speculative motive', M_2, which 'mainly depends on the relation between the current rate of interest and the state of expectation'.[2] But I am suggesting a distinction between the precautionary and speculative motives which deviates from Keynes' and, according to my treatment, it is not possible to say how much of the total quantity of money is held on account of the one motive and how much on account of the other. Sir Dennis Robertson criticises Keynes for failing to link up 'the rate of interest with what Mr Keynes, including it somewhat paradoxically under the heading of "active" money, calls the money held for "precautionary" purposes' and says that 'in this respect the older Cambridge theory is kinder to "liquidity preference" than is Mr Keynes himself'.[3] I am in the sad position of wanting to frustrate Sir Dennis Robertson's effort to find a firmer basis for the liquidity preference theory than he feels the speculative motive provides.

To say that the precautionary motive operates in a manner which is completely inelastic to the rate of interest is not to say that it plays

---

[1] W. Fellner, *Monetary Policies and Full Employment* (1946), p. 182.

[2] Keynes, *General Theory of Employment, Interest and Money* (1936), p. 199.

[3] D. H. Robertson, 'Mr Keynes and the Rate of Interest', *Essays in Monetary Theory* (1940), p. 25. See also H. G. Johnson, 'Some Cambridge Controversies in Monetary Theory', *Review of Economic Studies*, no. 49 (1951–2), p. 102, and Sir Dennis Robertson's reply, 'Comments on Mr. Johnson's Notes', *ibid.*, p. 109.

no part in the monetary determination of the rate of interest, any more than the same would be true of the transactions motive. Given the total quantity of money, both determine how the speculative motive has to operate in order to ensure that there is a demand for all the money in existence. But we have to look to the speculative motive for the interest-responsiveness – the elasticity of substitution – which is the necessary basis for any determinateness in the monetary determination of the rate of interest.

Nevertheless the precautionary motive has an important part to play. Let us assume henceforth that the situation is such that the precautionary motive would, if it operated in isolation (i.e. if the best guess of the person or persons concerned was that the rate of interest was rising at a rate equal to itself), result in money being held as well as securities. In other words, we assume henceforth that the disposition to feel income risk does not for anybody completely outweigh the disposition to feel capital risk but that it is a matter of a balance between the two. Then what the precautionary motive does is to give the speculative motive something to bite on. The speculative motive, if prompted by a bearish best guess, causes an increase in the amount of money held. While if it is prompted by a bullish best guess, it causes the amount of money held to be so much the less, but *some* money will still be held unless either the degree of bullishness inherent in the best guess is great or this best guess is entertained with great conviction. Two important considerations emerge.

The first becomes clear if we visualise an economy in which each person estimates the behaviour of the rate of interest with complete conviction. There is no risk or uncertainty (though unless everybody thinks alike most persons are bound to turn out to be wrong) and there is therefore no precautionary motive. Each person holds all his wealth *either* in the form of securities *or* in the form of money, unless he happens to be marginal between the two (because he happens to believe that the rate of interest is rising at a rate equal to itself). If everybody is alike in his views about the behaviour of the rate of interest,[1] the demand for money is infinitely elastic: a change in the quantity of money has no effect on the rate of interest. A finite elasticity

[1] A *sufficient* condition for what follows. The *necessary* condition is a high concentration, measured in terms of wealth, in the neighbourhood of the margin, of persons with identical views: idiosyncratics can be ignored if their idiosyncrasies are based on complete conviction.

is associated with heterogeneity of opinion, and the elasticity is smaller the greater is the degree of heterogeneity.[1] The analysis is conveniently conducted in terms of Keynes' 'two views'.

Risk, and uncertainty, attaching to the behaviour of the rate of interest, by bringing into play the precautionary motive, create intensive margins, one to be imagined inside the mind of each person concerned, which operate alongside the extensive margin. Lack of conviction on the part of individuals has the same effect on the shape of the liquidity preference curve as heterogeneity among them. The elasticity of demand for money is a function of both.[2] It is as though 'two views' operated inside each person's mind, one being responsible for his holding securities and one for his holding money.

The other consideration emerging from our treatment of the precautionary motive is related to a difficulty of exposition of the Keynes theory if one tries to present it in terms of complete conviction. The difficulty is that once a person is a bull, so that in any case he holds all his wealth in the form of securities, it does not make the slightest difference to the rate of interest (given the quantity of money) how violent a bull he is, for he cannot do more for the price-level of securities than put all his wealth into them; and that he does anyway even if he is only a mild bull.[3] The same is true, on the other tack, of

---

[1] It depends on the extent of the change in views of the person on the margin when the position of the margin is shifted by a given amount measured in terms of wealth.

[2] The nature of the function is such that homogeneity and the elasticity of the curve exhibiting the principle of increasing risk supplement one another, the elasticity of the demand for money being greater than each of the magnitudes it would assume if only one of these factors contributed to it. It is a general proposition that diminishing returns which arise simultaneously on extensive and on intensive margins produce a net degree of diminishing returns which is less than either taken by itself.

[3] It is of course true that the more bullish he feels the more anxious he will be to hold securities on borrowed money. Such loans would obviously have to be short-term if they are to support his view that the long-term rate of interest is falling. They are excluded from our treatment by our arbitrary simplification, which perhaps here even more than anywhere else involves an unjustifiable deviation from the conditions of reality.

In allowing for bank advances we have been inconsistent – at any rate verbally. It is therefore worth noting that additional bank advances made to enable bulls to hold securities have no effect on the rate of interest if they involve an equal reduction in the banks' holdings of securities; and if they represent a net addition to the amount of bank credit the consequent fall in the rate of interest can be duly associated with the increase in the quantity of money.

bears who are completely convinced bears – the degree of their bearishness is then without significance. For these ideas to be applied to the community as a whole, an increase of bullishness or bearishness is to be interpreted – unless it is to be accompanied by a widening of the 'two views' – as not only increased bullishness, or bearishness, of those who were already bulls, or bears, but also as a conversion to the bull tack of some who were previously mild bears, or to the bear tack of some who were previously mild bulls. Increased bullishness, in this sense, will, however, have the effect of lowering the rate of interest only so long as there are still some bears to be converted to the bull tack. After the rate of interest is already so high that practically nobody believes that it is going any higher (at least not at a rate greater than itself), everybody is already a bull and increased bullishness of the community as a whole is, like increased bullishness of individual bulls, without effect on the rate of interest. This is the case in which the quantity of money is so low that it is fully looked after by the transactions motive, the speculative motive does not operate, and unless and until the monetary forces are moulded by the real forces the rate of interest can be anything.[1] A determinate monetary explanation of the rate of interest depends – in the case of complete conviction – not only on there being expectations about the rate of interest but also of the expectations taking the form, for an appreciable part of the community, of a belief that the rate of interest is going to be *higher* than it is. So long as an appreciable part of the community expect that the rate of interest is rising (at a rate greater than itself), the greater or lesser prevalence of the belief that it is going to fall can be deemed to show itself in the number of persons who, although by way of exception to the general attitude, take this bearish view, and is thus (if the quantity of money is an independent factor) instrumental in determining the actual rate. But in a situation in which nearly everybody expects the rate of interest to be falling, interest-responsiveness becomes very low – the rate of interest becomes unstable except in so far as the real forces mould the monetary forces in such

[1] Similar indeterminateness prevails when nearly everybody is a bear. But this situation – in which all members of the public hold all their wealth in the form of money – is reached only when the banking system holds or finances all the community's securities, and is therefore more unrealistic, even regarded as a tendency, than the opposite one, in which the banks' assets are no greater in magnitude than the active circulation.

a way as to impose constraints; – and the link between the expected rate and the actual rate becomes tenuous.

All this is altered if the behaviour of the rate of interest is subject to risk and uncertainty – if the bullish expectations are entertained with a lack of complete conviction – as will be the case, for example, if the rate of interest is, as a matter of experience, moving on a downward trend but is subject to unpredictable fluctuations about the trend.

Bullishness, expressed in terms of a best guess, can now manifest itself as a diminution from the money balances which the precautionary motive evokes. While asymmetry inevitably arises from the fact that money balances cannot be negative (except in the light of embellishments which are ruled out on a simple presentation), the operation of a precautionary motive for the speculative motive to bite on enables bullishness to exert a negative effect on the quantity of money held under the combined influence of the two motives acting together and this restricts the degree of asymmetry. A general view, subject to risk and uncertainty, about the future of the rate of interest can influence the current rate even though the view is that the rate of interest is likely to be lower than it now is. Monetary determination of the rate of interest does not, under these conditions, have to be completely abandoned. It is only when the point is reached at which bullishness is so great as completely to outweigh the lack of conviction that the conventional asymmetry, which in varying measure is present at all stages, becomes completely re-established.

IV

Sufficient has been said to demonstrate the unsuitability of thinking of a schedule of liquidity preference as though it could be represented by a well-defined curve or by a functional relationship expressed in mathematical terms or subject to econometric processes. Keynes himself often gave way to the temptation to picture the state of liquidity preference as a fairly stable relationship, despite his intuitional horror of undue formalism, but his treatment at least can be justified by the need at the time for a forceful and clear-cut exposition if it was to carry any weight at all.

The idea of an at all stable relationship is further undermined when we come now to enquire what underlies the interest-responsiveness inherent in the operation of the speculative motive. In discussing what happens to the amount of money demanded when the rate of interest alters, it is convenient to distinguish analytically between a minor influence and a major influence. The minor influence arises simply because a change in the rate of interest means a change in the degree of sacrifice involved in holding money rather than securities. The smaller is that sacrifice, the further will a given speculative incentive push the margin in the direction of holding money. But if that is the only factor at work, the resulting elasticity of the liquidity preference curve will be quite small. The monetary forces determining the rate of interest will leave the rate of interest rather unstable in response to changes in the quantity of money or, with a given quantity of money, to changes in economic activity, except in so far as they are rather drastically moulded by the real forces. Inasmuch as experience suggests a fairly high elasticity of the liquidity preference curve, quite apart from any influence of the real forces, this must come from the effect of a change in the rate of interest on the rate at which it is expected to change – in other words, on the actual degree of the speculative incentive itself. This depends on the magnitude of the effect of the change in the rate of interest on the expected rate. The smaller the extent to which a change in the actual rate causes a change in the expected rate, the bigger the effect on the expected rate of change and the greater the extent to which the major influence on the elasticity operates. If the expected rate moves fully in the same proportion as the actual rate, the expected rate of change does not alter and only the minor influence is at work.

An important question is the point of time in the future to which the relevant expectation about the rate of interest should be related. The exposition so far has been based on the idea that it is the instantaneous rate of change which matters. If costs of dealing in securities could be ignored, this would be the correct basis so long as expectations were regarded as held with complete conviction. While a person's immediate expectations will be related to his beliefs about the more distant future, the only thing which is directly relevant is what he expects the rate of interest to be at the next moment of time – say to-morrow. His behaviour is determined by what he expects to happen between to-day and to-morrow, and expectations about later dates do not become directly relevant until to-morrow, when behaviour is decided afresh in the light of to-morrow's expectations about the day after to-morrow. When the device of complete conviction is abandoned, as a move towards reality, the problem becomes much more complex – quite apart from complications due to the costs of dealing in securities. A person will have more conviction about his best guess as to to-morrow's rate of interest then about the rate likely to rule, say, six months hence. But the same absolute error in his estimate of the expected rate of interest will have about one hundred and eighty-two times as much effect on the estimate of the rate of change in the rate of interest if it is governed by the one-day view as if it is governed by the six-month view. The question of the relevant date does not lend itself to any definite answer, but it can be answered very roughly as the earliest date which is consistent with a rate of change the estimate of which can be relied upon without too much lack of conviction.

This is very relevant to the question of the degree of responsiveness of the expected rate of interest to a change in the actual rate. If nothing very definite is looming up in the future to provide a fulcrum on which expectations can rest, the present will exert a strong influence on the operative expectation. How strong that influence will be depends enormously on the period of time over which a particular rate of interest persists. As Keynes put it, 'public opinion can be fairly rapidly accustomed to a modest fall in the rate of interest and the conventional expectation of the future may be modified accordingly; thus preparing the way for a further movement – up to a point'.[1] One of the great difficulties about liquidity preference lies in trying to evaluate the manner in which and the extent to which expectations about the rate of interest are influenced by the actual rate itself and by its past behaviour. The difficulty is illustrated by the contrast between the passage just quoted from Keynes and his reference elsewhere to a 'psychological minimum',[2] or indeed his statement that the rate of interest 'may fluctuate for decades about a level which is chronically too high for full employment; – particularly if it is the prevailing opinion that the rate of interest is self-adjusting, so that the level established by convention is thought to be rooted in objective grounds.'[3] More recently Sir Dennis Robertson,[4] Mrs Robinson,[5] Mr Johnson[6], and others have discussed the question whether there is really any limit to which in the light of experience, given sufficient

[1] *General Theory*, p. 204.
[2] *Ibid.*, p. 306.　　　　　　　　　[3] *Ibid.*, p. 204.
[4] 'Mr Keynes and the Rate of Interest', p. 35.
[5] 'The Rate of Interest', p. 18.
[6] 'Some Cambridge Controversies', pp. 101–2.

time, views about the future of the rate of interest will not gradually crumble, provided that the experience is of an economy in which the dying embers of bearish sentiment are not from time to time rekindled by unexpected and sharp upward jolts to the rate of interest.

What it comes to is that the extent to which the speculative motive operates, and the degree of interest-responsiveness which results from this operation, depends on the circumstances of the particular situation, and, in general, is less the longer is the period of time allowed for adjustment.

V

Cases in which interest-responsiveness is zero are the cause of a good deal of perplexity. For example, Sir Dennis Robertson[1] complains that Keynes apparently contemplates 'that, even if "idle money" were zero, there would still be some (unexplained) way for total money to be increased and the rate of interest to fall, the growth of incomes following as a consequence'. Such a case is properly examined as a *limiting* case rather than as a quite separate type of case. As a matter of mechanism and of causation, the Keynes analysis is valid, though it does leave the rate of interest indeterminate except to the extent that the monetary forces at work are moulded by the real forces so as to impose the restraints with which the operation of the real forces is associated. But for the expansionist repercussions of a fall in the rate of interest, the slightest increase in the total quantity of money would drive the rate of interest down to zero, or lower. This is what Keynes tried to make clear.[2] Sir Dennis Robertson, on the other hand, prefers the 'common-sense' view that the expansion results from 'the banks performing the primary function of banking, i.e. lending money to people who want to make productive use of it'.[3] He makes a good case against Keynes for 'being so taken up with the fact that people sometimes acquire money in order to *hold* it that he had apparently all but entirely forgotten the more familiar fact that they often acquire it in order to *use* it';[4] while elsewhere Sir Dennis Robertson draws an amusing picture of Keynes' banking system of which 'the only function...and the only way in which it could add to the

[1] 'Mr Keynes and the Rate of Interest', p. 12.
[2] E.g. to mention a passage which Sir Dennis Robertson actually refers to, *General Theory*, p. 209.
[3] 'Mr Keynes and the Rate of Interest', p. 12.
[4] *Ibid.*

supply of money, was the buying of gilt-edged securities from College Bursars and other persons who thought their price would fall later on'.[1] Here is a real issue. The pedantic Keynesian answer would be that when a business borrows from its bank it is merely an alternative to its issuing securities to the public, and the result is therefore the same as it would be if it did issue securities to the public and simultaneously its bank bought an equal amount of securities from the public. It has, however, to be recalled that Keynes himself, already in his *Treatise on Money*, attached great importance to what he called the 'fringe of unsatisfied borrowers'. The result is a lack of uniqueness in the correlation between the quantity of bank credit and its price. In his *General Theory* Keynes took little or no account of this since it would have detracted from the simple elegance of the theory. But it is undoubtedly an important fact that very often a business which is deterred from an act of investment by the high rate of interest or the large sacrifice of profits which its present owners have to suffer by issuing securities in the market, would be prepared to pay the rate which its bank would charge for an advance, but is unable to obtain the advance simply because of inadequacy of the bank's reserves. This means that the rate of investment is not simply a function of the complex of market rates of interest and prospective yields on shares. The readiness with which the banks can make advances to customers has an influence quite apart from the actual rates of interest which are charged and which rule. And it means that so long as an expansion of bank credit was going on, investment would be somewhat higher than it would be under the influence of the same market rate of interest if they were established with a constant quantity of bank credit.

This is, however, no reason for going to the other extreme and assuming that no investment which is actually financed by a bank advance would take place if an advance were not forthcoming from the banks. The point at issue involves a complication, and perhaps an important complication, but not a fundamental change of theory. How important the complication is can be assessed only from a knowledge, which at present is inadequate, of the extent and nature of the imperfection of the capital market, and in particular of the peculiar kind of imperfection which is here involved. It is hard to believe that the

---

[1] 'Some Notes on the Theory of Interest', p. 202 (*Utility and All That*, p. 107).

theoretical basis for the modern approach to the theory of the rate of interest which is alternative to Keynes' stands or falls by the factual importance of this market imperfection.

VI

In any case the alternative approach does exert a strong fascination. Even some of the staunchest defenders of Keynes are not immune to it. I will conclude by giving two examples of what seems to me to be this kind of heresy.

My first one is taken from Mr H. G. Johnson's article on 'Some Cambridge Controversies in Monetary Theory'. Under discussion between Mr Johnson and Sir Dennis Robertson is the Keynes proposition that an increase in thrift will tend to lower the rate of interest because of its effect in causing a contraction of activity in incomes, thus leading to a reduction in the demand for money. This proposition Sir Dennis Robertson regards as 'misleading'.[1] Mr Johnson, mesmerized by the serpent (the reference here is to ideas and not to persons) which it is his aim to scotch, makes an admission which seems to me quite erroneous. According to Mr Johnson, the Keynes proposition 'implictly assumes that the increased saving is being performed in order to build up cash balances – i.e., it relies on a hidden increase in liquidity preference'.[2] The implication is that but for this 'hidden increase in liquidity preference' the rate of interest would fall anyhow, quite apart from any contraction of activity.

My other example is taken from Professor A. H. Hansen's most helpful *Guide to Keynes*. In his chapter on 'Classical, Loanable-funds, and Keynesian Interest Theories', Professor Hansen defends the neo-classical school against Keynes' assertion that it 'had made a muddle of its attempt to build a bridge'.[3] A discussion of the nature of Professor Hansen's defence would lie outside the field covered by these notes. But there is one incidental point made by Professor Hansen against the Keynes theory which is relevant in a discussion of liquidity preference. Professor Hansen denies, what Keynes asserted, that liquidity preference and the quantity of money between them tell us what the rate of interest will be. Professor Hansen's

---

[1] 'Comments on Mr Johnson's Notes', p. 105.
[2] 'Some Cambridge Controversies', p. 98.
[3] A. H. Hansen, *A Guide to Keynes* (1953), p. 152.

denial is based on the grounds that 'there is a liquidity preference curve for each income level. Until we know the income level, we cannot know what the rate of interest is.'[1] But from this allegation of circular reasoning, the Keynes theory can be rescued by applying the device of simultaneous equations, as is indeed inherent in the treatments by Professor Hicks and Professor Lerner, of which in fact Professor Hansen makes use in the same chapter. Professor Hansen bases his attack on Keynes' attack on the classical theory. As formulated by Professor Hansen, Keynes' objection to the classical theory reads as follows: 'No solution, however, is possible because the position of the saving schedule will vary with the level of real income. As income rises, the schedule will shift to the right. Thus we cannot know what the rate of interest will be unless we already know the income level. And we cannot know the income level without already knowing the rate of interest.'[2] This is not, however, a complete account of the Keynes objection. Keynes' point about the classical theory is that whatever may be the rate of interest and the volume of investment, the position of the savings curve (relating the amount saved to the rate of interest) must be such as to cut the investment curve at a point the ordinate of which is equal to the rate of interest which happens to prevail. The rate of interest if left to the classical mechanism cannot be rescued from indeterminacy by applying the theory of simultaneous equations. It is not merely that the position of the savings curve depends on the rate of interest, in the same kind of way in which the position of the liquidity preference curve depends on the rate of interest, but it depends on it precisely in such a way as to involve indeterminacy, as the position of the liquidity preference curve does not.

These may be regarded as relatively trivial issues. But until there is agreement as to the correct manner of using the tool of liquidity preference for dealing with the simpler kind of problem, clarification of the more difficult issues is not going to be easy.

[1] *Ibid.*, p. 148. [2] *Ibid.*, p. 140.

5

FULL EMPLOYMENT AND BRITISH
ECONOMIC POLICY*

In 1931, and again in 1932, unemployment in Great Britain averaged over 20 per cent of the insured population. The average was only slightly below 20 per cent in 1933. It had been 10 per cent throughout most of the twenties. The recovery in the later thirties, despite the assistance given by rearmament from 1937 onward, never brought the average appreciably below 10 per cent. It is true that on the basis of the present classification of unemployment these percentages would work out at somewhat lower figures. But the difference is not really significant. For they would still be vastly in excess of anything experienced in recent years.

The ratio of unemployment has since the war (apart from a few weeks during the fuel crisis of 1947) never exceeded 3 per cent. For most of the period it has been under 2 per cent; for over two years it has been under 1½ per cent; and it is now 1.1 per cent. As has been recently stated in a British Government pamphlet, 'very few people before the war believed it possible to have so low a percentage of unemployment as this'.[1] The late Lord Keynes himself, the great protagonist of the view that the disease of unemployment can be cured, did not believe in as sensational a cure as this. In 1944 Lord Beveridge published his book, *Full Employment in a Free Society*, which was inspired by Keynes' ideas. Lord Beveridge suggested that it should be possible to reduce unemployment to not more than 3 per cent. This was made up of 1 per cent for seasonal variations, 1 per cent to allow for the fact that in a progressive society there is bound in any period to be a need for some workers to change their jobs and one additional 1 per cent to cover fluctuations of international trade. Lord Beveridge's battle cry was 'more vacant jobs than unemployed men'.

* *Nihon Keizai Shimbun*, 1956.
[1] *Must full employment mean ever-rising prices?*, (1956), This is a popular version of the White Paper mentioned below.

We now know, in the light of the experience of the past few years, that if the unfulfilled demand for labour is intense over wide sectors of the economy unemployment may be as low as 1 per cent, despite the fact that all the time some workers are changing their jobs. Under these conditions a worker will usually secure his new job before he loses his old one and there is no intervening period of unemployment, while at the same time seasonal variations are also levelled down.

What is interesting is the reactions at the time to Lord Beveridge's 3 per cent. Keynes, in welcoming his book, wrote to him: 'No harm in aiming at three per cent unemployment, but I shall be surprised if we succeed.' One of Keynes' followers, in a book published in 1948, wrote that 'some 4 per cent unemployment may well be the technical minimum to allow for the necessary turnover of jobs in a dynamic society'.[1] And yet it is only last February, when the unemployment ratio was slightly over 1 per cent, that Mr Harold Macmillan, the Chancellor of the Exchequer, in the Conservative Government, said to the House of Commons, with reference to Lord Beveridge's 3 per cent that it 'may sound very little in statistics, but I feel that there are grave dangers in this form of presentation'. 'There is a great deal of talk', he had said earlier in his speech, 'about the need artificially to create unemployment. I for one will never be a party to that.'

This does not mean that employment policy was at any stage consciously altered. Over the past few years people have become gradually more ambitious as to what should be aimed at, and the actual figures of unemployment are as much a cause as an effect of a modification of policy. With the realisation in the light of experience of what was possible has come a downward revision of what is acceptable in the shape of unemployment. The launching in January 1951 of the defence programme, which now presses with such severity on the economy, has had a lot to do with it. Partly as a result of this, the average ratio of unemployment fell from $1\frac{1}{2}$ per cent in 1949 and in 1950 to 1.2 per cent in 1951. It rose to 2.1 per cent in 1952 and this led in April 1953 to a rather expansionist budget, introduced by Mr Butler, the previous Conservative Chancellor of the Exchequer, who was anxious 'to bring out the full production of which we are capable'. And unemployment has until quite recently been falling steadily ever since.

In the course of 1955 the ratio of unemployment fell as low as 1 per cent. This was attributable to a strong upsurge in the desire of busi-

[1] J. E. Meade, *Planning and the Price Mechanism* (1948).

ness men to invest in industrial buildings and equipment and in fact, despite the general shortage of productive resources, the volume of industrial investment has increased substantially. Associated with this improvement of physical investment from what was generally regarded as an unsatisfactory position and associated also with the high level of activity, there set in a deterioration in the balance of payments. It is the state of the balance of payments which provides the immediate explanation of the measures introduced, with increasing force since the beginning of 1955, to restrict investment – by several rises of bank rate, restrictions of bank credit, and, in particular, restriction of bank advances, together with a pronounced modification in the character and magnitude of certain fiscal incentives to carry out replacement and expansion of industrial buildings and equipment.

There have also been introduced measures aimed more directly at consumption – particularly of durable goods, especially motor cars and household goods made of steel (imports of steel have had to be increased to supplement domestic production). Purchase taxes have been increased and hire-purchase regulations tightened up. Indeed it is only in this section of the economy that there has been any marked and positive reduction of output and employment in consequence of the measures introduced by the Government. In the case of productive investment the measures – so far at any rate – have not resulted in any absolute decline. They have no doubt put a curb on the rate of expansion and – also very important – on the accumulation of unfilled orders.

It has been made consistently clear on behalf of the Government that there was no desire to reduce in any absolute sense either industrial investment or the general level of activity and employment if it could possibly be avoided. The concern of the Government is with the balance of payments. And to an increasing extent since the latter part of 1955, the concern of the Government has been with the persistent rise of money wages, and the consequent effect on prices. The unsatisfactory position of the actual balance of payments is attributable in part to the progressive rise of British wages (though only to the extent that money costs in Britain go up faster than in competing countries). What is more important is that the prospect of the persistence of such a rise of wages would mean serious damage for the balance of payments of the future; and in other ways too a price

7-2

level which is known to be persistently and strongly rising fails to provide a secure basis for economic prosperity and progress.

The question is whether a satisfactory behaviour of money wages is compatible with the very low ratios of unemployment which have recently been ruling. On this issue there is a divergence of opinion. The Government is relying on an appeal for restraint. Apart from a few industries in which wages are determined by tribunals enjoying statutory powers, wages in Britain are settled between individual trade unions and bodies of employers by purely voluntary processes of negotiation. In the event of a conflict or of the threat of a conflict, the Government may in various ways provide the services of conciliators or arbitrators, but even then the decisions reached are not compulsorily acceptable (though usually they are accepted). Nor is there, as there is in the Scandinavian countries (where all the wage negotiations are conducted simultaneously once each year – or, as in Denmark, each two years), any co-ordination of wage negotiations by the Trades Union Congress or the British Employer's Confederation or by any other means. In the recently published White Paper,[1] the Government points out that 'a strong demand for labour, and good opportunities to sell goods and services profitably', mean that 'it is open to employees to insist on large wage increases, and it is often possible for employers to grant them and pass on the cost to the consumer... This is the dilemma which confronts the country... We all want full employment and we all want stable prices. But we have not yet succeeded in combining the two. The experience of the past ten years has shown that the fuller employment is the more liable prices are to rise; but the Government does not believe that there is any inevitable conflict between the two objectives.'

The appeal for restraint over wage movements would be more successful if it were simply a question of the rates negotiated between trade unions and employers. But success depends to a considerable extent on the attitude of employers who, faced with a shortage of labour, are under an incentive to bid wages up well above the negotiated rates. This is part of the explanation for so much importance being attached to the number of unfilled vacancies as a factor contributing to the upward pressure on money wages. In fact the number of unfilled vacancies at the beginning of May 1956 was 380,000, com-

[1] *The Economic Implications of Full Employment*, Cmd. 9725, March 1956.

pared with 425,000 a year previously. Over the same period unemployment rose from 223,000 to 237,000, bringing the ratio up from 1 per cent to a bare 1.1 per cent. These figures, which relate to the country as a whole, fail to reflect the extent to which pressure has eased in certain sectors. For example, in the Midlands – an important centre of the engineering industries – the ratio of unemployment rose over the year from $\frac{1}{2}$ to 1 per cent, largely as a result of the decline in the demand for motor cars. And generally the pressure on the labour market has eased to a degree rather greater than is suggested by the figures.

The justification of the Government's measures of restriction can, however, be sought simply in the fact that however little the pressure has eased, it has not in fact increased. This is despite the persistent upward movement in physical investment in industry, which the Government is far from deploring – as long as it is kept within bounds and so long as the balance of payments improves (as it has begun to do) and the movement of wages and prices is kept in check. The present movement is held to be a critical one from these points of view. To assist the appeal for restraint on wage movements industrialists – including nationalised industries – are asked to show restraint about raising prices. The Chancellor of the Exchequer recently said in relation to wages and prices: 'We are on a kind of plateau of stability for a year at least. We can stay there if we choose.'

In the same speech he had referred to the 'state of full employment, which the Government were so thankful to have and determined to preserve'. The Government's appeals may prove unsuccessful. But at least this seems a better line to explore than the line explored, without success, in Denmark. Unlike Norway and Sweden, Denmark has consistently accepted a relatively high level of unemployment. (The annual average is raised by large seasonal fluctuations but these would certainly be less if labour were less abundant.) Like Britain, Denmark has been faced with an adverse balance of payments and as in Britain measures have been adopted to restrain investment and consumption. But in Denmark the measures have gone much further. The country's output has fallen. The ratio of unemployment at the end of April was $10\frac{1}{2}$ per cent compared with $6\frac{1}{2}$ per cent a year earlier. Nevertheless when it came to the two-yearly wage negotiations early in 1956 the trade unions put in ambitious demands (and also demanded a reduction in the length of the working week). An intense conflict was precipitated and this was brought to a somewhat bitter end only by Parliament giving statutory force to the award of a state mediator.

There is no suggestion in Britain of a wages 'freeze'. Indeed it is generally accepted that if the workers are to gain their proper share in the fruits of economic progress money wages should generally rise with productivity and that this should allow room for some flexibility in relative wages. Subject to that – which is important – it is argued that the best hope for progressively raising the standard of living of the workers lies in the use of the fiscal system and in acceleration of the growth of productivity. The fiscal system has already contributed a great deal to redistributing income and building up the social services, and it is only on that basis that trade unions can be expected to refrain from pressing home the advantages offered by a sellers' market for labour. The growth of productivity depends very largely on securing a high level of physical investment. That is why it seems so important to find a means of reconciling high rates of investment and employment with an acceptable behaviour of the money-wage level and to avoid being driven into a policy involving really effective restraints on investment designed perhaps to bring the ratios of unemployment closer to Lord Beveridge's obsolete 3 per cent.

6

LORD KEYNES AND CONTEMPORARY ECONOMIC PROBLEMS*

I. Inflation

I am not intending in these talks to try to guess what Keynes would be thinking or saying if he were alive today. But one thing does seem certain and that is he would have been very surprised by present-day unemployment figures. In 1944 in a letter to Lord Beveridge, whose book about *Full Employment in a Free Society* had just appeared, he remarked: 'No harm in aiming at three per cent unemployment, but I shall be surprised if we succeed'. Today we have an unemployment figure of about one per cent.

I do not want to suggest that Keynes would have been unfavourably surprised by the lengths to which full employment has been taken. He always believed that we can and should adjust our ideas to the pressure of experience. 'Is it vain', he asked in an article published in America in 1940,[1] 'to suppose that a democracy can be wise and sensible? Must the poison of popular politics make impotent every free community? So much hangs on the issue that it is our duty to believe that we can do what we should, until the opposite is proved'. But he warned his readers that 'the new and unfamiliar aspects of the social scene' would present some 'strenuous brain-twisters'. And, towards the end of the war, in a letter to Mr T. S. Eliot, Keynes wrote that the maintenance of full employment required that we should be 'not only good but clever...It may turn out, I suppose, that vested interests and personal selfishness may stand in the way. But the main task is producing first the intellectual conviction and then intellectually to devise the means'.

Once a high level of employment began to present itself as a real possibility, it became obvious that the behaviour of money wages was going to offer a major problem. Here, wrote Keynes, 'a communist

---

* Two radio talks on the B.B.C. reprinted in *The Listener*, 3 and 10 May 1956.
[1] *New Republic*, 29 July 1940.

country is in a position to be very successful. Some people argue that a capitalist country is doomed to failure because it will be found impossible in conditions of full employment to prevent a progressive increase of wages. According to this view severe slumps and recurrent periods of unemployment have been hitherto the only effective means of holding efficiency wages within a reasonably stable range. Whether this is so remains to be seen. The more conscious we are of this problem, the likelier shall we be to surmount it.'[1] And, again: 'It is one of the chief tasks ahead of our statesmanship to find a way to prevent' money wages from forever soaring upwards.[2]

The inflation which the Government is at present so much concerned about is made up of two related but distinct elements. One element lies in the fear – or the fact – of money wage rates rising too fast. The other element arises from the possibility that, apart from rising wages, we are in purely physical terms extracting too much from the economic system, or at least trying to extract too much – that the pressure of the various demands on our productive resources is too heavy, with the result that we are liable to do relatively too much of one thing and too little of another. At the moment the Government is expressing concern both about wage inflation and about excessive demand, and in discussion the two seem to get inextricably mixed. But the wage inflation has been going on fairly steadily, not only in periods, like the present one, when demand can be said to be excessive, but also in periods when there was actually more slack in the system than was felt to be desirable. For example, Mr Butler in his 1953 Budget was not deterred by the thought of rising wages and prices from giving the system some boosts. This, I feel, was fortunate, even though one wished that he had concentrated more on direct boosts to investment and had done less, by means of taxation reliefs to boost consumption. If three years ago the regulation of the economy had been conducted with an eye to the behaviour of wages rather than to the level of activity, it would have meant not only the persistence but the aggravation of economic waste – of unemployment as a means of checking wage increases. (Denmark today provides an impressive indication of the amount of unemployment required to act as a moderating – and not so very moderating at that – influence on wage

[1] *Economic Journal*, June–September 1943, p. 187.
[2] *Ibid*, December 1944, p. 430.

increases. Denmark's restrictive measures have in fact added considerably to her unemployment, but nevertheless it has been necessary to resort to statutory action to control wages and prices.)

People sometimes talk as though the behaviour of money wages depends on the readiness with which the banks are prepared to supply the necessary money. In fact, Keynes himself talked exactly like that in 1925. But as his ideas developed he conceived of the wage bargain in common-sense, hard-headed terms of trade-union officials and employers' representatives. Credit conditions affect the outcome in so far as they affect the profitability of business and the superabundance or scarcity of labour, but not in any other way. In the Keynesian system the money wage is the fulcrum on which the price structure rests. The behaviour of prices depends on that of money wages rather than the other way round. And a movement of money wages brings about a more or less proportionate movement of prices, after allowance is made for improvements in productivity. Keynes worked it out for conditions of economic depression. The outcome of wage bargaining affected the price level, but not real wages or employment, except very indirectly.

The same idea was used by Keynes when he tackled the problem of inflation presented by the war. In his pamphlet, *How to Pay for the War*, published in 1940, Keynes argued that 'a demand on the part of the trade unions for an increase in money wages to compensate for every increase in the cost of living is futile, and greatly to the disadvantage of the working class . . . In their minds and hearts the leaders of the trade unions know this as well as anyone else . . . But they dare not abate their demands until they know what alternative plan is offered. This is legitimate. No coherent plan has yet been put up to them.'

What is the case today for offering some coherent scheme of thought to the trade unions as opposed to just nagging at them in the hope that nagging will do more good than harm? Keynes believed in treating the public as responsible beings, individually and collectively. And he believed in presenting to them the essence of the problem in common-sense physical terms rather than in the form of mystical claptrap. What would this involve today? First, one would want to enquire into the motivation of individual wage claims. There is the question of the part played by competitive bidding between employers at a time of labour shortage. It is curious that no reference is made to this in the Government's recent White Paper on *The Economic Implications of*

Full Employment; in a similar White Paper issued in February 1948, the Labour Government of the time appealed to industrial employers not to bid wages up competitively above the levels determined by collective agreements. More important, under our system of wage bargaining there is the constant competitive struggle going on between trade unions to keep up with one another. If any one trade union lags behind the other, the real wages of its members are liable actually to fall as a result of the rise of prices caused by wage increases secured by other unions. In this sense it is a matter of resisting a fall in real wages rather than of pressing for a rise. And this seems to point to the need for some co-ordination of wage negotiations in different industries.

This brings us to the crucial point – the need to get the trade unions' representatives to consider the wage level as a whole and not in terms of the sectional interests of individual trade unions or workers. No serious person is going to ask for a wage freeze: if real wages are to rise at all with increasing productivity it is better to rely on a slow rise of money wages than on a fall of prices, which are usually sticky. The extremely awkward problem of relative wages and wage differentials is then less difficult to handle. But when all that has been said and done, it remains broadly true that the standard of living depends on the physical realities of the situation and not on the behaviour of money wages. By the physical realities I mean the quantity of consumer goods which it is physically possible and worth while to produce, and the total amount of employment, including all the employment on things other than consumer goods – things such as defence and investment. These two quantities – the quantities of consumer goods and total employment – have to be fitted to one another, due allowance being made for saving. The fit is secured by the real wage being established at the necessary level. The process is the pressure of demand on the supply of consumer goods. This determines the extent to which prices are held up above money wages – the ratio of one to the other, rather than the absolute level of either – and it also determines the level of profits, which in so far as devoted to consumption reduce the amount of consumer goods available to support the real wage. And, of course, fiscal policy, taxation and so on, also plays a fundamental part.

The approach by the Government to the trade union leaders which I am visualising would be based on the belief that a proper balance between imports and exports can and must be established. This I shall return to in my second talk. Obviously, also, it would be aimed at ensuring that once a balance had been established it would not be disturbed, at least for some time to come, through our wage costs going up faster than costs in other countries. The object of the approach should be to investigate how far there was common ground on the question of the right use to make of the country's productive power. The heavy burden of defence would perhaps have to be taken as given, or reserved for discussion on some other occasion, and it might be thought right to apply the same procedure to the burdens of housing, the social services, and such-like. It then becomes a matter of the right division of what is left between consumption and productive investment in extending and improving the equipment of industry. One would assume a continued growth of productivity; one would be dealing mainly with the destinations of the growth of production in the immediate future rather than holding a *post-mortem* on the use of productive power in the immediate past.

This kind of picture is familiar to us. Ever since Sir Kingsley Wood's Budget of April 1941, about eight months after Keynes entered the Treasury, the Chancellor of the Exchequer, in presenting his Budget proposals, has dealt not only with the financial resources of the Exchequer but also with the physical resources of the nation. Dr Hugh Dalton has told us that this 'new approach to budgetary policy owes more to Keynes than to any other one man'; he says that 'what he launched was one of the intellectual revolutions of our time'.[1] The Budget statement has been assisted by the annual statistical publication, which also first appeared in April 1941, again as a result of Keynes' initiative, and which has developed, thanks to the work of Keynes' collaborators and their successors in Whitehall, into our magnificent annual statements of 'National Income and Expenditure'.

The trade-union leaders will point out that a considerable amount of consumption is done by classes of the community other than their own. If their co-operation is to be secured it will be necessary to satisfy them that this is adequately recognised in the incidence of taxation. In particular, they will need to be satisfied about taxation of profits, and probably about measures to control monopoly profits, including perhaps price control of essential commodities.

[1] H. Dalton: *Principles of Public Finance*, 4th ed. (1954), p. 221.

Granted all that, it then does become a matter of a choice on behalf of wage-earners themselves between consumption and investment – between the interests of the immediate and of the more distant future. The bigger the restraints which are imposed on investment, the bigger the possible rise in the immediate standard of living. But it is a once-and-for-all rise. It will be secured at the expense of productive investment and therefore of the growth of productivity, and it will mean that at somewhat more distant dates the standard of living will rise less rapidly, and will in fact be lower, than the levels which it would have attained had the restraints on investment been less severe. Any agreement which could in this sort of way be arrived at as to the best balance between higher investment and higher consumption could easily be translated into terms of a suitable wages policy.

This may sound unpractical. But it seems to me to make better sense than the present arrangement, under which the Government is working in the dark. Its policy is influenced by the threat of rapidly rising money wages, but it does not know how far this threat implies a definite desire to sacrifice future improvements in the standard of living to the interests of the present. Not that this question of the right balance between consumption and investment lends itself to dogmatic assertion. In 1943 Keynes was discussing this point with Mr Josiah Wedgwood and wrote: 'It would be in the interests of the standard of life in the long run if we increased our capital quite materially. After twenty years of large-scale investment I should expect to have to change my mind.'

The statistical record of our productive investment in recent years is not in fact impressive. We are cruelly hampered by the heavy burden of defence, falling with particular weight on the metal industries, on which we have to call for so much of our investment as well as of our exports. But it is not only a question of having the physical resources available for investment. What is also necessary is the urge on the part of business men to expand and re-equip. So much depends on what Keynes, in his *General Theory*, called 'animal spirits – a spontaneous urge to action rather than inaction'. The business man is a sensitive animal. That is why it is so important at the present time to try to take advantage of the buoyancy of his spirits rather than to suppress them.

But to do so investment must be allowed to increase, and if this is to happen without additional inflationary pressure it means restraint on consumption. This is where taxation plays a vital part, taxation designed to build up a Budget surplus. Mr Macmillan is budgeting for a fine 'above the line' surplus – to the tune of about £450,000,000 a year. But this magnificent result is an inheritance, the automatic effect of prosperity on the yield of existing taxes. It was unthinkable that he could have given any substantial part of it away. Some of us feel that he should have added to this surplus by imposing yet more drastic taxes. But at least we can all agree that the decision to keep public saving going on this scale is a tribute to Keynes' teaching, even though Mr Macmillan describes 'public saving' as 'a hateful phrase'. The lapse of ten years has not dulled the edge of at least this tool in the Keynes apparatus of thought, about which the White Paper on *Full Employment* of May 1944 was half-hearted, suggesting, in typical civil-service jargon, that 'it might well become a matter for consideration whether in prosperous times rather more taxation should be raised than was necessary for the Budget requirements of the year'.

'Clearly the effect of high taxation in discouraging outlay should be tried before recourse is had to a high rate of interest', Keynes wrote in July 1939.[1] Even then, with the war clouds gathering, he thought it for the time being right 'not to discourage private enterprise...more than is necessary'. Today so much turns on increasing our productivity, and this calls for a high rate of investment. Credit restriction means restraint on investment – that is how it works.

This is the hard truth which Keynes first started preaching in his *Treatise* of 1930. Even today attempts are still made to escape from the harsh physical realities which Keynes emphasised back into the old-fashioned world of mumbo-jumbo, in which the economy yields to a few waves of the magic wand of credit. Such attempts to avoid the awkward implications of a policy of credit restriction and dear money usually involve recourse to some manifestation of what is called the quantity theory of money, the idea that inflation is the direct cause of expansion of credit rather than physically too much investment and consumption, no matter how brought about. The quantity theory supports the comfortable notion that restriction of credit is an end rather than merely a means and that it will do the trick without the necessity, which on the face of it seems paradoxical, for dealing with rising costs and foreign competition by restraining business men from extending and improving their productive equipment. The quantity

[1] *The Times*, 24 July 1939.

theory mentality is far less common today but the subject is one on which Keynes was involved in continual controversies. One of them was in 1940 with the editor of the *Financial News*, to whom, in a published letter, he offered the following advice: 'If you are not too old, as to which I have no information, I strongly recommend an operation. By modern methods an inflamed Quantity Theory can be removed with much less danger than formerly.'

Nowadays, the rational approach to these problems is the normal one and the magic wand has been largely discarded. As an example of the rational approach, I would quote Mr Macmillan's appeal, made in the House of Commons on February 17, to business men who are not directly hit by the credit squeeze to restrain their investment as though they were. That is a frank admission of what the need for a credit squeeze really entails and of its arbitrary incidence. Keynes taught the importance of being purposive in policy and action – of having a rational view of aim and purpose and method. To Keynes the credit instrument was just a means.

As the war approached he successfully persuaded the authorities to place their reliance on other means, more suited for the purposes of war, of directing and controlling the economy. As Mr Harrod puts it in his great *Life of Keynes*: 'He had indeed the right to claim that his theoretical work between the wars had revolutionised the modes of thinking of economists upon inflation. They had long ceased to regard inflation primarily as an over-issue of notes or even an over-expansion of bank credits.' It was the physical use of resources which mattered. Under Keynes' influence the rate of interest was actually lower in the war, and for a time after the war, than it had been before. In 1942 Keynes was able to claim, in a broadcast, that 'the Treasury is borrowing money at only half the rate of interest paid in the last war'.[1]

Another important benefit of the era of cheap money accrues to the occupiers of the houses built in the post-war years. And at the back of Keynes' mind was always the thought that it would need a low, and falling, rate of interest to stimulate the investment needed under normal peace-time conditions, after the ravages of war had been made good, to take full advantage of our productive powers. One of these days – we hope and pray – normal peace-time conditions may be realised. We should then be able to see how necessary it was to get the

---

[1] *The Listener*, 2 April 1942.

rate of interest down again. Keynes' fear always was that the fact that the rate of interest had been high would lead people to be afraid that it might in the more distant future become high again. Keynes argued that this would seriously interfere with the process of making money cheap at a time when cheap money was again needed as a stimulus. But we could scarcely expect Keynes to foresee that the burden of defence would weigh so heavily long after the war was over and that the problems would for the time being remain the problems of shortage rather than plenty.

In his preface to his *General Theory* of 1936, Keynes said that the composition of the book had been for him 'a long struggle of escape and so must the reading of it be for most readers if the author's assault upon them is to be successful – a struggle of escape from habitual modes of thought and expression'. He went on: 'The ideas which are there expressed so laboriously are extremely simple and should be obvious.' By now they seem so obvious that one has to be reminded what so much fuss was about. In the same preface, Keynes, referring to his fellow economists, said: 'Those who are strongly wedded to what I shall call the "classical theory" will fluctuate, I expect, between a belief that I am quite wrong and a belief that I am saying nothing new. It is for others to determine if either of these or the third alternative is right.' After the book appeared he aimed at a less professional public. His main vehicle was *The Times*. Just before the war he wrote yet another memorandum, aimed this time at the Chancellor of the Exchequer and the Governor of the Bank of England, as well as subsequently at readers of *The Times*. In a letter about this memorandum to Lord Brand, he said: 'It is difficult to make progress against the weight of tradition or to get people to consider the problem afresh in the light of modern conditions and modern thought.'

In a curious way it was the war, although its economic problems were so entirely different, which brought victory to Keynes in dealing with the traditional economic problem of peace – the problem of waste of resources. Keynes was singing a very different tune when he addressed the House of Lords in 1944 on the subject of the proposed International Monetary Fund: 'Sometimes almost alone, in popular articles, in the press, in pamphlets, in dozens of letters to *The Times*, in text-books, in enormous and obscure treatises, I have spent my strength to persuade my countrymen and the world at large to change their traditional doctrines and, by taking better thought, to remove the curse of unemployment.' And now, he said, he was speaking 'at the very moment of the triumph of these ideas'.[1]

Keynes' analytical framework, although aimed at the problem of unemployment in peace-time, did, in fact, provide the basis for his handling of the problems of shortage of resources in wartime. And it does in fact provide the basis for most of what is said – perhaps I may be excused for saying 'for most of the sensible things which are said' – about the problems of inflation in peace-time, though we have ceased to be conscious how much of the manner of present-day exposition we owe to Keynes. Perhaps the war lent itself more readily to Keynes' emphasis on an approach based on a common-sense appreciation of physical realities and to his horror of dogma and mystique, and perhaps that is partly why it was in the war that his ideas about the economics of peace-time gained so much ground.

Keynes himself was fond towards the end of his life of saying that one thing and only one thing was certain and that was that the problems which we should be faced with would be strange ones and not the familiar ones. I think that he was getting bored with his triumphs and, without the burden of defence particularly in mind, he wanted to give up feeling that it was going to be the same kind of thing over again. In *How to Pay for the War*, he had dealt with the problems of inflation by the use of measures some of which would be acceptable only under the pressure of war. He had no time to write any similar handbook directly applicable to our present problems. But the analytical framework is there. Different people may use it to arrive at different recommendations of policy – according to their judgement and feelings about the relative importance of the present and the future, about the relative importance of different classes of the community, and about everything else to which differences of judgement and feelings properly relate. But what we owe to Keynes is to use it as an apparatus of rational thought and to think in terms of physical realities, and when it comes to policy to be self-conscious and purposive as to what it is intended to achieve and how it is expected to work.

[1] House of Lords, 23 May 1944.

II. The balance of payments

Early in 1944 the House of Lords was debating the Anglo-American proposals for setting up the International Monetary Fund. Keynes, who had been working in the Treasury since 1941, commended the proposals which are so closely bound up with his name. Their Lordships would wish to consider, he said, whether by accepting them, we would be 'surrendering anything which is vital for the ordering of our domestic affairs in the manner we intend for the future'.[1] He hoped that their Lordships would trust him not to have turned his back on all that he had fought for. 'Public opinion is now converted to a new model, and I believe a much improved model, of domestic policy. That battle is all but won.'

If Keynes can be said to have devoted his life to anything it is to liberating internal policy from the domination of external factors. How Keynes would have detested, for example, the argument advanced in favour of currency convertibility in an American Report two years ago, that it 'would tend to impose a discipline on countries by inducing them to follow appropriate internal financial policies'.[2] But objection to discipline imposed from outside carried with it a need for self-discipline. In the same House of Lords speech Keynes not only said: 'We will not accept deflation at the dictates of influences from outside.' He also said: 'We intend to prevent inflation at home'. It is in the light of that observation that it is necessary to read his statement that the plan for the International Monetary Fund provides that the 'external value' of a currency, that is to say, a country's rate of exchange, 'should be altered if necessary so as to conform to whatever *de facto* internal value results from domestic policies, which themselves shall be immune from criticism by the Fund'. 'Whatever results from domestic policies', and not from *lack* of domestic policies.

This brings me back to Keynes' statement, which I quoted in my previous talk,[3] that we must find a way to prevent wages from forever soaring upwards. It would be unthinkable to have to look forward to an unending series of devaluations. Keynes never contemplated such a prospect. But it is a counsel of despair to say that constant devalua-

[1] House of Lords, 23 May 1944.
[2] *Staff Papers* presented to the Randall Commission on Foreign Economic Policy, 1954, p. 469.
[3] Above p. 104.

tion can be avoided only by maintaining a higher level of unemployment, and a lower level of activity than would be desirable apart from the balance of payments. Keynes disliked any idea of having to influence the behaviour of wages in this kind of way. Hence the vital necessity for an understanding with trade unions and employers.

At the present time, the issue which is uppermost in people's minds is how rapidly the balance of payments will respond to the restraints imposed by the Government. But perhaps the better question to ask is by what process of cause and effect an improvement might occur.

The first point is that the Government's restrictive measures by abating the demand for labour will have some effect in slowing down the upward movement of money wages. The effect is likely to be inadequate unless the measures are carried to the point of real unemployment, and even then they may not be very successful. And such success as they have will soon be lost if the measures are relaxed. There is, therefore, as we have seen, every reason for seeking a wages policy as an alternative which does not involve the same restraints on investment and activity.

But the behaviour of wages is only one element in the inflationary situation. The other element, which logically is quite distinct, lies in the heavy pressure of the various demands on our productive resources. This has adverse repercussions on our imports and exports, even if the level of wages costs can be taken as given. It is partly a matter of the relationship of output and employment taken as a whole to the balance of payments. If production is less, less imported raw materials are needed and export markets are more readily cultivated. If people's real incomes are less, they buy less imported goods. Are we looking, to put the matter in moderate terms, to losing part of the normal growth of output which increasing productivity makes possible, and to a corresponding small increase in unemployment? If we reach a point of time – perhaps we have already reached it – at which output is no greater than it was in the previous year, will that be a cause of jubilation, because of some favourable effect on the balance of payments, or for despondency, as it was when a similar position was reached a few years ago? And will it be necessary to continue indefinitely to keep a damper on the growth of production? The importance of these questions is underlined by Mr Macmillan's decision to leave out of his Budget statement the customary attempt to indicate the specific influences on the economy which the measures are designed to exert. The difficulty of forecasting can be readily admitted, but is it not possible that added to that is a certain obscurity as to objectives?

If we cannot afford the imports needed to match the level of output and real income which from other points of view would be desirable, it means that we are in danger of having to allow the balance of payments tail to wag the dog. This is just what Keynes was always fighting against. 'If higher earnings lead us to import more bananas than we can afford, this cannot be remedied by the Treasury chastising itself with a high rate of interest.'[1] That was written in July 1939. His remedy, apart from higher taxation, was: 'putting obstacles, such as would certainly be necessary in a war, in the way of the public buying what they want'.

I said in my previous talk that I was not intending to try to guess what Keynes would be saying today. But on the subject of the use in peace-time of import control, he has left some clues. In a speech in the House of Lords delivered a few months before his death, he referred to 'the disastrous consequences of a *laissez-faire* system which pays no direct regard to the preservation of equilibrium and merely relies on the eventual working out of blind forces'.[2] In an article written at the same time, he did make a startling reference to 'the invisible hand...operating towards equilibrium', but before the end of the article he was again running true to form: 'I must not be misunderstood. I do not suppose that the classical medicine will work by itself or that we can depend on it. We need quicker and less painful aids, of which exchange variation and overall import control are the most important.'[3]

This does not mean that Keynes would overlook the effect on overseas suppliers. What has to be realised is that in any case in our present situation we have to get our imports down except in so far as our exports can be encouraged. It is a choice of means. Either we import less as a result of a slight intensification of our import restrictions and maintain our domestic activity, or our domestic activity has to be damped down and that is why we import less. In either case there is the same adverse effect on overseas countries taken as a whole – with differences, one way and the other, for individual countries and

[1] *The Times*, 24 July 1939.
[2] House of Lords, 18 December 1945.
[3] *Economic Journal*, June 1946, pp. 14, 15.

8-2

for individual interests. But the one method is far more favourable than the other to ourselves. At any rate, this is an argument which could be given an airing in international discussion. And it could be reinforced by a reminder that, as is now all too clear, we liberalised and relaxed our import arrangements rather too fast and too far. We were lulled into doing so by a sense of false security about the balance of payments, failing to realise that it appeared to be satisfactory only because we were content with a rather lower level of activity than is now seen to be feasible and desirable. It would have been better if instead of so much liberalisation of imports we had established a larger, if temporary, surplus of exports over imports and built up, while the going was still good, larger monetary reserves.

All this is on the assumption that the wages question is being looked after. If every time we achieve a high level of activity money wages are going to go shooting up, it is of course hopeless anyhow.

So much, for the moment, for the relation of the balance of payments to total output and employment. It may be objected that I am presenting the situation in too tragic a light. What Mr Macmillan in his Budget statement talked about was redeployment of labour, rather than an overall decline in activity. The reason why he could talk in this way is that there is at present a widespread shortage of labour, so that labour which is released from one line of activity will be largely absorbed in others. Under such conditions, restriction of imports would be less effective. Unless it was highly selective, it would intensify the already excessive pressure of demand, and so result in indirect damage to the balance of payments which would partially offset the direct benefit. The question is how far internal restraints will improve our balance of payments before they become so great as to cause the shortage of labour more or less to disappear and to bring the argument back to general slackening of activity as a means of securing any further necessary improvement.

The point at issue is that the balance of payments does not depend only on how much we produce. It depends also on the extent to which we are using resources – what our national expenditure is as opposed to our national income. If the sum of our consumption and our domestic investment exceeds our production, the excess must take the form of an excess of imports over exports. That is a proposition which seems obvious enough today, but was far from obvious when Keynes worked it out in his *Treatise* published in 1930. It is in fact a tautology like many propositions in economics. Like many economic tautologies it is very useful. But being a tautology it cannot establish any indisputable chain of cause and effect. That applies to the claim that the balance of payments will improve by pretty well the full amount by which investment is limited. That is certainly a possibility which is consistent with the tautology. But it assumes that if investment takes less of the available labour supply, almost the whole of the labour released will help to expand production of goods for export and of goods which replace imports. Admittedly the production of these goods is being held back by shortage of labour. But plenty of other kinds of industries and services are short of labour and will help mop up any that becomes available as a result of internal restraints. If the restraints are applied only to investment and not to consumption, a considerable part of the curtailment of investment will in practice accrue to consumption, so long as the curtailment is modest and employers producing consumer goods are still held back by shortage of labour. They will eagerly absorb what labour is released to them and their production will increase. I say what labour is released to them because one of the difficulties is that a reduction of output is not nowadays accompanied by a corresponding release of labour: employers hang on to redundant labour for fear that when they need it again it will no longer be possible to recruit it. But in so far as the production of consumer goods does benefit from restraints on investment and from the consequent easing of the labour market, the inflationary pressure on prices will lessen, profit margins will fall and real wages rise. While there will be some reduction of imports, there will also, as I say, be an increase in consumption. In many ways, of course, this will be welcome, but it is not the object of the operation. It means that part of the investment is needlessly sacrificed without helping the balance of payments.

What it boils down to, I think, is that restraints on investment – designed perhaps to keep it from expanding further for the moment rather than to bring about a decline – combined with additional taxation of the consumer and additional import restrictions, would do the trick without any one of these measures having to be at all heroic. (Once more, this is always granted an adequate wages policy.) The import restrictions would be fairly effective if the other two measures had sufficient impact on the shortage of labour. But in so far as we rely on restraints on investment, they will serve only to prevent the balance of payments from getting worse unless they are applied sufficiently vigorously to bring about an absolute decline in investment. An absolute decline is likely to be disappointing in its effect on the balance of payments if it is small, and if it is large enough to produce an adequate effect it will probably have to be large enough to cause a general decline in activity, with the waste which that involves.

The order of magnitude of the problem is therefore very relevant. I suppose that if our balance of payments improved by £200,000,000 a year, we should for the moment feel reasonably satisfied. That amounts to about £4 a year for each man, woman and child. As problems go, our problem does not sound a particularly tough nut. Are we, perhaps, relying too much on the steam-hammer? It is a matter of about one and a half per cent of total consumers' expenditure. But, on the other hand it is a large proportion of our net investment (net of depreciation, as Keynes was in the habit of measuring it: gross investment is a flattering but deceptive concept, beloved of politicians because it sounds a lot and of statisticians because it avoids some awkward difficulties).

Looked at in this way our problem sounds fairly trivial. But I want now to consider the behaviour of other countries. This will bring me to an important additional reason why it would be preferable to combine direct action on the volume of imports – it would not have to be taken far – with indirect action operating on internal demands.

We depend very much on what happens in world markets. If our balance of payments is to improve it can do so only if the balances of payments of some other countries are allowed to deteriorate. There is the rub. Some of the other countries have had unfavourable balances, too, though usually to a less serious extent than ours, and they too want to put them right. And even some of the countries with balances of payments which look reasonably satisfactory are taking steps to make them even better, or, what comes to much the same thing, are afraid of deterioration and are taking steps prompted by that fear. One of the troubles is that so many countries depend for a satisfactory balance of payments on what is called extraordinary expenditure by the United States – expenditure of various kinds but largely military in origin. Rightly or wrongly, countries which benefit from such United States expenditure have no confidence in its being maintained. The result is that although in many cases they are actually accumulating monetary reserves, they tend to behave as though they were losing reserves. The existing reserves often seem far from adequate – even though in relation to needs they are far more adequate than ours. The result of all this is that many other countries have taken steps to protect their balances of payments by much the same measures – credit restriction and dear money – as we have adopted. And despite exchange control there is sufficient mobility of funds between international centres to add considerably to this competitive upward pressure on interest rates. In a certain sense and over certain fields, countries can be said to be using credit restriction and dear money as means for competing both for trade and for international funds – and so on both tickets for monetary reserves. It is only to the extent that our measures of internal restraint are stronger and more successful than those of the others and to the extent that the competitive struggle for monetary reserves which I describe is not yet world-wide that we can hope to improve our balance of payments and replenish our reserves – that is, if we rely on internal restraints alone.

The way Keynes always put it is that there is usually much more reluctance to lose monetary reserves than to receive them. The result of this asymmetry is that a deflationary bias is introduced into the world system. Keynes set out to remedy this in his plans for a new international monetary institution.

The International Monetary Fund represented, both in scale and in concept, enormous concessions from Keynes' original vision. But Keynes' recently awakened enthusiasm for Anglo-American co-operation withstood every disappointment (Mr Harrod described how it was only at the very end of his life that he was assailed by doubts – at Savannah, at the first meeting of the Fund, and of the International Bank, on which, too, he had built such high hopes). In the outcome the Fund has not even fulfilled its limited promise. It might be argued in defence that avoidance of a deflationary bias is the last thing that the world system needs at present – that whatever may be the character of the problems which face the world, they are not the problems which Keynes was concerned about: the problems associated with the threat of serious unemployment. While that is true, it does not dispense with the need for international co-operation of an active kind. Admittedly there are countries – the United States is one – which find it desirable at a time like the present to impose a certain restraint by making money somewhat dearer, and by other restrictive measures, for reasons which are purely internal and imply no concern about the balance of payments. But elsewhere, as I have said, there is much concern about the balance of payments, resulting in a competitive struggle between countries for monetary reserves. This takes the form of credit restriction and dear money, and must mean unnecessary sacrifices of capital accumulation and of activity the effect of which on balances of payments largely cancels out, and all that is left is a loss of trade in both directions. And the interests of the undeveloped countries need to be brought into this picture. It all calls for co-operation in a far more purposive sense than is at present provided for. Also the danger of momentum carrying these restraints to the point of real trade recession can by no means be ignored.

In the place of international co-operation at the present time there seems to have been substituted a craze for dogma. Keynes grew to hate dogma. Lecturing in 1933 on the subject of national self-sufficiency, he said that he was '... brought up, like most Englishmen, to respect free trade... I thought England's unshakable free-trade convictions, maintained for nearly a hundred years, to be both the explanation before man and the justification before Heaven of her economic supremacy. As lately as 1923, I was writing that free trade was based on fundamental truths which, stated with their due qualifications, no one can dispute who is capable of understanding the meaning of the words.'

In the early 'thirties when Keynes was arguing in favour of tariffs, his critics charged him with inconsistency. But he was never ashamed to admit that his ideas on a subject had benefited from thought. 'I seem to see the elder parrots', he wrote, 'sitting around and saying: "You can *rely* on us. Every day for thirty years regardless of the weather, we have said 'What a lovely morning!'"' But this is a bad bird. He says one thing one day and something else the next.'[1]

So Keynes took pride in advancing his understanding of a problem. On occasion, also, a change of view might be a reaction against the too ready acceptance (to Keynes sometimes tiresome rather than flattering) of his teachings by his followers – there is a biting reference in that last article of his to 'how much modernist stuff, gone wrong and turned sour and silly, is circulating in our system, also incongruously mixed, it seems, with age-old poisons'. And very often a change of Keynes' ideas reflected a change in the prevailing conditions.

[1] *New Statesman and Nation*, 4 April 1931.

Both factors are illustrated by his attitude towards trade discrimination of the more extreme types – barter agreements, or something approaching them, rather than just the Imperial Preference of the Ottawa Conference. In 1938 he was advocating an arrangement for making 'sure that those from whom we buy spend a reasonable proportion of the proceeds in corresponding purchases from us'.[1] That was a time at which international co-operation did not exist. As Mr Harrod has put it, Keynes' 'instincts were for international co-operation. If these instincts had been dormant in the years before the war, that was because such co-operation seemed impracticable.' The war completely altered the outlook. Referring to a system of bilateral and barter agreements, Keynes said in his earlier House of Lords speech: 'As a technique of little Englandism, adopted as a last resort when all else has failed us, with this small country driven to autarchy, keeping itself to itself in a harsh and unfriendly world, it might make more sense.'

Nevertheless, in putting the case for currency convertibility as provided under the plan for the Monetary Fund, he was careful to make it clear that it would not rule out discriminatory commercial practices. 'The Bretton Woods plan would be consistent with our requiring a country from which we import to take in return a stipulated quantity of our exports.'[2] But that statement was confined to the question of fact. It was a question which he hoped would not prove material. But it might. 'If we gain less assistance from other measures than we now hope, an agreed machinery of adjustments on the monetary side will be all the more necessary', even if the ideal of commercial non-discrimination has to be discarded. This is an important point. The currency convertibility which is inherent in the Articles of Agreement of the International Monetary Fund is something far less than the convertibility which is nowadays in people's minds – or which at least should be in their minds if any sense is to be made of the discussions of the past few years. For these imply non-discrimination in trade as something closely bound up with the idea of convertibility.

On the trade issue Keynes was being hard-headed on the whole. Had we not more to gain by discrimination against us being outlawed than we had to lose by forgoing discrimination in our favour? This, of course, raises the question of our arrangements in the sterling area.

[1] *The Times*, 7 October 1938.
[2] *Ibid.*, 24 August 1944.

Here it should be recorded that Keynes had been fighting hard for a settlement covering the sterling balances and was relying on success. After his death the matter was dropped. This means that the abandonment of discrimination in the sterling area's import control would now impose a heavy drain on our monetary reserves.

I should mention also that Keynes' ideas about currency convertibility depended on a stricter recognition of the distinction between income account and capital account than is today fashionable on the part of experts on exchange control.

To some it may appear that in these two talks I have made too light of balance of payments difficulties as an influence on policy. But I would draw attention to the familiar point – so crucial to much that Keynes taught – that every unfavourable balance must have its counterpart in a favourable one somewhere else. For the world as a whole there can be no balance of payments difficulties. That is a simple point but from it follows the submission that countries acting independently and competitively will adopt internal policies which are more restrictive than is consistent with their interest, when they are looked at as a whole.

Actually, it has not been too bad – far less bad than Keynes often feared – at any rate so far. The reason lies partly in heavy expenditure on defence. In my previous talk I referred to our own defence expenditure as a burden. But defence expenditure elsewhere – and especially in the United States – has on the whole been a helpful factor to us by supporting overseas demand. And apart from that it is now at long last believed that an incipient recession can be effectively dealt with if the Government is prepared to intervene with suitable measures. This has had the important result that, particularly in the United States, the animal spirits of business men have become far less volatile than when Keynes discussed them. It is an open question how much this stabilising element owes to defence expenditure. But it seems clear enough that it owes a great deal to Keynes' teaching. Early in my previous talk I mentioned that in 1940 Keynes was asking himself whether, as a result of war, the United States would make the 'grand experiment' which would prove his case. Six years later, shortly before his death, he felt able to write: 'Whatever vicissitudes one may foresee for American prosperity, it is certain that the public demand for vigorous government action to meet any serious or prolonged unemployment will be intense.' He had worked out the basis of that last article of his before his disappointing visit to the Savannah Conference. It is written in a more than usually optimistic vein, and also in a strangely complacent vein.

Much now depends on whether Keynes' optimism on this issue of the avoidance of serious recession in the American economy – a new-found optimism, which he entertained with legitimate pride – stands the test of the future as well as it has of the past few years.

7

MEMORANDUM OF EVIDENCE
SUBMITTED TO
THE RADCLIFFE COMMITTEE*

The Ends in View

1. A good test of any proposition relating to monetary theory is whether it represents the behaviour of the monetary and credit mechanism as a means or as an end. Doctrines and ideas which are objectionable are those which suggest that definition of the manner in which the machine should operate is more important than identification of the objectives which are sought and of the causal processes by which monetary measures are calculated to achieve them. So long as the objectives can be depicted as having an independent being, irrespective of the character of the means employed for controlling the system, there is no reason for belittling the importance of the monetary mechanism as a component of the whole economic system, with a vital part to play side by side with other mechanisms, including especially the budgetary mechanism. It is when the end is subordinated to the means that economic progress is in danger of becoming the victim of monetary *mystique*.

2. There are two important ends which in this purposive sense require to be defined. One is the general level of economic activity, the other the balance between consumption and investment.

3. It is possible to discuss – as a problem in itself – what degree of pressure it is desirable that demand should exercise on the available productive resources – primarily manpower and equipment – so as to secure the best possible use of them. The pressure of demand originates from various sources, each of which can be influenced in various ways. If Government expenditure, including defence expenditure, is, for the purpose of discussion, taken as given, the question resolves

---

* Committee on the Working of the Monetary System, *Principal Memoranda of Evidence*, 1959. H.M.S.O. [Written 27 May, 1958].

itself mainly into the behaviour of the forces governing *consumption* and of the forces governing *investment*.

4. Consumption can be largely influenced through the instrument of taxation, the weight of which determines the extent to which the incomes of taxpayers are available for spending. A rough measure of the restraint imposed by taxation on consumption (relatively to the weight of Government expenditure) is the 'above the line' surplus on income account – the surplus of tax revenue over Government current expenditure.

5. On the other hand, the monetary and credit mechanism operates mainly on investment, and especially on the rate of fixed investment.[1] Investment can also be influenced by certain forms of budgetary policy, and monetary policy has some direct effect on consumption, especially if motor cars are included under the definition of consumption rather than of investment. For present purposes, however, it is useful to distinguish between budgetary and monetary policy in terms of the distinction between consumption and investment.

Monetary Versus Budgetary Policy

6. This brings me to the second important end of purposive policy which also requires to be defined – the balance between consumption and investment in contributing to any particular level of economic activity. Budgetary and monetary restraint are often referred to as alternatives. This is misleading. They could be regarded as alternatives if the overall level of activity was the only consideration. This it is far from being. Therein lies the danger of thinking vaguely in terms of an expansionist or deflationary influence (a danger which is sometimes intensified by regarding budgetary influences as monetary in character). If it is desired to restrain, or to stimulate, economic activity it

---

[1] I have been allowed to see the Memorandum on 'The Scope and Limitations of Monetary Policy' submitted to the Committee by I. M. D. Little, R. R. Neild and C. R. Ross (*Memoranda of Evidence*, Pt. XIII, No. 23, pp. 159–67). It is helpful to my own exposition to be able to express my strong agreement with the authors of this Memorandum, both in general and on most points of detail. I am assuming that I may take it as read. I do, however, attach more significance than do the authors of this Memorandum to the effects of monetary policy on investment. I agree that to secure an appreciable influence on total demand requires a big change in monetary policy. But that is the reason why big changes are apt to occur. The effects in the narrow field of private industry I judge to have considerable importance.

matters enormously to what extent budgetary and to what extent monetary measures are employed.

7. On the balance struck between them depends the growth and economic progress of the economy. It is true that the choice between consumption and investment ultimately represents a set of political decisions. But while the natural reluctance of taxpayers to pay taxes, and of Governments to impose them, ensures that the case for consumption does not suffer from neglect, there are in operation the following additional factors, such as should unquestionably be resisted, which reinforce the bias of a democratic society towards an ill-considered short-sighted preference for immediate consumption at the expense of investment – and so at the expense of additional consumption in the future:

(a) Monetary policy can be modified at a moment's notice whereas budgetary changes are normally introduced only once a year. The need for restraint usually presents itself as more urgent than the need for relaxation or expansion. There is a tendency, therefore, to rely on monetary policy on the restrictive tack, but when the time comes for giving the economy a 'shot in the arm' – perhaps as a result of earlier monetary restraint having been overdone – to take advantage of the opportunity of making tax concessions, even though it means waiting till Budget Day.

(b) Once tax concessions have been made it is politically difficult later on to withdraw them. Expansionist monetary policy can be reversed quite easily.

(c) The imposition of restrictive measures by budgetary means involves an invidious selection of taxes to fall on particular classes of individuals. Monetary restriction is anonymous; and even though in fact it involves some delegation of authority to bank managers, the Government do not feel that they are responsible for its incidence, and for this reason they are inclined to prefer it.

(d) Rightly or wrongly, monetary measures are generally thought to be more effective on the restrictive tack than on the expansionist tack, and are therefore more readily resorted to when restraint is called for. Whether this view is well founded or not, monetary measures certainly are slow, as well as unpredictable, in exercising their full effects, which, as they come into operation, are imbued with considerable momentum. When the monetary screw is turned on and the results appear for the moment disappointing, the impatient reaction is frequently to turn it tighter, with the final result that the squeeze is overdone. But disappointment with the effects of monetary *expansion*, applied at times when a stimulus is called for, is likely to result in budgetary concessions as much as in greater resort to monetary expansion.

(e) Rightly or wrongly, vested interests seem to favour keeping money on the dear rather than the cheap side.

(f) Restrictive measures are usually called for at times when the country is losing monetary reserves, or having suffered heavy losses is trying to replenish them. This itself calls for dear money, on account of its influence on capital movements, quite apart from its effect in reducing the pressure of demand on the country's productive resources. A favourable balance of payments does not exert the same pressure in the opposite direction in favour of cheap money, because it is far less important to avoid gaining monetary reserves than to avoid losing them. Furthermore, a favourable balance of payments is, up to a point, likely to be taken out in relaxation of import and exchange controls rather than in pushing down rates of interest.

8. Over any term of years the economy is inevitably subject to fits and starts. For the reasons which I have enumerated, there is some tendency for the fits to be nursed by budgetary rather than monetary relaxation, and for the starts to be moderated by monetary rather than budgetary restraint. To the extent that this tendency operates – and it may become somewhat more pronounced than it has so far[1] – the proportion of consumption becomes larger, and the proportion of investment smaller, than is desirable on the pure merits of the choice between them. The natural downward course of rates of taxation tends to be accelerated at the expense of monetary tightness. The remedy lies in greater consciousness of what is involved in the choice between monetary and budgetary measures. It also requires that budgetary policy should be capable of being modified more frequently than once a year. This is already to some extent possible with purchase tax, and such flexibility could easily be extended by statutory

---

[1] See paragraph 67,

provision and should then be taken ready advantage of; while autumn Budgets are already not unknown.

The Influence of Monetary Policy

9. It will be clear that I attribute to monetary forces a substantial influence on investment, though I regard it as slow in coming into effect and unpredictable in its results. At the same time I certainly take the view that there are other methods of influencing investment when it needs to be influenced. While considerable reliance should be placed on these other methods, this does not mean that monetary forces should remain completely impassive in the face of changing circumstances. There always must be a monetary policy. Whatever its expression, it would be absurd for it to take no account of the economic climate. It is best expressed in terms of rates of interest on loans of various maturities and of the amount of bank advances. The authorities must have a view as to what they want these to be. As regards rates of interest, I accept the usual opinion that they are directly influential mainly on investment in durable capital, including housebuilding, more particularly in the private as opposed to the public sector. This does in fact account for quite an appreciable part of total investment. For private industrial investment the availability of bank advances has a direct significance. In addition I attach importance here to a less direct influence – to the reaction of changes in interest rates, and in the availability of bank advances, on the state of the stock exchange – measured not only by the prices of shares, as well as of bonds, in relation to returns on them, but also by the ease with which individual companies can issue shares without turning the prices against themselves.

10. The high earnings yields which are offered on some shares – and especially on the shares of the companies which follow a conservative distribution policy and of the smaller companies – must serve as a check on issues of ordinary shares, and so on the total of industrial investment. The narrowness of the market in the shares of all but the really large companies tells in the same direction. The effect is not large in relation to the total of investment, but it may be large in relation to net investment in private industry, which is such a small proportion of total net investment and such a very small proportion of total gross investment.

11. It may seem perverse to insist on this view at a time when for some years the problem has been generally presented as one of restraining and not as one of stimulating the growth of investment. But to my mind it is the most alarming feature of this country's economic position that it has been thought necessary – or indeed that it has been necessary, as I would to some limited extent admit under the circumstances which ruled – to impose a check as soon as business men's spirits began in 1955 to recover from the doldrums. The level of net industrial investment which business men were aiming at represented a considerable improvement but only if it had been achieved would investment have been running at what would, in my opinion, have been a satisfactory level. In taking this view I am not just thinking, in conventional economic terms, of the worthwhileness of temporary current sacrifice for the sake of more rapid economic progress. I am thinking also in comparative terms – if we do not keep pace with other countries our balance of payments problems may become aggravated and our people will be disappointed with our relative level of progress, such as is already manifest.[1] The wages problem is one with which I deal below but it can be said now that there is inevitably a certain natural inertia about the progress through time of the money-wage rate, which follows a remarkably similar course in a large number of countries, and that to lag behind in the growth of productivity is almost bound to mean forging ahead of other countries in the rise of costs and prices.

12. The need for restraint on investment has been conceived to arise partly on account of the development of an unduly heavy demand for labour – very low unemployment and many unfilled vacancies. So far in the development of my argument my answer to this would be that greater use could have been made of budgetary restraint of consumption. But the need for restraint on investment has arisen also – and in large degree – from the inadequacy of the productive equipment available for producing capital goods. In particular, it has been

[1] One of the most recently published 'league tables' is truly terrifying. I refer to Table 1 of Chapter III of the *Economic Survey of Europe in 1957*. From 1953 to 1957 the gross national product of the United Kingdom measured in real terms rose at an average annual rate of 2.9 per cent. In western Europe only Turkey, Denmark and Eire did worse. For West Germany the figure is 7.7 per cent. In the metal-using industries the average annual rate of increase of production in this period was 4.3 per cent for the United Kingdom. Only Sweden and Eire did worse. For West Germany the figure is 13.2 per cent.

necessary to restrain the growth of domestic retention of the products of the engineering industries, on which the defence burden falls so heavily, in order to safeguard the growth of exports of similar products, and in order to keep down imports of the steel needed to supplement domestic steel-producing capacity. In other words, it has been necessary to restrain the growth of the country's productive capacity in the engineering and steel industries precisely because it is inadequate. If confronted by any complacent suggestion that the country has not done too badly in productive investment, I would strongly urge the Committee to keep in mind the unsatisfactory state of the country's balance of payments, when taken in relation to the monetary reserves and to the pressures which must be expected to originate from the economic development of some of the sterling-area countries. Both in terms of productive capacity and in terms of productive efficiency, it is surely clear that the outstanding need is to avoid discouragement of investment.

13. I myself go further and believe that *stimulus* is a better expression of the need than mere avoidance of discouragement. Immediate and overwhelming exigencies have enforced discouragement. There is a danger that the measures calculated to restrain investment, partly intentionally and partly unintentionally, will have been relaxed too late and that natural momentum – so slow in getting built up in the first place – will carry the discouragement deeper in degree and further in time than is intended by the authorities. The planning of investment is a lengthy process. And business men's spirits, remarkably resilient though they have shown themselves, cannot just be turned on and off at will.

The Desirable Level of Activity

14. So far my discussion has been conducted in terms of a high rate of investment being an alternative to a lower rate of consumption, and *vice versa*, both being geared as a result of a suitable combination of monetary with budgetary policy so as to achieve some particular level of overall activity. I have, in other words, confined myself to the second important end which I mentioned of economic policy – the achievement of the best possible balance between consumption and investment. Introduction of the first end – the attainment of the right level of economic activity – adds force to the immediately foregoing considerations. Investment now has to be considered as an important

influence on the total demand for productive resources. What I have argued so far is, in effect, that any desirable raising of demand should as far as possible be effected by stimulating investment, through an expansionist monetary policy as well as by othei means; but that any necessary restraint on demand, if it is really necessary, should so far as possible be effected, by budgetary means, through restraint on consumption. But there are political as well as economic limits to such a principle, and provided that restraint on demand really is necessary it will, I readily admit, call for monetary restraint (and other restraints on investment) as well as for budgetary restraint (on consumption). And, more generally, the manner in which monetary policy at any moment finds expression, in terms of rates of interest and the behaviour of bank advances, will and should be determined by levels of activity current and prospective, as well as by the behaviour of investment, actual and prospective, and, more generally, by indications of the state of business men's expectations, including the behaviour of the stock exchange.

15. The underlying question is how high is the pressure at which it is desirable or safe to aim at driving the economic system. Loss of potential output is particularly serious if it includes – being the result of – loss of potential investment, less serious if it is the result of restraint on consumption. And, in either case, the damping of markets in industrial products will take the edge off the urge to invest, over and above the direct effect of monetary restraint; and revival of this urge by monetary expansion will be more difficult if confidence in the steady growth of demand has been undermined.

16. It is difficult to say to what extent at the present time the flattening out (and in my opinion probable decline) of industrial investment in the private sector can be attributed directly to monetary restraints and to what extent to the failure of demand to keep pace (largely as a result of these and other restraints) with the growth of productive capacity and technical knowledge. In any case the record of the last three years is depressing. Production has scarcely increased. Those who take the complacent view have either to argue that net investment in industry has not been very substantial in any effective sense or that a great deal of potential productive capacity is now being temporarily wasted. Neither argument is encouraging. If the results of the policy are measured in terms of the behaviour of costs and prices during the period it is not encouraging either.

The Balance of Payments

17. A policy which has had the result of depriving the economy of the natural growth of output over a period of three years, and of the extra investment which might have formed part of the growth, will, however, be defended, I suppose, by reference to the balance of payments on income account. There is, of course, no doubt that if overall demand remains more or less stationary while productive capacity grows, the slack which thereby develops will have the effect of causing the balance of payments to become more favourable than it would have been had the growth of demand been sustained. It is partly a matter of the relationship between the behaviour of demand and the behaviour of money wages, costs and prices. That important issue I will come back to. But quite apart from possible effects on the behaviour of money wages, the pressure of demand has a direct influence on imports and exports. Levels of activity lower than might have ruled mean smaller imports of materials. This effect will be especially prominent where the domestic production of the material is almost but not quite adequate to requirements – the steel-using industries provide the outstanding example. Restraint of personal income means to some extent smaller imports of consumer-goods. A less active domestic market enhances exports, both by reducing the actual domestic offtake and by rendering domestic sales relatively less profitable compared with overseas sales (business men will often argue the opposite, and indeed it does partly depend on the actual situation and on the length of the period under consideration). And importers too find the domestic market less profitable.

18. If investment is to be sacrificed in the interests of the balance of payments, the important question arises how much benefit to the balance of payments is likely to be afforded by any given cut in the rate of domestic investment and by the resultant effect on overall demand. In indicating the nature of the answer to this question I continue for the moment to disregard possible influence on the behaviour of money wages.

19. Let me first take a case in which the level of overall demand is so high in relation to productive resources that a moderate reduction will exercise its influence primarily in causing the prices of goods to be quoted at less high scarcity levels under the influence of demand and in alleviating actual shortages of goods (partly revealed in poor

delivery dates), and only to a small extent in reducing the volume of overall domestic production. Under such conditions of scarcity, a cut in the rate of domestic investment which is not so large as to nullify these conditions will have a relatively large effect in improving the balance of payments. But even under such conditions of scarcity the improvement of the balance of payments will usually be considerably less than the cut in the rate of domestic investment. For, provided that the scarcity takes its origin in an overall shortage of manpower, there will be a switch to production of consumer-goods and, at the lower level of prices, consumption will share with the balance of payments the benefit of a reduced rate of domestic investment. In so far, however, as the scarcity lies in a shortage of equipment for the manufacture of capital-goods, there is a more direct impact on the overseas trade in these capital-goods themselves – exports of machinery are promoted and imports of steel fall off – and the improvement in the balance of payments will be a correspondingly high proportion of a cut in the rate of domestic investment.[1]

20. At more normal levels of demand, such as do not provoke scarcity prices or shortages, the impact of a cut in the rate of domestic investment will fall mainly on production. Imports will be reduced only to the extent that a lower level of production requires less materials for purely physical reasons and to the extent that out of lower personal incomes less will be spent on imports. To some extent exports may also be stimulated by positive unattractiveness of the domestic market (though business men will often argue the opposite). Under such normal conditions a cut in the rate of investment will have a relatively small effect on the balance of payments and its main contribution will take the form of a reduction in the country's production and employment below what is physically possible. Such a reduction is of the kind, in my opinion, that the country has been experiencing recently – in the form of a failure of production to expand with the growth and improvement of productive equipment and with technical progress. It is a very serious thing if activity has to be curtailed because the country cannot afford the imports entailed in full production. It is especially serious if the curtailment takes the form quite largely of curtailment of investment, including investment in capacity designed to enable more goods to be exported at more competitive prices and to reduce dependence on imports.

[1] Cf. paragraph 12.

21. It must be emphasised that on the present basis of my argument – which excludes effects on the behaviour of money wages – a temporary slackening of the economic tempo does not go to the roots of balance of payments trouble. To the limited extent that the trouble is alleviated, the alleviation marches with the treatment – and no further. As soon as restraint is relaxed, and activity recovers, the trouble will start up afresh. Indeed, permanent damage will have been inflicted by the loss of potential improvements in productive capacity and efficiency.

22. A country can very easily get into a position in which *it cannot afford* to use its resources to the full – i.e. to the full extent that would be feasible and desirable if its exporting capacity was greater – simply because its imports would then be more than its exports would pay for (after allowance for other necessary provisions, actual and contingent, out of the country's receipts of overseas currency). I believe that this is the position of Britain to-day. While I agree that a most urgent problem is to improve the balance of payments and build up monetary reserves, I do not agree that it is either desirable or necessary to do this at the expense of the growth of productivity.

23. The problem to be faced is one of a chronically insecure balance of payments position and it should be faced firmly and squarely. The first question to which an economist directs his mind when faced with such a situation relates to the exchange rate. I am not impressed by the argument that in fact British prices have in recent years gone up no faster than those of competitors. While on the pure facts there is much, though not everything, in the basis of this line of argument, one over-riding plain and brutal fact is that the country's balance of payments is utterly unsatisfactory in relation to the needs and dangers of its position,[1] and would be still more so but for the restraints imposed on the level of activity. Adjustment of the exchange rate has, however, to be laid on one side so long as there is so little hold over the wage position.

24. Other, less orthodox, measures have to be considered. Liberalisation of imports was taken somewhat too far, under the influence of ill-timed optimism about the state of the balance of payments, and the

---

[1] Here I can express my hearty agreement with the Council on Prices, Productivity and Incomes when they suggest that in this context it is 'better to examine the actual behaviour of the balance of payments...than to pay much attention to these interesting historical studies of prices and costs' (*First Report*, Appendix VII, p. 70).

balance of payments position now calls for some restoration of import control. Incidentally, it can serve as a flexible instrument of policy and its use in this way would also make it easier to deal with any future exchange crisis. The necessary restriction of imports, which is not large, could be secured mainly at the expense of imports from dollar sources. There is after all nothing very novel in the idea that in so far as the United States, in consequence of her own protective measures and of failure to maintain domestic activity, is causing balance of payments trouble elsewhere, the appropriate response is for other countries to tighten up their restrictions on imports from the United States. This is the idea inherent in the famous Bretton Woods 'scarce currency clause,'[1] which has proved such a snare and delusion, and in the matching provision in GATT.[2] But nowadays West Germany must also be regarded as a cause of strain in international payments, such as could be relieved by some degree of discrimination against her goods as well. Such discrimination would, no doubt, be contrary to OEEC rules,[3] while in any case a reversal of liberalisation would be contrary to OEEC policy. But an adjustment both of the rules and of the policy would be in the interest too of several other western European countries, which find themselves in much the same position as Britain.

25. The mild control of imports which I here advocate as a means of improving the *balance of payments position* will operate at the expense of other countries' exports to us, taken as a whole, only in so far as it improves the *actual* balance of payments and in so far as this is taken out in a faster re-building of the country's holdings of gold and dollars than would otherwise have been possible. But the main object would be to enable a higher level of activity to be sustained without positive deterioration of the balance of payments. It is the *composition* of the country's imports which would be affected more than the total *volume*: as a result of some cutting down on imports of the less essential goods, and of goods which can easily be replaced from domestic sources, it would be possible to pay for the bigger

[1] Article VII of the Articles of Agreement of the International Monetary Fund.
[2] General Agreement on Tariffs and Trade, paragraph 5 (a) of Article xiv.
[3] O.E.E.C. Code of Liberalisation, Article 7. It may turn out to be a source of strength for the Common Market that no attempt has been made to write the doctrine of non-discrimination into the 'escape clause' – Treaty establishing the European Economic Community, paragraph 3 of Article 108.

imports of raw materials which higher production requires and which would take place with the withdrawal of restraint.

26. In general, countries cannot import more than their exports will pay for and if the import bill is not trimmed by direct control it has to be trimmed by the wastefully inefficient process of cutting down domestic production. When several countries get into such a position, as they are now beginning to, a beggar-my-neighbour process is started which might have been avoided by selective import control designed to relieve the strains on the system of international payments so that economic activity would not need to be restricted.

27. I want to emphasise that it is a matter only of degree. This country, like many other countries, still places some reliance on quantitative control of imports. Though it may not amount to much, few would feel happy about abandoning it completely at the moment. That being so, the question does at least arise whether this control should not be operated more flexibly.

28. So long as, in the interests of the balance of payments, a lessening of the pressure of domestic demand is called for to alleviate conditions of scarcity, I would not dispute the desirability of restrictive action. And indeed under such conditions of scarcity restriction of imports, by contributing to the scarcity, would exercise a somewhat nugatory effect on the balance of payments position. It is only when the impact of a reduction of demand would fall mainly on production rather than on prices and shortages that I would urge that there are less objectionable methods of improving the balance of payments.

29. What does seem clear in any case is that such restriction of investment as may be called for on account of balance of payments difficulties should be highly discriminatory. The desirable course would be, if it were possible, positively to stimulate investment in the exporting industries and in those capable of replacing imports, especially where productive equipment is the bottleneck – while discouraging investment everywhere else. Monetary restriction can only with difficulty, and within rather narrow limits, be imbued with discriminatory bias. Here *par excellence* arises a strong case for some of the alternative methods of discouraging investment, and especially for those which operate by way of direct control.

The Price Level and the Role of Wages

30. The primary concern of monetary policy is often thought to be the price level. A rising price level may be serious because of implications for the balance of payments. Or it may be regarded as objectionable for reasons independent of the balance of payments. Usually the motivation is mixed – at any rate in those countries which are liable to balance of payments trouble (unlike the United States and West Germany, in both of which nevertheless there is much concern about the behaviour of the price level). But it makes a good deal of difference to what extent it is the one motive and to what extent others. For the maintenance of balance of payments equilibrium, all that is necessary, roughly speaking, is that prices should not rise faster than they do on the average in other countries. Purely internal considerations may call, on the other hand, for something approaching stability of prices – and are often said to call for absolute stability of the average level of prices.

31. The level of prices at any moment of time can be regarded as mainly the outcome of three factors: – the level of money wages, the state of productive equipment and technical knowledge and efficiency, and the level of demand. Demand is in a direct sense an unimportant influence on prices unless it is so high as to strain the available productive resources and to result in scarcity prices. When it does become as high as this, prices are forced up relatively to money wages. (Real wage rates suffer in consequence. With higher levels of demand aggregate real wages may nevertheless be higher as a result of somewhat greater employment and of overtime, but eventually the aggregate real wages bill as well as real wage rates will suffer from demand being too high.)

32. The *movement* of prices, as opposed to the actual level of prices in relation to money wages, depends on how money wages move. Broadly speaking, the price level will rise to the extent that money wages rise faster than productivity, as determined by improvements in the state of productive equipment and technical knowledge and efficiency.

33. This raises the question of the relationship between the state of demand and the behaviour of money wages. Generally it is true that the greater the pressure of demand on the available productive resources the more rapidly, *ceteris paribus*, will money wages rise. So

137

much is fairly common ground. The important questions, however, are (i) the extent to which this influence is quantitatively important, (ii) the implications generally of *ceteris paribus*, and (iii) in particular whether the rate of growth of productivity, which is equally important on the other side in determining the course of prices, is not adversely affected by an attempt to curb the rise of wages by operations on the demand side.

34. At this point I want to suggest to the Committee that they avoid resort to the distinction between 'demand inflation' and 'cost inflation'. It is a distinction which I believe to be unhelpful and mis-leading. (This is quite apart from the troubles inherent in the use at all of the words 'inflation' and 'deflation'. These are illustrated by the fact that in the United States economy, which is subject at the present time to what some people would describe as a deflation – if they had to use this method of description – the price level is still rising: a symptom in another sense of inflation if not inflation incarnate.)

35. It is the rise in wages which is the cause of prices rising. In that sense all price inflations are 'cost inflations' (or wage inflation). But the speed at which wages, and therefore prices, rise is likely in some degree to depend on demand. In that sense there is nearly always some measure of 'demand inflation'.

36. A state of pure 'demand inflation' might be conceived as one in which the pressure of demand on productive resources is very heavy and there is such an acute general shortage of labour that employers are progressively bidding wages up against one another to levels which bear no relation to negotiated wage-rates. The rate at which wages are rising will then be independent of the outcome of wage negotiations, and will depend exclusively on the level of de-mand. A level of demand which was so high as to produce such a result would in any case be ruled out as too high on account of direct repercussions on the balance of payments[1] and its effect in stimulating a progressive upward movement of wages which was not in any way anchored to the results of wage negotiations would be an important additional reason for restricting it.

37. The normal situation is, however, one in which the behaviour of prices is determined by the course of wage negotiations, so that any progressive rise in prices is a 'cost inflation' – if the term has to be used. The fact that the rate at which it proceeds depends in some

[1] Paragraph 28.

measure on the level of demand has led to the dangerous conclusion that the appropriate remedy is to operate on demand. This dangerous conclusion is embodied in the use of the term 'demand inflation' to cover far too wide a range of possible situations. The parties to wage negotiations seem to be pictured as passive cogs in a machine. And attention is diverted from the vital part played by the wage bargain to the influence of the pressure of demand. If reliance is placed on regulation of demand in order to secure a tolerable behaviour of prices, it must almost certainly mean maintaining unemployment at a level which would represent very serious economic waste as well as political unacceptableness. This is certainly so if complete stability of the price level is aimed at. It is liable to be so, though in much lesser degree, if the objective is merely to prevent prices rising faster than in other countries (especially as in West Germany the strong belief in the virtue of complete stability of prices is likely to persist while in the United States, and other countries too, it has recently become a wide-spread article of faith).

38. The economic waste involved in such a policy is particularly great if demand is regulated by restricting productive investment, as will be the main result of relying on monetary policy. Not only is there the loss of potential investment. But the growth of productivity is thereby curtailed, thus narrowing the limit on the permissible rate of rise in wages and increasing the amount of unemployment required to secure observance of the limit.

39. Allusion is here again called for to the country's record over the past three years. The price level has in fact risen considerably as a result of wage increases; and whatever may have been achieved in avoiding a still faster rise it has been at the cost of losing the whole of the normal growth of productivity over the period. One reason why the results have been disappointing is that unemployment has increased so little. Stagnation of output is expressed in uneconomic use of employed labour more than in positive unemployment, such as might at least have exerted some favourable effect – not in my judgment at all large – on the course of wage negotiations.

40. The failure of the cost of living to fall is particularly significant over the last few months, during which there has been a marked fall in prices of materials as a result of deterioration in world conditions. In the United States the cost of living has continued to rise in recent months despite the strong recession; and though this may be partly

attributable to the behaviour of the prices of certain foodstuffs, some prices in the industrial sector are continuing to rise and fears are still being expressed about the danger of too strong an upward trend of wages.

41. It would, I submit, be a grave mistake for the Committee to accept the view that it is the proper function of monetary policy, together with budgetary policy and the like, to secure a tolerable behaviour of prices. One can readily admit the advantages of a stable price level, taken in isolation. It does not follow – very far from it on my submission – that the right aim of monetary policy is to secure a stable price level. The real solution lies elsewhere. It lies in the realm of wage negotiations. In making my submission I am not denying some influence on the behaviour of wages and so of prices from monetary and budgetary restrictions. It can, however, be so secured to the extent desired only at an economic cost which far outweighs the economic advantage which is aimed at.

42. It may be that discussion of better methods of settling wages would be held to lie outside the Committee's terms of reference. That, I would venture to suggest, should not prevent the Committee from attributing the evil to its proper origin and from suggesting that the remedy should be sought there, by appropriate procedure.

43. Even so the Committee would be concerned with the implications for monetary policy of inevitable delay in devising a more proper remedy for the evil and of lack of complete success in securing its application (and for my own part I would not expect complete success). I would not deny that such prospective delay and such probable lack of complete success have some implications in terms of monetary measures (though one would hope that the implications would show themselves mainly in budgetary measures and other alternative means of restraining demand). The more unbridled are the procedures for negotiating wages, the less feasible is it to run the economic system under really full pressure. But in the absence of anything like what might be called a wages policy, it would, I am convinced, be economically expedient, as well as politically inevitable to abandon any idea of stability of the price level. The only relevant question would be in what degree a progressive rise in prices should be tolerated for the sake of avoiding undue restriction of demand. And in view of the poor response of the behaviour of wages to restriction of demand, I do not believe that it would be desirable to go

beyond avoiding such positive shortage of labour as could, in moderate measure, be usefully tolerated if an effective wages policy was being operated. (Here, as elsewhere, I am unable to recommend the adoption of any mechanical rule, based, e.g., on the difference between the number of unfilled vacancies and the number of unemployed.)

44. An important question presents itself. In so far as development of slack in the economic system does have some effect in moderating the behaviour of wages, is the effect a lasting one which will persist even if the slack is subsequently taken in? Or will the course of wages resume its former course with the restoration of demand to the level required to take full advantage of productive capacity? For example, it is said that 'what we are aiming at now is a short pause before we take on the forward march again'. But will the trouble with wages and prices start all over again once the forward march is resumed? Is this another respect in which alleviation marches with the treatment and no further?[1]

45. I can try to answer this question only in terms of such small part of the improvement which seems recently to have occurred as I feel can reasonably be attributed to the existence of slack in the system, as opposed to others factors to which I shall allude.

46. In so far as the vicious spiral takes the form of money wages trying to catch up the cost of living, which itself goes up with money wages, it is true to say that an alleviation of the fever will persist even after the remedy ceases to be applied.

47. But where creation of slack is most effective in moderating the rise in wages is in respect of what is known as the 'wage drift'. In many industries, particularly where piece rates have to be fixed for a multiplicity of operations, the wages actually paid are to a considerable extent in excess of the minimum called for as the outcome of wage negotiations. If labour is scarce the gap between actual wages and negotiated rates may become progressively wider. While the behaviour of actual wages is influenced by the course of wage negotiations, they may be bid up by employers under the influence of high demand faster than the negotiated rates. This is not 'demand inflation' in the full sense,[2] which will occur only in extreme cases of acute shortage of labour, but it shows some of the characteristics of such a demand inflation. A reduction of demand will lead to a less rapid rise of actual wages by reducing or eliminating the 'wage drift'

[1] Cf. paragraph 21.   [2] See paragraph 36.

quite apart from any influence on the course of wage negotiations. It is clear, however, that with the taking in of the slack the drift would be fully resumed, and the trouble, so far as it takes this form, would start all over again.

48. Apart from periods of marked shortage of labour, I would attribute major responsibility for the upward movement of wages in this country to the competitive struggle between trade unions, and inside some of the trade unions between various sections of labour. Restraint displayed by any one section of labour taken in isolation operates at the expense of their real wages, which are reduced as a result of wage increases secured elsewhere. The general rise in wages arises very largely from the competitive need of individual sections to protect their standards of living against encroachment by rival sections. If at any moment wages could be frozen, all would then be well provided that the national wage structure which happened at that moment to exist was generally acceptable. But that never is the case. There is no agreement about *relative* wages. The conventional use of the word *leap-frogging* is highly appropriate. Even if some moderation in the manner in which the competitive struggle manifests itself is attributable to the development of slack in the economic system, it will break out again with full vigour when demand resumes a buoyant course.

49. At this point I should perhaps indicate to what I attribute the improvement which is apparent in the outcome, actual and prospective, of this year's wage negotiations compared with those of recent years. I do not believe that much of it is due to the damping down of demand, and I do not believe in any monetary influence operating otherwise than by damping down demand. (The damping down of demand will, however, have had an important and probably – so long as the damping continues – decisive, effect on the 'wage drift,' as opposed to the course of negotiated wage rates.) What I do believe is that the Government have succeeded in creating a state of alarm about the progressive fall in the value of money and, more successfully than on previous occasions when restraint has been appealed for, have brought about a state of general awareness of the role of wage negotiations in bringing about that fall. An atmosphere has been created in which trade-union leaders feel self-conscious on this account, perhaps more acutely than ever before. And the employers are more confident of Government backing. The independent persons who serve on the

multiplicity of Courts, Tribunals and Councils which are called upon to deal with claims and disputes have become somewhat clearer in their minds that the national interest can properly enter into their findings.

50. That all this should be so is in a way peculiar. For at any rate at the outset the Government's approach was directed by an economic theory according to which the behaviour of wages was merely an outcome of the monetary situation. It was denied that they were appealing for restraint or that they desired any interference with collective bargaining, and it was pointed out that they were not attempting to instruct arbitration tribunals.

51. But there has been a considerable improvement in the state of awareness of the importance of restraint over wage increases. A further important factor has operated. By reason of its being nationalised the railways industry, with a deficit and a development programme which can be financed only at the will of the Treasury, provides an influential expression of the Government's determination. For the Government to show its determination in this way does not require the exercise of monetary restraint. It is true that a higher level of economic activity would mean a smaller deficit for the British Transport Commission and that it might point to an increase of charges as a means of recovering a rise in the wages bill. But clearly it would still be possible for the Government to exercise the same pressure by adjusting the amounts of money involved and by using its legal and moral authority to prevent any undesired increase of charges.

52. These then are the factors which rather than monetary policy I believe really are contributing to moderation. To recite them is to invite attention to the inadequacy and precariousness of their hold. It is likely to become relaxed in the course of time unless the atmosphere of crisis is constantly renewed. But the mere fact that the fever has been somewhat abated is likely to prove of some help for some considerable time to come.

53. Nothing, however, has been done, apart from the attempt over the London omnibus men, to deal with what I have suggested as the major cause of the progressive rise in wages – the competitive struggle between trade unions and different sections of labour, exacerbated by the absence of agreement about *relative* wages. I believe that negotiation of some kind of national wage structure, conceived in terms of relative wages, at least for the most important sections of labour, is an

essential pre-requisite to securing over any term of years a tolerable behaviour of the absolute wage level. I do not, I think, under-estimate what is involved. Essentially it would be a matter for negotiation between trade unions, and to some extent within trade unions. It would involve a clear departure from the traditional system of wage negotiations and would call for strong central direction inside the trade-union movement.

54. If the *relative* wage problem could be solved – even perhaps only on a skeleton basis – it should not be too difficult to secure that the *absolute* wage level followed an acceptable course with the passage of time. For the most part uniform all-round increases could be called for, with such particular slight adjustments of relative wages as were indicated by changing circumstances. There seems to me to be much to recommend the successful Swedish and Norwegian system of synchronising all wage negotiations, with a good deal of central co-ordination, and restricting them to perhaps two-yearly intervals.

55. The 'wage drift' would still remain a problem. If the possibility of statutory control, of the kind which operates in the Netherlands, is dismissed, one is thrown on to the employer's sense of solidarity and on his recognition of the national interest.[1] This does not offer a very firm basis. The degree of its efficacy as a restraining influence would determine to what extent it was expedient to run the economic system so hard as to involve a marked overall shortage of labour.

56. This rough sketch of a possible reform of the system of wage negotiation will appear to many to present an unattainable ideal. The relevance of my sketch arises from my strong belief that stability of the price level must be regarded as equally attainable or unattainable.

57. I would add a few comments on the whole concept of an absolutely stable price level as an objective, without repeating what I have already indicated about the desirability or feasibility of trying to secure any such objective. The really important thought which underlies

---

[1] In the appeal for restraint issued by the Government in which Sir Stafford Cripps was Chancellor of the Exchequer, strong stress was laid on the importance of 'the strictest adherence to the terms of collective agreements,' so as to avoid 'competitive bargaining...and unjustifiable increases in wages' (Cmd. 7321, February 1948). A similar appeal was made when Mr Harold Macmillan was Chancellor ('the plateau policy') but this White Paper did not include any similar admonition to employers against bidding up wages above negotiated rates (Cmd. 9725, March 1956).

advocacy of price stability relates to the harm which is done to the economic system once it becomes generally recognised *as a certainty* that the price level will go on progressively rising without interruption and without limit. It is continuous and complete confidence in that *expectation* which does the harm. But to break that confidence it is not necessary to achieve absolute stability. Provided that there are periods of time during which prices of a considerable number of commodities fall somewhat in a manner that cannot altogether be foreseen, so that the direction of the course of prices at each moment of time cannot be predicted with certainty, it will not seriously matter if it turns out *ex post* that over a number of years the trend of prices has been upward.

58. Advocacy on doctrinal grounds of the merits of absolute stability of prices is highly prejudicial to the country's interests. It would certainly help in solving its balance of payments problem if it were possible, without sacrificing investment and production, to secure stability here while prices continued to rise elsewhere. But it would add seriously to the country's balance of payments difficulties if the result of propagating the doctrine was to secure its successful application in the creditor countries. 'The goal of price stability, seemingly so obvious right from the national point of view, may not in all circumstances be consistent with good creditor behaviour from the point of view of the outside world.'

59. Finally, there is the fact – so very simple but unpalatable to many business men – that absolute stability of prices means that some prices have to fall while others rise. Business men, especially those who produce or handle branded products which are ultimately bought by members of the public, are much readier to increase prices with a rise in wages which outstrips the rise in output per head than they are to lower prices where output per head rises more than wages.

The Role of the Quantity of Money

60. This exposition has been aimed at dealing with the operation of the monetary and credit mechanism as a matter of straightforward cause and effect, expressed in terms of physical realities. It differs fundamentally from those treatments of the subject which attribute to the quantity or supply of money a direct influence on prices, or a direct influence on wages and so on prices. My contention is that

the quantity of money operates on the system in three, and in only three ways:

(a) Other things equal, a larger quantity of money means lower interest rates, because it means that the banking system is taking a larger quantity of securities off the market, is assisting in greater measure in financing the holding of securities, and is reducing the extent to which securities have to be issued on the market in order to secure finance. It is the lower level of interest rates, not the larger quantity of money, which exercises an expansionist influence. For the purpose of securing a given end, in terms of investment, the rates of interest provide the means, and it is immaterial what changes in the quantity of money have to occur as part of the process of securing a particular desired behaviour of rates of interest.

(b) This is subject to a qualification, which involves an important issue of machinery, but does not affect the principle. Bank advances are at most times – and not only when they are limited by Government admonition or direction – subject, in greater or smaller degree, to a process of rationing. In other words, banks do not habitually charge to their customers the highest rates of interest which the traffic will bear. There is normally what Keynes called 'a fringe of unsatisfied borrowers'. The result is that the behaviour or bank advances exercises an influence on investment which is separate from that exercised by rates of interest.

Although the volume of bank advances bears some relationship to the total volume of bank assets, which is roughly equal to the total quantity of bank deposits, the relationship is not a fixed one. It is quite possible for example, for bank advances to increase without any increase at all in the total quantity of bank assets, other types of assets being reduced to the same extent. Such an increase would exercise some favourable effect on investment and this could not be attributed to the behaviour of the supply of money, which would, *ex hypothesi*, have remained constant.

(c) The operation of the forces indicated under (a) and (b) has an effect on the state of the stock exchange, and this affects the readiness of business men to finance investment by issuing ordinary shares and this has some influence on investment.

61. My contention that it is not the quantity of money in itself which determines the size of the stream of total demand requires that the velocity of circulation of money should be regarded as a purely passive factor. Bank deposits are held not only as a means of exchange but also as a way of holding wealth which for the moment the owners do not desire to put into other forms. The quantity of money held in the latter 'inactive' form is closely related to the level and structure of rates of interest, but the relationship is not at all a stable one, so much depending on expectations about the future. The velocity of circulation, as normally conceived, is an entirely bogus concept. It is a weighted average of the velocity of the 'active' circulation and of the velocity of the 'inactive' circulation – the latter happens to be zero. The weights are the quantities of money held 'actively' and 'in-actively' respectively – as a means of exchange and simply as a way of holding wealth. If the quantity of money is increased, this means that the banks have increased their assets, and in doing so they will have bid up the prices of securities, i.e. lowered rates of interest. Until this fall in rates of interest (and any expansion of bank advances) has influenced the level of demand, and so of activity, by its effect on investment, the whole of the additional money will be held in inactive form, the rise in security prices and the fall in interest rates having precisely to be such as to induce the public to make the necessary swap with the banks of other forms of holding wealth for deposits. It is obvious that the change in the *weights* is exactly such as to cause the *weighted average* velocity of circulation to decline in the same pro-portion as the total quantity of money has increased. The quantity of money multiplied by the velocity of circulation is exactly the same as before. The proportion held in 'inactive' form – with zero velocity of circulation – has gone up and this pulls down the weighted average velocity. If and when the quantity of money multiplied by the velocity of circulation does alter, it alters *because* the reduction in interest rates, and the other influences mentioned above,[1] have operated on demand and so on activity and perhaps prices and wages. It is an effect and not a cause.

62. I stress this elementary proposition beause I believe that the Committee should view with suspicion any line of argument which attributes to the behaviour of the supply of money a significance of its own, apart from its relationship with rates of interest and bank

[1] Paragraph 60.

10-2

advances. This is no mere hair-splitting matter. To regard it as such is to deny the importance of taking a purposive view of the ends of economic policy and of adopting means which, through some recognisable process of causation, are designed for the sake of the end in view and not for their own sake.

The Structure of Interest Rates

63. Those who do think in terms of the importance of keeping down the quantity of money, *as an end in itself*, thereby create quite unnecessary headaches for themselves – and for others. For example, the problem of the structure of interest rates is much discussed. Monetary policy finds its expression in the whole complex of interest rates, ranging from the Treasury Bill rate to the rate on irredeemable Government securities (not to mention other types of securities). Many complicated considerations properly enter in. Quite apart from effects on investment, there are the questions of the interest charges on the National Debt and of interest charges on local authorities and nationalised industries, of the charge on the balance of payments of interest payments to non-residents, and of the part played by interest rates in influencing the movement of funds to or from London (a wide and very important subject with which I do not deal in this Memorandum). The interplay of these considerations will point in any particular situation to a desirable structure of interest rates. At one time it may be desirable to push up short-term rates of interest in order to keep funds in London against the competition of high rates of interest in overseas centres, and perhaps in the face of fears about the sterling rates of exchange. But it may be felt at such a time that there is no case on that particular occasion for reducing the level of domestic demand for the country's output, and that long-term rates of interest should be kept relatively low. Alternatively, it may be desired on some other occasion to push up long-term rates, because demand is proving too buoyant and needs to be restrained, when there is no need for high short-term rates.

64. Within wide limits it is possible to achieve any desired structure of interest rates by a suitable combination of monetary policy with management of the National Debt. The Exchequer, by issuing short-dated securities in the place of long-dated, or *vice versa*, can secure the desired shift in relative rates of interest against the background of

a monetary policy which operates on rates in general. Of course, the interest charge on the National Debt will thereby be affected and this consideration will play an important part in determining the objectives of policy.

The 'Overall' Deficit

65. The headaches arise only for those who are not content to leave the quantity of money to look after itself. A great deal has been written and said about the 'overall' deficit of Government revenue in relation to total Government expenditure (including 'below-the-line' capital expenditure and financing). It is claimed that this results in an undesirable expansion of the banks' assets and in the quantity of money. The reason appears to be that it is only if the banks are enabled to expand their assets that a home will be found for the Government securities which have to be issued in order to finance this 'overall' deficit. What is meant by such a statement is that if the quantity of money did not expand, higher rates of interest would have to be offered on Government securities in order to find a home outside the banking system for those newly issued. Higher rates of interest may or may not be undesirable in a particular situation. If they are undesirable then there is no harm in an increase in the quantity of money. It is the behaviour of interest rates which matters and their influence on the level of demand, not the behaviour of the quantity of money. Either interest rates are dangerously low, in which case they should be raised, or they are not dangerously low, in which case there is no harm in the increase in the quantity of money which is called for to keep them down.

66. Some of those who worry about the 'overall' deficit go even further. They take it for granted that it can be financed only by increasing the floating debt (and that the whole of this increase has to be found a home inside the banks). But there is, of course, absolutely no reason why the Exchequer should not issue precisely the same kind of securities (though on cheaper terms) as the local authorities which are now denied access to the Public Works Loan Board. If the 'overall' deficit *were* financed entirely by issuing Treasury Bills, the reason would presumably be that it was desired to raise the Treasury Bill rate (in which case incidentally some interests outside the banks would be attracted into holding more of them, and bank assets would not need to expand by the full amount of the increase in the floating

debt). Actually the value of 'tender' Treasury Bills outstanding was on the average less in 1957 than in 1956 and less even than the sum of tender Bills and Treasury Deposit Receipts in 1948.

67. To my mind the 'overall' deficit is of no significance. But perhaps I make a serious mistake of tactics in complaining of the seriousness with which it is often viewed. It does provide – most providentially though irrationally – an argument for restraint in making concessions to taxpayers. It is a fortunate thing that, most of the local authorities having been cleared out from 'below the line,' the nationalised industries were brought in. The danger is that they too may be sent back into the market and that on that account the Chancellor of the Exchequer, faced with an 'overall' surplus in the place of an 'overall' deficit, will be expected to reduce taxes, at the expense of the 'above-the-line' surplus, which is what really does matter.

68. This confusion is often derived from the idea of a rate of 'real savings' which is apt to fall short of the rate of investment, being supplemented by credit creation. Any such concept should be suspect. Thrift is what matters – in the sense of refraining from physical consumption. But that has nothing to do with the behaviour of the quantity of money (though the rate of interest may exert some influence on the exercise of thrift).

A Minimum Liquidity Ratio

69. The proposal of a compulsory minimum liquidity ratio, which could be altered from time to time, is usually prompted by the ideas which I have been criticising. It has, however, to be recognised that an expansion of the banks' assets which *includes* an expansion of the banks' advances may be objectionable, on account of the consequent stimulus to investment, whereas it would be unobjectionable without it, regarded merely as the condition for avoidance of a rise in interest rates. But though it will help towards the end in view, a minimum liquidity ratio provides a rather indirect and imperfect method of limiting the banks' advances, which are more competitive with the banks' investments than with their liquid assets. When, however, the Treasury Bill rate is being deliberately kept low in order to keep down the interest on the National Debt, a compulsory liquidity ratio will help very directly to maintain the floating debt, the benefit of the Exchequer being at the expense of the banks' profits.

70. In general, any such device, including a variable cash ratio, is to be welcomed if it provides better means for securing a purposive end. The danger of such devices lies in the end becoming subordinated to the means.

Regulation of Bank Advances

71. For example, if it is desired to limit the total of the banks' advances, there seems much to commend a direct approach, and to proceed by way of edict, as the Government are doing. The Government can be criticised, I feel, on the grounds that the actual quantitative limit imposed at present on Bank advances is too low but not on the principle involved by this type of direct regulation.[1]

72. In any case it is nowadays generally agreed that monetary control provides a very unreliable and clumsy method of regulating investment. The greater the onus that can be placed on other measures the happier will be the conduct of monetary control.

Control of Capital Issues

73. The Capital Issues Committee could play a more useful role if it still enjoyed the backing of Government Departments concerned with the administration of physical controls. As things are now, it cannot be easy to discriminate on merit between one project and another, and often it must be difficult or impossible to decide which particular elements in a company's plan of development would be prejudiced by a refusal. When the Committee are actuated by financial considerations, as opposed to the merits of the physical projects, they seem to me sometimes too ready to court criticism. Nevertheless, I believe that their scope should be widened by stopping the obvious loopholes.

74. One very serious loophole lies in the financing of hire-purchase finance companies. This is particularly serious in view of the relaxation of the hire-purchase regulations themselves and the Government's apparent unwillingness to increase their severity. It is anomalous also that these companies, by reason of not being clearing banks, should escape both the Chancellor's direction as to the banks' advances and the implication of the conventional minimum cash ratio.

[1] See *Minutes of Evidence*, Qn. 10993.

Building Licensing

75. As to physical controls, I believe that there is a very strong case for re-establishing the fabric of building licensing and administering this control in accordance with the changing needs of the situation. Usually there could be a great deal in the way of open general licensing for building work falling into stated categories, at some periods all building operations would be temporarily free of control.

Investment Allowances

76. My final suggestion, as another powerful instrument to work in with monetary control and lighten the load on it, is the restoration of investment allowances, in the place of initial allowances. They are capable of considerable flexibility. There is no reason why at times of heavy pressure of demand they should not be negative, so as to constitute a tax on investment. If they are to be altered according to the economic situation it is, however, important that such alterations should be capable of being announced at any time, and not only on Budget Day – if necessary, for administrative reasons, with retrospective effect. For anticipation of a change in the rates will cause it to have the contrary of the desired effect until the change is actually announced and effective.

77. Some differentiation of rates should be possible as between one industry and another and one type of investment and another. While such possibilities are limited, the thin end of the wedge of discrimination has already been inserted in the provisions for investment and initial allowances, and it could certainly be driven in harder.

78. Monetary restriction throws a burden on the Exchequer while cheap money reduces the cost of interest on the National Debt. With investment allowances, and to a limited extent also with initial allowances, it is the other way round. The expansionist policy is expensive, the restrictive policy is cheap and might even yield revenue. The two methods should thus make happy playmates.

8

THE PACE OF DEVELOPMENT*

I

'To him who hath shall be given.' In its negative implication that sums up the basic problem which faces an underdeveloped country. Production relatively to population is severely limited by lack of physical resources and of skill. Although the standard of consumption is therefore low, there is only a small margin of production over the necessary minimum of consumption. And yet it is this margin which, apart from the use of foreign capital and of foreign aid, limits the amount of investment, and so limits the rate at which productivity and productive capacity can be increased as a result of development. It is a problem of the take-off, to use Professor Rostow's analogy.[1] If only the margin could be increased, production would grow faster and this would enable the margin to grow faster. In other words, any immediate effort will have a pronounced cumulative effect over future years and any immediate sacrifices are likely to be generously rewarded in the years to come. The trouble is that it is just at the early stages of development that an immediate sacrifice is so onerous. As has been recently stated in the report of a working party on development in Asia and the Far East, an acute and important conflict lies in 'the choices between immediate consumption and rapid growth based on high levels of investment. The major conflict for the countries of the ECAFE region is the conflict between present and future consumption – to the problem of time preference'.[2]

This conflict arises, it is pointed out, 'because it is not possible for a country to use more than the total amount of resources available to

* *The Challenge of Development*, The Eliezer Kaplan School of Economics, The Hebrew University, Jerusalem (1958).
[1] W. W. Rostow, 'The Take-off Into Self-sustained Growth', *The Economic Journal*, March 1956.
[2] From the Report of the ECAFE Working Party of the Economic Commission for Asia and the Far East on Economic Development and Planning, *Economic Bulletin for Asia and the Far East*, November 1956, p. 3.

it'.[1] This method of presentation is useful when applied to a country in which the available labour supply as well as all physical resources – natural resources and capital equipment – are fully utilised. For a country in which there is reasonably full employment, more labour can be applied to development only at the expense of applying less to the production of consumption goods. Here a higher rate of development means less production of consumption goods, and therefore less consumption. It is under conditions of full employment of labour that it is possible to apply the classical idea of accumulation as involving a sacrifice to the present generation, incurred for the sake of the future. And since the working population can then be treated as fairly homogeneous and since their consumption constitutes a large part of the total, it is not altogether unreasonable to regard decisions about rates of development as involving, at least in part, 'the problem of time preference' on the part of the workers. For the same individual who suffers the sacrifice will secure the future benefit, or if he does not, his children will. This does not mean of course that other classes of the community, whose consumption is far from negligible, cannot, and should not, be called upon to pay heavier taxes and so share in the sacrifice involved in a higher rate of development, but the extent to which this is expedient and practicable depends on the social and political environment, and in particular on how far taxation of the wealthier classes has already been carried as a means of improving distribution of income independently of the rate of development.

This is the position in many developed countries today whose resources, including the labour force, are pretty fully utilized under the pressure of the various competing demands, including the demands originating from quite high rates of physical investment. And there are a number of countries or regions which would usually be described as underdeveloped in which there appears to be no important reservoir of surplus labour. For example, Professor Arthur Lewis' views about industrialisation in Ghana are largely based on the fact that 'there is a shortage of labour in the Gold Coast which rapid industrialization would aggravate'.[2]

I want to confine myself to the more typical case of an underdeveloped country in which the labour force is very far from being completely utilised. This is the position in a large part of Asia. It is

[1] Report of the ECAFE Working Party, p. 3.
[2] *Report on Industrialization and the Gold Coast*, Accra (1953), p. 65.

also of course the position in Israel. But at this point I must make it perfectly clear that my remarks are not directed at Israel. I do so with shame and regret. I do not pretend to have any detailed knowledge of any of the countries to which, in a very general way, my remarks might apply. One does, however, hear quite a lot about them. I wish that I could say the same about Israel so far as my part of the world is concerned. The result is that while I should hope that there will be some bearing on Israel's problems in what I have to say, I cannot pretend that it is directly prompted by them.

The main point which I want to make about the typical under-developed country, in which there is surplus labour, is that it is perhaps somewhat misleading to present the problem of forcing a high rate of development in terms of the sacrifice to 'the present generation as a whole', as it was put to the ECAFE Working Party by the Secretariat.[1] What is now involved is principally a redistribution of consumption between different classes of the community and not a reduction in the total. The sacrifice is confined to particular classes. They are important of course. But there is a danger of being too much concerned about 'substantial interference with the natural time-preference of the people as individuals',[2] and of forgetting that a high rate of development from the outset involves current benefit as much as current hardship, quite apart from the all-round benefit which gradually results from the improvement in the means of production. If we think too much of the time preference of those who make a temporary sacrifice we are apt to overlook the benefit to other classes.

The burden falls quite largely on those wage earners who would be fully employed anyhow; the benefit accrues quite largely to those who secure full employment in consequence of the high rate of develop-ment and to those who would otherwise have to support them. The factors introduced by the existence of peasant proprietors and of a surplus of rural population are fundamental to the problems of a typical underdeveloped country but they need not affect the main course of my argument at this stage, and for the time being I will only allude to them and reserve more detailed consideration for later treatment.

[1] From a working paper prepared by the Secretariat for the ECAFE Working Party, *Economic Bulletin for Asia and the Far East*, p. 23.
[2] *Ibid.*

I want to take as my basis a proposition which is so obvious that it seems sometimes to be overlooked. It is simply this. In principle there is no reason why under these conditions a higher rate of investment need necessitate a lower aggregate of consumption, as it would if labour were scarce. For this conclusion to be completely upheld it would be necessary to assume that no productive resources are used in common by the investment and the consumption sectors. On the face of it that may sound a rather wild assumption. One thinks at once of limited resources of foreign exchange, of raw materials produced at home, such as steel, of transport and power facilities, and of particular kinds of skilled labour, as important scarcities which involve a conflict between the rate of economic development and the supply of consumption goods, in the sense that more of one necessitates less of the other – if the accumulated development of the past is taken as given. The qualifications thereby introduced to my basic proposition are not really fundamental. My case here rests on the enormous flexibility of a properly conceived development scheme – and to a minor extent on some limited possibilities of applying to the pattern of consumption the methods of Procrustes – by means of discriminatory taxation and some use of controls. If a given amount of foreign exchange is available for importing capital equipment, this does not mean that the character of the equipment is also given – spades might be imported rather than bulldozers. And in an underdeveloped country there are plenty of things to be done which can be done, if necessary, in a manner that does not seriously encroach on the services of scarce resources. To quote Professor Arthur Lewis –

Roads, viaducts, irrigation channels and buildings can be created by human labour with hardly any capital to speak of – witness the Pyramids, or the marvellous railway tunnels built in the mid-nineteenth century almost with bare hands. Even in modern industrial countries constructional activity, which lends itself to hand labour, is as much as 50 or 60 per cent of gross fixed investment, so it is not difficult to think of labour creating capital without using any but the simplest tools.[1]

It seems to me that one of the big failures in some of the underdeveloped countries lies in not exploiting on a greater scale traditional methods of construction which, although primitive, could add substantially to the accumulation of capital wealth by harnessing surplus manpower.

[1] A. Lewis, 'Economic Development with Unlimited Supplies of Labour', *Manchester School*, May 1954, p. 160.

I want therefore to postulate that means are available for securing that development *could* take place, *insofar as it was thought desirable*, in such a way as to take full advantage of the profuse availability of general labour and to take fully into account the scarcity of other productive resources. At any moment of time the problem is then one of trying to secure a greater redistribution of consumption. For additional employment means that those who would otherwise have been unemployed or imperfectly employed would add to their consumption and that additional consumption would have to be at the expense principally of those who would be fully employed anyhow. And over any period of time the problem is one of trying to secure a more rapid growth in the production of consumption goods. In considering the possibilities of improvement, the basic questions to be asked about any development plan are these:

1. At any and each moment of time could the more privileged, including those who enjoy full employment anyhow, consume less, so that the available supply of consumption goods could be spread out more evenly, with the result that total employment could be greater, and the rate of development speeded up?

2. Could the technical character of the equipment and improvements in which the development is expressed be modified in such a way as to take fuller advantage of the fact that, in one sense, labour is a more or less free good?

3. Could development in the consumption section be speeded up, so as to accelerate the growth of output of consumption goods – apart from any improvement secured under 2:

(a) as a result of the gradual speeding up of the rate of development secured under 1?

(b) as a result of attributing rather more importance to aggregate consumption in the fairly near future and rather less importance to the build-up for the more distant future?

Such comments as, in my ignorance, I am venturing are comments on certain habits of mind into which, I believe, it is easy to drop. I do not suggest that any of the considerations which I am advancing are not familiar to those who have been concerned with these matters. I am not, I am afraid, claiming to say anything new. Indeed, I should prefer to feel that I was not stating anything, but was simply asking some questions, by way of reassurance. But if I am giving way to the temptation to make rash assertions, it is because I have the feeling that certain methods of presentation, which are not necessarily wrong in themselves, encourage habits of mind which are to some extent wrong, and result in the considerations which I am stressing, becoming to some degree a subject for not much more than lip service.

II

I want to spend some considerable time on my first question – that of the distribution of the available supply of consumption goods. There are at least three familiar methods of presenting the problem which is here involved. One is the method which I have already illustrated – that of a conflict between present and future consumption. I have already explained why that method lends itself to overlooking completely the fact of surplus labour. There is a further objection to it – the concept which it implicitly introduces of a homogeneous working class, each member of it enjoying much the same standard as other classes. Such consumption is quantitatively extremely important. It comprises the consumption not only of capitalists in the ordinary sense, few perhaps in number but often substantial in terms of aggregate income and consumption, but also of the poor but numerous peasant proprietors and small landlords. Quite apart from the question of securing a contribution from these classes, so as to divert more of the available consumption towards those who would otherwise be unemployed, there is the serious fact to be faced and dealt with that the consumption of these classes is actually enhanced by reason of a higher rate of development, which, so far from imposing a sacrifice, confers a benefit.

Neglect of the consumption of other classes is a tendency which arises equally from the other two familiar methods of presenting the problem of the redistribution of consumption which I am now coming on to, and I will not repeat the point. The second method which I want to mention involves the familiar idea that what limits investment is the excess of production over consumption in the consumption sector, because this has to provide the consumption of those employed in the investment sector.[1] This, of course, subject to various important

---

[1] See, for example, M. H. Dobb, *Économie Appliquée*, 1954, p. 303 (translated in his *On Economic Theory and Socialism* (1955), p. 138) and 'Second Thoughts on Capital-Intensity of Investment', *Review of Economic Studies*, 1956, p. 35. Mr Dobb is careful to point out that he is presenting 'a very simplified two-industry model'.

qualifications, is perfectly correct as a statement. My objection to it is that it seems to make it natural, rather than highly unnatural, that the amount of labour which can be employed in any situation is strictly limited. It lends itself all too easily to calculations of the amount of employment which the system can stand. Of course, anybody who makes that sort of calculation realises that the excess of production over consumption in the consumption sector and the progressive development of that excess, depend on the success with which consumption is restrained as well as on the success with which production is expanded. But the formulation seems to me to encourage discussion in terms of aggregates and in terms of ratios, and the overwhelmingly fundamental question of the minimum consumption per head which can be tolerated for those who are fully employed seems to me to be overshadowed. Indeed it is often extremely difficult to discover what is assumed about this.

This difficulty arises especially over the prospective influence of the carrying out of a development plan on the growth of consumption per head of those who are fully employed anyhow. For example, under the Indian Second Five Year Plan it is visualised that the rate of total consumption may increase by some 21 per cent and the long-term plan appears to provide for it to increase over the next ten years by something like 50 per cent.[1] If one makes due allowance for the prospective growth of population and of industrial employment it would appear – though this is not, I think, stated – that a very considerable rise in the standard of living of those who are fully employed throughout is visualized. This may be politically desirable or necessary. If so the case is not presented – and above all it is not explained why it is politically desirable or necessary to achieve such a substantial improvement in the standard of living of those who are fortunate enough to enjoy full industrial employment. It is expected that the carrying out of the Indian Second Five Year Plan will 'not have any significant impact on the carry-over of unemployment of the earlier period'[2] (although it will relieve underemployment in agriculture and in village and small-scale industries).[3]

It is perfectly true that, with a growing population, the increase in

[1] *Second Five Year Plan*, Government of India Planning Commission (1956), p. 74 and chart facing p. 11.
[2] *Second Five Year Plan, A Draft Outline*, Government of India Planning Comission (1956), p. 8.
[3] Indian *Second Five Year Plan*, p. 74.

the labour force over the five year period is expected to amount to ten million and that the addition to employment should keep pace with that, a result which, if achieved, will be an improvement on the First Five Year Plan, the execution of which failed to increase 'employment opportunities *pari passu* with the increase in labour force'.[1] In the disappointing character of the growth of employment in relation to the growth of population, development in India, both realized and prospective, suffers from the same characteristics as development in many other countries with growing population. This defect of development and of development programmes is widespread. The carrying out of the programme for Greece, with a less rapid growth of population than that of India, 'will leave a major part of the excess labour supply, roughly anticipated at about one million at the beginning of the period, unabsorbed in effective production by 1960'.[2] With an even less rapid growth of population, the four year plan for Italy is expected to leave unemployment at over one million, but this would represent halving the figure over the period of the plan and the Italian *Ten* Year Plan enjoys the distinction of aiming at the virtual elimination of surplus labour by 1964.[3]

It does seem *prima facie* that the need to allow a fairly rapid rise in the standard of living of the fully employed is not sufficiently questioned. The same growing volume of consumption, if spread out more evenly, would not only mean less human misery, because the growth of employment would be more rapid, but would actually mean a more rapid growth of development. A rise in the standard of living with any rise in productivity of the fully employed worker seems sometimes to be regarded as an economic law, rather than something acceptance of which puts a serious brake on economic development and prevents full advantage being taken of the availability of surplus labour.

I suspect that part of the trouble arises from the use of global investment coefficients, coupled with capital–output ratios, without a sufficiently detailed and specific enquiry into the underlying relationships. It sounds impressive when we read that in India the investment coefficient – the ratio of saving and net investment to the national income – is expected to rise from about 7 per cent in 1955–6 to about

[1] *Ibid.*, p. 5.
[2] *Report of the Expert Group on the Economic Development of Southern Europe*, United Nations Economic Commission for Europe (1956), p. 16.
[3] *Ibid.*

11 per cent in 1960–1, to 14 per cent in 1965–6, and to 16 per cent in 1970–1. But the question is why the rise to the ultimate level of the coefficient is so slow. A more rapid rise could be achieved if it were possible more effectively and rapidly to harness surplus manpower, by diverting to those who would otherwise be unemployed and imperfectly employed more of the additional supplies of consumption goods. An important proviso, insofar as reliance is placed on private enterprise, is that by fiscal means the extra profits and agricultural incomes which are the result of high rates of development are prevented from absorbing more than a limited amount of the additional supplies of consumption goods.

Granted that proviso, the severity of which I do not wish to underestimate, my suggestion is that there is an undue readiness to regard the investment coefficient as simply part of the data. In India, we are told, the rate of economic development depends, apart from other considerations, on 'the proportion of the current income of the community devoted to capital formation'.[1] It seems to me to be as true, and perhaps more illuminating, so say that the proportion of the current income of the community devoted to capital formation depends on the rate of economic development. The fulfilment of a more ambitious programme would mean that consumption would grow even more rapidly, but that the consumption per head of those fully employed throughout would grow less rapidly, employment would grow more rapidly, and the growth of non-wage incomes – profits and agricultural incomes – would be more rapid. The scope of any such improvement is clearly subject to severe limitations.

III

The temptation is, as I say, to take it too easily for granted that the amount of employment which the economy can stand must be severely limited. This is the reason, I suggest, for the unadventurous spirit in which the question of rates of taxation is approached in many of the reports about development plans. It is astonishing how little space is devoted to the subject and how very unspecific and feeble are the remarks made about it in reports which on many other aspects of development are extremely specific and detailed.[2]

[1] Indian *Second Five Year Plan*, p. 7.
[2] In *The First Five Year Plan, 1955–60 (Draft)*, issued by the Planning Board

ESSAYS ON EMPLOYMENT AND GROWTH

The Italian Four Year Plan and the Greek Economic Development Programme provide rather extreme examples of the kind of attitude which I have in mind. It is assumed that taxes will not be raised at all.[1] It is true that in both cases reliance is placed on a diminution of tax evasion. But in the main the substantial growth in government revenues shown in the plans is the result simply of the projected growth of national incomes. In the case of Italy it is actually estimated that government savings will increase proportionately less than national income.

While in all such various reports lip service is normally paid to the need for restraining consumption it is seldom realised with sufficient force that unless *rates* of taxation are progressively raised, or new taxes are introduced, consumption will grow with real income, and that the growth of government revenue based on pre-existing rates of tax does not represent any positive contribution to the problem. One might have thought that if the Italian and Greek Plans do not call for any revision of taxation policy, that is a very good reason for trying out more ambitious plans. The Pakistan First Five Year Plan involves an 'increase between the first year and the final year of the Plan period in the annual amount of public revenue available for development purposes' of 'about 13 per cent of the increase in the estimated gross national product'. It is stated that 'an increase of this magnitude appears to be quite within the country's means'. But if this is so, why not try out a plan which the country could not quite so easily take in its stride? It is true that in the Pakistan Plan reliance is not placed entirely on 'the automatic result of expansion of production' but 'a series of positive measures will be needed to augment revenues'.[2] The Indian Second Five Year Plan aims at securing by means of additional taxation measures, including higher rates of tax, an addition to Central and State Government revenues which represents an addition of only 16 per cent to existing revenues.[3] One half of this addition is based on the recommendations of the Taxation Enquiry

of the Government of Pakistan (1956), seven pages are, however, devoted to 'some suggestions in very broad terms about possible changes in taxation' (vol. I, pp. 162–169).

[1] *Economic Development Programme for Italy*, United Nations Economic Commission for Europe (1956), p. 111 ;*Report of the Expert Group on the Economic Development for Europe*, p. 22.

[2] Pakistan – *The First Five Year Plan*, p. 143.

[3] Indian *Second Five Year Plan*, pp. 78, 91.

Commission and the other half was left to further investigation. I hope that I do not show lack of appreciation of the problems of increasing taxation in countries like India and Pakistan.[1] I certainly do not wish to support my case by undue emphasis on the facts that in the one country the ratio of tax revenues to national income is only $7\frac{1}{2}$ per cent,[2] and that it is rather less than that in the other.[3] But I do find it remarkable that the ratio of public to total saving visualized for the next five years is only 25 per cent in India[4] and 20 per cent in Pakistan.[5] This leaves 75 per cent and 80 per cent respectively to private savings.[6] These seem extravagantly high proportions for countries in which the great mass of the population live at standards of living which preclude personal saving. In the light of such figures the phrasing of the statement of the ECAFE Working Party that 'it is important that public revenues shall grow appreciably' might, one feels, have been more robust without danger of exaggeration.[7] Public revenues do in fact automatically grow more than 'appreciably' with the growth of national product. The point at issue relates to the tax *rates* and to the possibility of introducing new taxes.

Some misleading habits of thought perhaps prevent the attack on this problem from being as forceful as it might be. First of all there is the close association which one finds in some of these reports and documents between the fact of *public* investment and the need for *public* saving. In addition to covering all current expenditure out of current revenue, governments should, we are told, 'with the assumption of increasing direct responsibility for investment...also endeavour to finance a significant part of such investment by public saving'. In the light of this quotation from the Report of the ECAFE Working Party,[8] it seems fortunate that in fact so much of the investment in these programmes *is* to be undertaken by public bodies. On the other hand, there may be some reluctance to exacerbate the opposition which is inevitable anyhow against the intrusion of the

---

[1] For a study of the possibilities of collecting more revenue in India from personal and business taxes, see N. Kaldor, *Indian Tax Reform* (1956).
[2] Indian *Second Five Year Plan*, p. 90.
[3] Pakistan – *The First Five Year Plan*, p. 161.
[4] Indian *Second Five Year Plan*, p. 77 *et seq.*
[5] Pakistan – *The First Five Year Plan*, p. 17.
[6] External finance is planned to supplement total saving by 22 per cent of total saving in India and by 56 per cent in Pakistan.
[7] From the Report of the ECAFE Working Party, p. 8.
[8] *Ibid.*

11-2

State into the field of enterprise by attaching to it a case for more drastic taxation.

The presentation of the Indian plan relates the need for public saving, and so for additional taxes, not only, on the one side, to the amount of public investment to be undertaken, but, on the other side of the account, to the amount of borrowing to be secured from the public.[1] It is thus made to appear as though borrowing and taxes are equally good ways of raising finance for the public authorities, provided that the borrowing is from the public and not from the banking and monetary system. Instead of the proper contrast being drawn between taxes and all forms of borrowing a most misleading contrast is drawn between taxes and borrowing from the public, on the one hand, and borrowing from the banking and monetary system – deficit finance – on the other hand. The case for additional tax revenue is much less impressive if it is derived purely from an esti- mated failure, which might turn out unduly pessimistic, to borrow enough funds from the public.[2] These defects of presentation are avoided by the Planning Board of Pakistan, which adds public and private investment together and balances the total against public and private saving taken together, neither borrowing nor deficit finance entering into the picture.[3] One hopes that this presentation will assist the Pakistan Government in resisting 'the overriding pressure...for relief of one kind or another' which their Planning Board anticipates as soon as a surplus of current revenue over current expenditure is revealed.[4] In Greece, on the other hand, where public investment is to play a much smaller part, the complacent view towards taxation is no doubt associated with the statement that 'it is estimated that the funds required to finance the Public Investments in local currency will be readily available to the State'.[5]

I want to mention a further reason why the case for additional

[1] Indian *Second Five Year Plan*, pp. 77 *et seq.*
[2] Even Mr Kaldor accepts this line of approach and bases the need for additional taxation on his view, which would, he thinks 'be shared by most economists' that over the five-year period of the second Indian plan 'the amount of deficit expenditure which the economy can absorb is not likely to exceed...Rs 800 crores', as opposed to Rs 1,200 crores envisaged under the Plan (*Indian Tax Reform*, p. 1).
[3] Pakistan – *The First Five Year Plan*, p. 150.
[4] *Ibid.*, p. 162.
[5] *The Greek Long-Term Programme of Economic Development*, United Nations Economic Commission for Europe (1956), p. 44.

taxation appears to be put forward with lack of vigour. It is very much mixed up with the idea of securing a more equitable distribution of income and wealth. So long as this is confined to meaning an equitable distribution of the burden involved in a rapid growth of employment under an ambitious development programme, there is no need to cavil. Quite the contrary. Equity, so interpreted, would mean that the interests of those who would otherwise remain unemployed or imperfectly employed would come first in the scale of priority. The case for having public saving is based on considerations of equity in this sense. But this is not how it is interpreted. 'A reduction in inequalities has to proceed from both ends', we are told in connection with the Indian plan. 'On the one hand, measures have to be taken to reduce excessive concentration of wealth and incomes at higher levels, and, on the other, incomes in general, and particularly at the lowest levels, have to be raised.'[1] As to the excessive concentrations of wealth, we have been told by Mr Kaldor that without 'an efficient system of progressive taxation on the small minority of the well-to-do who in India number only about one per cent of the population...the rise in expenditure during the plan will inevitably increase the wealth of the richest classes disproportionately'.[2] It is about the ideal of raising incomes at the lowest levels that I am expressing doubt. Presumably this does not refer exclusively to those who secure additional employment. In the minds of some people there may be the idea of a more equitable distribution of the existing burden of taxation, but the early stages of an ambitious development programme, designed to overcome the problem of the 'take-off' and to start the cumulative process of 'to him who hath shall be given', is the wrong time for *redistributing* the burden of taxation. Additional taxes should be aimed at increasing budget surpluses. This they cannot do if they are used for tax remissions. And if they are so conceived the adverse repercussions on private saving provide a very convenient argument for anybody who wants to obstruct, on classical lines, the attempt by such means to secure greater equality. To aim at a general transfer of income downward through the social scale is not helpful to economic development except insofar as it results from economic development. On the other hand, if the disparities which were causing concern were those which exist between those who are imperfectly employed and the rest of the

[1] Indian *Second Five Year Plan*, p. 35.
[2] *Indian Tax Reform*, p. 1.

community as a whole, including in heavy measure large numbers of workers as well as of peasants, the concern could usefully show itself in more ambitious development programmes, facilitated by ambitious taxes all round. I doubt whether these disparities were in mind when the Pakistan Planning Board wrote that 'existing levels of consumption are already austere for the vast mass of people, and it is neither desirable nor practicable to depress them any further. On the contrary, it is urgently necessary to raise them.'[1] There is a widespread tendency to regard the unemployed as outside the community with whose interests one is concerned. When one reads, in the same report, about 'the ideals of a free society', one is forced to wonder whether the neglect of unused productive power, combined with the misery which goes with that neglect, are purposively justified by reason of the enjoyment by the more fortunate majority of a higher standard of consumption than would be compatible with more rapid development.

Neglect, insofar as it is neglect, of the interests of the unemployed and imperfectly employed goes hand in hand with neglect of the question how in fact they live. The answer is of course that in a country which has no state scheme for their support they live on their relations. When an unemployed man is provided with work or an imperfectly employed man moves into more effective employment, the rest of the family are relieved of the burden of supporting him. Their standard of living rises even if their real earnings do not rise, and if their real earnings rise progressively through time their standard of living rises faster. This is, so to speak, an uncovenanted benefit, and if it is allowed to be fully realized the rate of capital accumulation is deprived of the progressive acceleration with which the gradual elimination of extreme poverty should be capable of cumulatively endowing it. The remedy is, in determining the future course of the rate of investment, to have regard to *standards of living* of the mass of the workers rather than of real earnings per head. But the trouble is that the burden of supporting the indigent is distributed between families, and between regions, in a far from uniform manner. If policy is based on the relief to the average or typical family, some families may suffer a progressively falling standard of living, and for many families the improvement may appear inadequate. But the roughness of the justice therein involved is considerably less than the

[1] Pakistan – *The First Five Year Plan*, p. 75.

roughness of the justice involved in some families being much poorer per head than others.

What I am really pleading for is a more purposive and conscious set of decisions about the desirable – in the sense of minimum necessary – growth of the standard of living of the fully employed wage-earners. That will then determine how far the pace of development can be gradually accelerated. An improvement in the rate of development other things equal, means higher profits, and higher agricultural incomes, as well as lower real wage rates for those fully employed, than would prevail under the same conditions with a lower rate of development. This will mean higher consumption for the capitalists and the agriculturalists, and this will be at the expense either of the improvement in the rate of development or of the real wage rates of those fully employed. And apart from the effect of higher capitalists' incomes on the distribution of consumption, they are likely to give rise to political objection and will tend towards a concentration of the private ownership of capital. That is the case for combining an ambitious development programme with a progressive programme for drastic taxation of profits and other incomes which benefit in real value from a high level of investment instead of, like real wage rates, being kept down. The profits accrue in increasing measure but if a considerable part is diverted into the surplus of state revenues over current expenditure, the additional saving which has to match the additional investment can take the form of public saving and does not necessitate the growth of private consumption which goes with a growth of personal saving.

On this line of argument it does not matter how large gross profits become because it is the size of profits net of tax, not of gross profits, against which objections arise. The argument is, however, subject to severe limitations. As taxation becomes more drastic the temptation to evade it, and to avoid it, becomes bigger. The disincentive effects become more and more serious, and the political obstruction more and more obstinate.

Beyond a point it may be preferable to keep down the gross profit rather than to allow it to grow and rely on keeping down the net profit. The question is how this can be done without sacrificing economic development itself. The answer is by raising indirect taxation.[1] This too contributes to public saving. It enables a given rate of investment

[1] Cf. N. Kaldor, *Indian Tax Reform*, p. 4.

to be matched by a rate of saving of which a smaller amount is private saving, which means that it involves smaller profits. The prices received by the producers, net of additional indirect taxes, are depressed because consumers are provided with no additional purchasing power with which to pay the taxes.

The normal argument against greater reliance on indirect taxation, apart from taxes on luxuries, is that it falls on the poor and tends to be regressive. That is not inconsistent with its falling also on the producers – and keeping down profits. In general it will fall partly on the one and partly on the other. A further argument against additional indirect taxation then might be that a reduction of profit margins will mean loss of output – high-cost production will be cut out and physical resources used less intensively. These two arguments are not, however, independent. It all turns on the elasticities of supply. If these are very small, indirect taxes fall almost entirely on the producers and the question of loss of output scarcely arises. When I say that 'beyond a point' it may be preferable to keep down the gross profit, what I have in mind is the possibility that the pace of economic development may be sufficiently great for the pressure of demand to elicit almost the maximum output which the available natural resources and equipment are capable of yielding even though unlimited labour is available to work with them. If, and insofar as, that point has been reached, indirect taxes can be used to supplement direct taxes – provided that they do not curtail profit margins to levels at which production begins to be seriously affected. The curtailment of profits will result in curtailment of capitalists' consumption and even if it operates at the expense of some loss of output of consumption goods, there will – if this loss is only small – still be a net gain of consumption goods available for increasing investment. (The situation here depicted is one in which, with a *given* rate of investment, the imposition of indirect taxes would cause prices paid by consumers to fall relatively to wages: more than the whole of the taxes would fall on profits.)

The decision as to which commodities could stand indirect taxes of this kind therefore turns not only on the elasticity of supply of the products of each type of physical capacity but on the extent to which curtailment of profits would result in a curtailment of the capitalists' demands for the products of the same type of capacity. Commodities which constitute the staple consumption of the poorer classes do not qualify unless their supply is highly inelastic.

Indeed, these somewhat paradoxical possibilities for the use, and for the effects, of indirect taxation are not inconsistent with the introduction of subsidies on the bare necessaries of life to help meet the shock resulting from any sudden inauguration of a bolder development plan. The point is that subsidies will succeed in keeping down prices against the pressure of a rise of demand only to the extent that the supply of the necessaries has some appreciable elasticity and only because additions to capitalists' incomes are not to any appreciable extent devoted to them. It is only under these circumstances that the use of such subsidies can be justified, and clearly the justification must be strong and the use restrained. Some of the foodstuffs which are important in the diet of the poor may in this way lend themselves to subsidies, provided that the response in the supply does not merely reflect substitution for other important crops. But if there is to be a sufficient elasticity of supply to justify a subsidy, it is almost certainly necessary that most of the consequent improvement in agricultural prices should be syphoned off by securing greater revenues from land taxes or the like. Otherwise, the result will be to increase the food consumption of the agricultural population – conceivably by more than the increase of production.

The elasticities of supply to which I refer here are elasticities of short-period supply – within the limitation imposed by given amounts of physical resources – though in the case of food a year or so must be allowed for the full short-period adjustments to be made. It is, however, necessary for the argument that the imposition of indirect taxes, and the resulting curtailment of profits, should not prejudicially influence the manner in which new investment takes place in the production of the taxed commodities. The curtailment of profits should not go so far as to bring the desire to invest below what is required to absorb the physical resources which can be made available. Furthermore, reliance may have to be placed on profits for some of the finance needed to pay for the investment (though such reliance, if at all extensive, points to dangerous deficiencies in the financial system). In other words, some of the disincentives which result from heavy taxation of profits result also from the curtailment of net profits which is the effect of curtailment of gross profits; and when indirect taxation has been carried so far as to begin to have serious consequences of this kind, additions to it can no longer be justified as a form of taxation which avoids all the defects of heavy taxation of profits.

What is especially important is to ensure that investment is not directed to the less desirable ends, and in particular that additions to productive capacity are calculated to expand the production of the necessaries of life of the poorer classes. This will certainly not be achieved with any success except under some system of allocation and control, but so far as concerns the influence of indirect taxation, it will be of positive assistance if it falls with greater severity on the less essential commodities. The difficulty is, however, that for administrative reasons it will usually be necessary to confine indirect taxation to a limited number of classes of commodities and that a wide range of the less essential commodities and services will escape. This, it must be admitted, would add considerably to the weight which has to be placed on any system of allocation and control for avoiding waste of investible resources in private industry and trade.

There is one very important form of discrimination which is easily secured. One of the great problems in a rapidly developing economy is to prevent diversions from export to domestic markets. The imposition of a sufficient indirect tax, with exemption of exports, can secure for any commodity that the total rate of output and its division between export and domestic trade are unaffected by reason of a rise in the domestic demand.

The question, on which I have touched, of short-period elasticity of supply raises some issues of principle which I will mention in passing. I took as my basic proposition that it is possible to organize a higher rate of investment without thereby physically necessitating a lower aggregate of consumption, so that the economic problem is one of redistributing consumption rather than of enforcing a net over-all reduction. But if there is some elasticity of supply, a higher rate of investment will, by raising demand, lead to a higher output of consumption goods and, therefore, to a greater aggregate of consumption. The consumption of those who benefit will increase by more than the reduction of the consumption of those who suffer. My argument is then imbued with *a fortiori* force. Instead of dealing with a limiting case, to which Keynes may be thought by some to have little to contribute, we are now dealing with a case of Keynesian unemployment which differs from the conventional case only in the degree of the inelasticity of the supply curves. The only really acceptable reason for forgoing both the development and the additional output of consumption goods which a higher rate of investment would entail could be the unwillingness of those who are anyhow fully employed to accept a lower standard of living. That seems on the face of it a poor reason for failing to take maximum advantage of the physical possibilities for stepping up the production of consumption goods. What I have said so far can be regarded as a challenge to the wages system rather than to the operation of the profit motive. But if elasticity of supply is admitted, the challenge is widened and can be directed also at the system under which the volume of production depends on profits. An economic welfare theorist could devise a wonderful method of getting the systems to produce better results, under which the unemployed would bribe the employed to accept lower wages and both parties could then be better off with higher activity in both the investment and the consumption sectors. My suggestion of subsidies belongs, on the other hand, to the realm of practical politics, even though it is capable of useful application only in severe moderation.

The existence of appreciable elasticity of supply may mean that employment has not been carried to as high a level as the system is capable of 'standing', and that a higher rate of development would be perfectly feasible even without the introduction of special measures such as additional taxes. If the possibilities of production which exist even with the limits imposed by wage and profit systems, and by existing policies, are not being fully exploited, the immediate defect lies with the programme or with the execution of the programme. It may be premature to discuss the changes required to facilitate more rapid development if, up to a point, development could be speeded up without any important changes. Some authorities are inclined to take the view, about particular countries which are undergoing development, that the limiting factor is not at all the supply of consumption goods. It seems fairly clear that this was not the limiting factor during the period of the Indian First Five Year Plan. At the end of it 'prices...were lower by 13 per cent than when the plan started; in fact, they were slightly below the level on the eve of the Korean war'.[1] Foreign exchange reserves fell by less than was envisaged in

[1] Indian *Second Five Year Plan*, p. 5. It is noteworthy that in a letter by Mr Eugene Black, Governor of the World Bank, to the Indian Finance Minister in the autumn of 1956 on the subject of the Second Five Year Plan, the record of the period of the First Plan is favourably contrasted with the prospects for the Second Plan unless the programme for the public sector is cut down.

the Plan. 'The severe fall, by about 10 per cent, in Indian food prices in 1954–55' which 'caused considerable distress in rural areas', is the reason why Dr Balogh, in discussing the Second Five Year Plan, welcomes the inclusion of labour-using public works; for the consequent increase in 'the income of the lowest wage earner' will 'increase demand for food grains, which are relatively abundant'.[1]

If Dr Balogh is right about this it means that the Plan, or its fulfilment, fails to comply with even the most conservative and unambitious criteria. As Mrs Joan Robinson has put it: 'If it is not fear of the unemployed eating too much when they are given work that prevents full employment from being the objective, there must be some other hidden snag which the planners are trying to steer past, and it would surely be best to find out what it is and seek for means to root it out.'[2] Dr Balogh tells us that in India, 'the two main bottlenecks are: first, organizing capacity, and, secondly, foreign exchange for essential (machinery) imports. It is not as if food imports at this juncture represented an important burden.'[3] And one is often told much the same about other countries too when one tries to find out what really are the factors which are limiting the rate of economic development.[4]

[1] T. Balogh, 'India's Plan under Scrutiny', *The Banker*, July 1956. With his implicit criticism of the Plan for failing to take full advantage of existing resources, Dr Balogh combines the rather different criticism that 'investment in agriculture seems inadequate'. He is clearly thinking both of the possibility of speeding up the pace of development with existing agricultural resources and of the possibility of speeding up the growth of development by more rapid expansion of these resources. Similarly: 'The commodities that India needs most to prevent an increase in investment and income from leading to a monetary breakdown are the goods that are in heavy surplus in the United States – sugar, butter, cotton, wheat and rice.'

And elsewhere, in 'Problems of the Second Five Year Plan', *Capital*, Calcutta, 1956, Dr Balogh refers 'to the unusually long series of favourable monsoons, a recurrence of which over the second five year plan period can surely not be counted upon with any assurance'. The vagaries of the weather have, of course, to be reckoned with. The proposal of the Indian Planning Commission for the building up of buffer stocks is presumably put forward as something to be done in the event of exceptionally favourable weather rather than at the expense of the rate of development calculated to absorb normal harvests (Indian *Second Five Year Plan*, p. 39).

[2] Joan Robinson, '*Unemployment and the Second Plan*', Supplement to *Capital*, Calcutta, 1956.

[3] Balogh, 'Problems of the Second Five Year Plan'.

[4] Serious doubts as to the criteria which underlie development plans are raised by the following passage, relating to redistributive tax measures,

It certainly does seem to be a fact that investment is often held up by shortage of the foreign exchange required to pay for imports of equipment. The availability of foreign exchange must of course impose a decisive limitation on the maximum rate of development which can be carried out at any particular stage of the development process. This arises because imports supplement domestic production of consumption goods and because exports compete with consumption for the use of physical productive resources. In basing my argument on the hypothesis of a given total supply of consumption goods at any moment of time, I have implicitly been ruling out the possibility of improving on the planned rate of development at the expense of bigger imports and smaller exports of consumption goods. But this does not mean that the allowance of foreign exchange for imports of equipment should be allowed to dominate the rate of investment. If it does so it is because of failure to make sufficient allowance for the possibilities, referred to earlier in this paper, of importing equipment involving more capital-saving techniques and of carrying out part of the development by primitive methods requiring the use of very little capital per man employed. This brings into prominence Dr Balogh's other main bottleneck – organising capacity. The fact that some techniques are less capital-intensive does not mean that a deviation towards them is easy to make. And, in general, it requires more organising power, and not less, to cope with larger bodies of men endowed with smaller amounts of capital per head. But in a different sense the trouble is too *much* organisation. There is, I feel, too premature a desire to ape the elaborate capitalistic processes of advanced industrial economies. There is also perhaps too much emphasis on the idea of balance in the development programme. The result is an unduly rigid relationship between the amount of foreign exchange available for importing the equipment and the amount of employment in the investment sector.

The shortage of organising capacity is, of course, an extremely

from the Secretariat working paper prepared for the ECAFE Working Party: 'To the extent that a redistributive fiscal policy shifts purchasing power and real income from the rich to the poor, it tends to raise the effective demand for domestic products, reduce non-essential imports and provide greater inducement to invest in the domestic private sector. At the same time, redistributive finance, if applied too far in the form of high marginal tax rates, can impede the entrepreneurial effort and restrict further investment' (*Economic Bulletin for Asia and the Far East*, p. 47).

173

serious factor. This is not, however, a reason for unadventurous planning. In all countries development suffers from difficulties of organization. But the difficulties are faced more effectively where the targets are ambitious, and more effective steps will then be taken to improve and expand the available organising capacity. It is important also that the system of allocation and control, required to prevent wasteful use of resources, should not be so elaborate and detailed as to frustrate the natural response to prosperity in socially constructive directions of the spirit of enterprise. Production will often be impeded by some rather simple physical bottlenecks which will yield fairly easily to treatment under the influence of 'natural forces', without involving heavy investment.

Poor organization, combined perhaps with the use of primitive methods of construction, does in a sense mean waste of resources. It means waste in a *real* sense if the resources in question are consumption goods which might be used to provide more useful alternative employment in the investment sector. It may also mean waste in a real sense if it involves squandering foreign exchange, in the purchase of equipment and in increasing the supply of consumption goods, which might have been conserved and used to better purpose later on when time allowed better organisation to be built up. But unlike foreign exchange the services of surplus labour cannot be conserved. Failure to use them currently entails carrying into the future nothing but human deterioration and degradation, misery and unrest. The most that can be demanded is that the value of the work carried out – with 'bare hands' or however it may be – represents compensation from the social point of view for the adverse effect on the standards of living of those who would be fully employed anyhow, after allowance has been made for the saving in cost of supporting indigent relations, and after such allowance has been made as society, so to speak, wishes to make for the consequent improvement in the standard of living of those who secure the additional employment, and of other classes of the community. My case certainly rests on there being plenty of useful work to be done within the limits which I have imposed – I am far from advocating public works undertaken almost entirely for the sake of the employment provided.

The case for driving the system rather harder than it appears willing to go derives support from other considerations as well as from difficulties of organisation. The difficulties which stand in the way of an adequate system of taxation are partly administrative and partly political. Both kinds of difficulty are very powerful when it is a matter of preparing proposals in cold blood – at a time when the need arises purely from paper calculations about the future and not from the pressure of present-day facts. Mr Kaldor was invited to investigate 'the Indian Tax System in the light of the revenue requirements of the Second Five Year Plan',[1] as actually published. We shall discover fairly soon whether, under the pressure of the execution of the Plan, Mr Kaldor's proposals, or their equivalent, are put into effect. What I suppose we shall never know is whether, had the plan been more ambitious, Mr Kaldor would have felt able to formulate correspondingly more ambitious proposals.

The same considerations apply to the use of controls. It was only when towards the end of 1956 the Indian foreign exchange reserves started falling with unexpected rapidity that it had to be accepted that a considerable amount of the less necessary imports could be excluded. The India Planning Commission stresses the need for 'preparedness to adopt physical controls and allocations as necessary... Controls on essential consumption cannot be ruled out in particular situations.' But it 'would be desirable on psychological as well as administrative grounds to avoid as far as possible control and rationing of the necessities of life',[2] and no doubt other controls as well.[3] But the way to reduce the risk of being forced to introduce additional controls is to exercise appropriate restraint in planning and execution. What one would really like to know is whether, in the secret minds of the planners, any ultimate resort to additional controls will vindicate the plans as adequately bold or condemn them for undue rashness.

I do not feel that, speaking in Israel today, there is need further to labour the point that the end plays a decisive part in determining the means.

In considering the possibilities of more rapid development, I have been admitting that a sacrifice is involved – to a particular class of the

[1] N. Kaldor, *Indian Tax Reform*, p. i.
[2] Indian *Second Five Year Plan*, p. 39.
[3] For a similar indication of reluctant apprehension, see the report of the ECAFE Working Party, p. 12. The Pakistan Planning Board are naturally more unqualified on the issue. 'Extensive and rigorous controls on the use of resources... would be repugnant to the national ideals which have been enshrined in the Constitution recently adopted... We must... give full consideration to the environment within which private enterprise can flourish.' (Pakistan – *The First Five Year Plan*, p. 75.)

community – and so far I have on the whole been at pains to confine the possible sacrifice to the forgoing of part of the year-by-year improvement in standards of living rather than to call at any point of time for an absolute fall in standards. It must, however, be admitted that the improvement on the development plan to be secured in this way will begin by being very small, and though it will increase cumulatively through time it may be a long time before it is at all considerable. The cumulative implication of 'To him who hath shall be given' could be applied far more fruitfully if it was possible to face some small absolute fall in the immediate standard of living of the fully employed, resulting from a sudden jump in the rate of development. It is this, rather than the more modest attack confined to the rate of improvement, which involves the really serious political difficulties. They could be lessened by providing in the Plan for a fairly rapid restoration to something rather better than the pre-existing standards, the rate of improvement being severely restricted only after that has been achieved. It would be easier too, politically, if the rise of prices accompanying a sudden improvement in the rate of development could be associated with additional indirect taxation, so as to avoid a sudden increase in profits. This would have advantages from the economic point of view, subject to the considerations advanced earlier, and it would also help to allay apprehensions of a progressive rise of prices if the rise could, in people's minds, be attributed to extra taxes.

IV

I must deal very briefly with the third familiar method which I want to refer to of presenting the problem of the distribution of the available supply of consumption goods. It is the method which involves the use of that bewildering and misleading word 'inflation'. It is misleading because, as commonly used, it suggests that the weight of heavy demands on resources is dangerously onerous only in so far as monetary factors can be said to contribute to it.[1] Above all, it distracts attention from the part played by the wage bargain in fostering a progressive upward movement of prices. I will not here

[1] For example: 'There is the danger that the amount of deficit finance proposed in the Second Plan will prove to be well beyond the capacity of the Indian economy to absorb without excessive price increases' – from the letter, already referred to, addressed to the Indian Finance Minister by the President of the World Bank.

elaborate my views on the topic of deficit finance as we are, I believe, having a separate session on the monetary aspects of development. I will content myself now with saying that in my view the fundamental issue is not monetary but physical, as presented, for example, by the available supply of consumption goods and the question of their distribution. But I would not for a moment deny that a rapidly rising price level presents a serious obstacle to a country's development and that it is perfectly possible that as a result of trying to do too much a country may succeed in doing too little. Nor would I deny that, especially in underdeveloped countries, the speculative indulgence in hoarding of commodities and gold, and in wasteful forms of building, leads to misdirection of resources. These anti-social methods of holding private wealth call for strict controls and stringent penal measures. Their extent does also depend, among other things, on the general state of credit and on levels of rates of interest. This is a sense in which monetary policy is very important. But monetary policy must be conceived and developed in terms of the total stock of money in relation to other forms of private wealth, and some compromise has to be struck between the desire to promote socially constructive investment in the private sector and the desire to discourage anti-social methods of holding wealth. No assurance of correct monetary policy can be derived from matching the expansion of the monetary medium with the growth in the use of money for the purposes of day-to-day transactions.[1] This growth is a factor in determining the rate of investment which should be aimed at, because it requires restraint of consumption to build up the stock of money used for the purposes of day-to-day transactions. But the extent to which investment is financed by the monetary and banking systems will not determine whether the rate of investment is or is not dangerously high. The usual rule for the safe amount of deficit finance provides no assurance whatever that monetary policy starts off right and even if by some

[1] One is often told that a monetary theory which is applicable to advanced countries has no place in the underdeveloped countries. I have indicated in the text the importance in underdeveloped countries of anti-social forms of holding wealth. But on the main point of difference which is often stressed, the Pakistan Planning Board takes precisely the contrary view: 'Money is accumulated beyond transactions needs as one of the major methods of storing or holding wealth. In this respect, of course, the situation differs radically from that of highly-advanced industrial economies' (Pakistan – *The First Five Year Plan*, p. 155. It has been hinted earlier in the text that the usual *mystique* about deficit finance is avoided in this document).

happy chance it starts right there is really very little assurance that it will be kept right by adherence to this rule.

This observation has perhaps more application to Israel than most of my paper. And in going on to my next point I have Israel especially in mind, and I will not shirk being blunt. The behaviour of money wages is the key to the behaviour of the price level in Israel, as in advanced industrial economies. In a country like India, on the other hand, the proportion of the working population which lives on wages is small. Even there, however, the wage system provides some sort of a base, small and uncertain though it may be, for the very large pyramid of the price structure, though obviously other important elements contribute to the danger that the system of prices will move progressively higher in an unsuccessful attempt to achieve stability. My main objection to the word inflation, in the sense in which it is commonly used, is that it seems to grant some partial absolution to the parties to the wage bargain. If only one was permitted to take the rather simple view that the vicious spiral was due to the unsuccessful attempt of wages to catch up prices, or something of that kind, and leave the quantity theory of money out of it, responsibility would be more clearly attached where it belongs. When labour is organised its leaders should be able to say to what extent their policy takes into account its full implications – in terms of a brake on economic development, of a drag on the growth of employment, and of postponement of the date at which surplus manpower will finally have been absorbed into full and effective employment and the benefits of capital accumulation can be more handsomely displayed in the form of rising standards of living as opposed to a rising volume of employment. If the carefully considered view of the representatives of organised labour is that the Government is trying, in the interests of absorbing immigrants into the economic life of the country and of its economic development generally, to impose too heavy a burden on those who are already well established in industrial employment, and if that view brooks no discussion or argument, one would have imagined that in a country like Israel there must be less heavy-handed and destructive methods of influencing the Government's policy than by operating through the wage bargain. I put it like that because I believe that a calm, scientific appraisal of the implications of a high rate of development will be conducted with a public spirit which is broader and more farsighted than the public spirit which serves as

178

a drag – an effective drag, but only up to a point – on wage movements. But, of course, it is quite essential that, for political and sociological reasons, as well as economic, the taxation of other classes should be severe, in application as well as intention. I have already mentioned the part which might be played by subsidising some of the bare essentials of life. I need not expand on the futility of tying money wages to a cost of living index, but stabilisation of an index based on the prices of a few bare necessities could serve a useful purpose.[1]

Employers also need to be asked to exercise restraint in bidding up wages. This is not a very palatable view but I do not see how it can be avoided. It is especially important in countries in which there is no strong trade-union movement, and in which therefore the vicious spiral may result from the actions and attitudes of the employers as much as from those of the workers.

I am touching here on the tricky field of social psychology, and of the possible influences of education and propaganda in communities with which I am entirely unacquainted. All I will say is that I am not convinced that nothing could be achieved if the issues were presented on a straightforward and commonsense sort of basis. It is not merely the usual argument that wage increases defeat their own purpose. It is a question of securing some appreciation of the idea that wage increases retard economic development and that the benefits associated with development are not only those which lie in the future but also take the current form of less risk of unemployment and a smaller burden in supporting relations who are unemployed or imperfectly employed. It is particularly important in a country like India, where wage labour is a small proportion of the total, that this small tail should by every possible means be discouraged from wagging a very large dog.

V

Having dealt now, at rather considerable length, with three methods of presenting the problems involved in the distribution of the

---

[1] It is worth noting that the last round of Swedish wage negotiations, which will result in very modest increases over the ensuing two years, has led to agreement that an escalator clause, which becomes effective if the cost of living rises by more than a certain critical amount, will not operate if the rise in the cost of living is attributable to special taxes imposed for anti-inflationary purposes.

12-2

available supply of consumption goods, all of which I regard as misleading – though not necessarily as erroneous – I suppose that I should at least indicate a method which I would myself prefer. Granted the kind of economic system which rules in the countries which I have in mind, the problem, it seems to me, is best presented in terms of a vested interest on the part of a large majority of the population in a standard of living which, though low enough in all conscience, represents more than their share of the available supply of consumption goods, with the result that the minority have to live on a standard which is very much lower. The vested interest is partly the result of physical necessity. A man needs more food, and more clothes too, if he is doing hard work than if he is idle or doing only occasional light work. It is conceivable that, in particular countries at particular times, the total effective power of the whole labour force would be less if consumption was divided equally – just as shipwrecked sailors in a lifeboat might be well advised to concentrate dwindling rations on those who man the oars, the rest being kept alive on a starvation basis. I doubt, however, whether the economic system could usually find full justification purely in terms of expediency. It is a system under which, to put it crudely and brutally, some must live on a starvation basis so as to enable those who are in effective and full employment to enjoy the higher standard which, for a mixture of reasons, they are able to maintain. The problem is how to secure that the starvation standard, which has to be the lot of some, is, progressively through time, the lot of as few as possible.

The problem is also to secure that it is the lot of those who are least able to make a useful social contribution by being in employment. This is the answer to those, like Dr Balogh, who argue that, in a country like India, 'a cut in private consumption expenditure', resulting from heavier taxation of the rich, 'will not...necessarily produce the desired results. A large part of this expenditure is devoted to servants or goods produced by handicraft. A nondiscriminating cut in expenditure might, in fact, easily result in increased unemployment rather than increased investment.'[1] But if servants and craftsmen become unemployed it becomes possible to employ others instead who would otherwise have to remain unemployed. Granted that some have to starve, it is better that it should be the parasites of the rich rather than those capable of constructive work.

[1] Balogh, 'India's Plan under Scrutiny'.

The solicitude which I appear to invite on behalf of the unemployed should not be allowed to suggest that I am urging the case for 'work for work's sake'. The case for taking advantage of the existence of surplus labour to increase output is not to be confused with any suggestion that greater employment should be secured at the expense of smaller output.

But the rejection of 'inferior' techniques does not rule out the possible adoption of more capital-saving methods, so as to secure a larger output, with the aid of the limited amount of capital that is available, by employing more labour. The natural bias against any deliberate encouragement of inefficient methods sometimes becomes a very wrong-headed bias in favour of highly capital-intensive methods which are appropriate only to economies in which labour is scarce and dear. From this confusion there appears to have developed in some quarters a feeling of intellectual snobbery against taking into account the fact that labour is abundant. This is combined with the feeling that 'the most important single factor in promoting economic development' being 'the community's readiness to develop and apply modern technology to processes of production',[1] this entails using the same processes as are used in the most advanced countries.

There are of course great difficulties in the way of adjusting the application of modern technology, which has been developed in advanced countries, so as to take account of the relative scarcity of capital and abundance of labour in underdeveloped countries.[2] And of course imported plant is more likely in its character to be appropriate to the economic circumstance of the supplying country than of the importing country.

A more valid consideration arises with plant which is highly durable or which takes a long time to get into production. It is then necessary to consider to what extent during the life history of the plant labour is likely to become scarcer.[3] Hence the importance of finding an answer to a question put, in the context of the Indian Second Five Year Plan, by Mrs Joan Robinson: 'By the time the basic industries', on the importance of building up which strong emphasis is laid, 'are ready to produce machinery, will the surplus of labour have been digested,

[1] Indian *Second Five Year Plan*, p. 6.
[2] Cf. *Analyses and Projections of Economic Development*, prepared by the Economic Commission for Latin America, (1955), vol. I, p. 8.
[3] On this, and the related issues, cf. *The Greek Long-Term Programme of Economic Development*, p. 24.

so that the time will be ripe to begin mechanising industry and agriculture in earnest?'[1]

The question of the right choice of technique is vast and baffling and I will confine myself to a few comments. First, the choice of technique in the production of consumption goods. This has become a familiar problem. Low wages in themselves ensure that under the influence of private enterprise relatively capital-saving techniques will be used – i.e. more capital-saving than would be used if wages were higher.[2] But the industrial wage is not so low as would be necessary to reflect the fact that, in those countries of which I speak, labour is more or less a free good.[3] Does this mean that it would be desirable to deviate in the direction of even less capital-using techniques than will be adopted under private enterprise? Or, on the other hand, is it possible to rest on the idea that 'to the extent that the competitive market system is operating effectively, the need for any special policies for allocating resources among different purposes is obviated'.[4]

The usual answer is that private enterprise will promote the socially desirable technique provided that the social objective is to maximize the current rate of accumulation.[5] The reason is that the maximization of profit will maximise saving, including the contribution to public saving made by taxes on profits. This rule has in fact to be modified – even for operation on its own ground. It does not take into account the contribution to public saving made by indirect taxes. If the system of indirect taxation is such[6] that a substantial additional contribution is made to the revenue when more men are employed in producing additional consumption goods, this should be brought into account but is not brought into account by the calculations of private

[1] Joan Robinson, 'Unemployment and the Second Plan'.
[2] But it is efficiency wages which matter and as against a relatively low wage per head has to be set any relatively low intrinsic efficiency of the labour.
[3] It is sometimes objected that in such countries the proper social cost of labour is the additional consumption which is required for physical reasons to enable a man to work efficiently, over and above what he has to keep alive on when he is out of work. This would be valid, however, only if no account were taken of this additional consumption in considering economic objectives. The normal procedure is based on the view – which seems justified – that a man derives satisfaction from the additional food which he can afford when he is in work, including that part of it without which he would be physically incapable of working.
[4] From the Report of the ECAFE Working Party, p. 3.
[5] See, for example, M. H. Dobb, *On Economic Theory and Socialism*, p. 3.
[6] In accordance with the argument advanced earlier in the text.

enterprise (which is influenced by the ruling rate of profit and not by the high rate of profit which would rule if indirect taxation were abolished but the rate of investment nevertheless maintained). Allowance also has to be made for the fact that a man who is provided with additional employment increases his consumption by less than the wage which he is now paid. Insofar as the saving to his relations of the cost of maintaining him in unemployment, or in imperfect employment, becomes reflected in a higher rate of investment[1] (and a corresponding narrowing of the gap between real wage rate and standard of living of those who were already in full employment), this again is something which is not allowed for in the calculations of private enterprise. Private enterprise, in its search for maximum profits, fails to make allowance for the existence of surplus labour, except insofar as this is reflected in the wage rates which are paid, and for both the foregoing reasons this failure implies that it adopts a technique which, from the social point of view, is too capital-using even if the social objective is to maximize the current rate of accumulation, i.e. it would be desirable to use a technique requiring more labour and less capital for a given output.

The deviation in this direction called for by the two reasons which I have stated is limited. It would still be possible, by further deviation in this direction, to secure, for given current investment in the production of consumption goods, a more rapid growth of output, and with it a more rapid growth of employment. The argument against this is that the more rapid growth in the fairly immediate future of output of consumption goods, of consumption, of national income, and of employment, would be at the expense of investment in the fairly immediate future, and therefore of consumption and income in the more distant future. To secure the objective of maximum rate of accumulation it is necessary to employ the available capital in a relatively inefficient manner, i.e. less productively than it would be employed if it were used with more labour. The reason can best be seen in terms of the function, as I have described it, of starvation in regulating the economic system. A more efficient use of capital would entail 'too' rapid a diminution of the number of those who, unemployed or imperfectly employed, live on a starvation basis.

The question of the right social objective is of course crucial. Do we necessarily accept the view put forward by the ECAFE Working

---

[1] As was urged earlier in the text.

Party that 'the basic principle in economic development is the optimum use of resources, so as to maximise the rate of growth over
time'?[1] Although the Indian Planning Commission refers to 'an
attempt to work out the implications of the development effort in
terms of factor allocations and product yields so as to maximize
incomes and employment',[2] and although they state that 'it is imperative that in a country with an abundant supply of manpower,
labour-intensive modes of production should receive preference all
along the line',[3] in the outcome it is difficult to infer to what extent
the maximization of the rate of accumulation is not an overriding
objective, insofar as the future course of the rate of accumulation
depends on the pattern of current investment.

In advocating boldness in the planning of development, I have tried
to throw doubt on the validity of the conventional idea of a conflict
between the interests of the present and of the future. I have argued
that, in a country with surplus labour, a high rate of development
need not involve such a conflict. The conflict is all in the present –
between the interests of those who are fully employed anyhow and
those who could secure employment from a higher rate of development; but in terms of the current rate of consumption regarded as an
aggregate there need be no conflict. In this sense stepping up the rate
of development can be of benefit in the present as well as in the future.
When, however, it comes to the choice of technique for the production of consumption goods, and to the influence of that choice on the
rate of development, there is a genuine conflict. It is a conflict between
the interests of the relatively near future and the interests of the
relatively more distant future. These interests can be expressed in
terms of income, and also of consumption, taken as aggregates; while
if full employment can be assumed anyhow for the more distant
future, there is a conflict between employment in the near future and
standards of living in the distant future.

A choice of technique which sacrifices everything to the interests of
the distant future is entirely without justification. It may seem feasible
to ignore the simple political and psychological fact that people are

---

[1] Report of the ECAFE Working Party, p. 3. The Working Party mentions as
a conflict which does arise in practice that 'between such aims as the
desire for full employment and maximum growth' but this is not expressed
in the form of a conflict between *output* at near and at distant dates.
[2] Indian *Second Five Year Plan*, p. 15.
[3] *Ibid.*, p. 27.

more interested in benefits which they will enjoy rather early than late – and perhaps only vicariously enjoy through their children; although neglect of this simple fact is impossible to reconcile with the respect which is paid, in the name of liberty and democracy, for the interests of those who are relatively fortunate in being fully employed anyhow as against the unfortunate who are unemployed or imperfectly employed. But what cannot be ignored is that an addition to consumption of given size means more when people are very poor than when they are less poor, and that the implication of development is that the people are gradually going to become less poor as time goes on. It seems reasonable to add that an addition to consumption of given size means more at a time when it accompanies extra employment than at a time when conditions of full employment have been achieved anyhow.

The real conflict, therefore, arises over the possibility of securing an addition to the consumption, and to the employment, of the present generation over the immediately coming years at the price of forgoing, in the more distant future, a larger amount of consumption. How the appropriate rate of discount should be evaluated is a nice question. But it is clear that the right technique is a less capital-using one than the technique which is calculated to maximize the rate of accumulation.

What is here advocated is some sacrifice in this way of the rate of development for the sake of using capital more efficiently and for the sake of avoiding a nonsensical neglect of the interests of the near future as opposed to those of the distant future. This does not mean abandonment of the claim that rates of development are capable of being higher than in fact they are, as a result of greater restraint on consumption per head, or on the growth of consumption per head, of those who are fully employed anyhow and of the recipients of profits and agricultural incomes. What it means is that on the basis of the physical resources available at each moment of time, the highest possible rate of development should be achieved; but that the form in which physical resources are expanded with the passage of time should not be determined solely with an eye to securing maximum rates of development. In other words, there is a limit to the extent to which, for the sake of the rate of development, capital should be embodied in an inefficient form – by which I mean a form in which it results in a smaller output than it would be capable of if combined with more labour.

There is another aspect of the pattern of investment which also involves the same sort of conflict between consumption and employment in the near future and consumption in the distant future. But this time a bias towards consumption and employment in the near future is favourable, and not unfavourable, towards the rate of accumulation in the near future, though a higher rate of accumulation in the near future can be secured only at the expense of accumulation in the distant future, and ultimately of course of the accumulated stock of capital. These conflicts are involved in the choice between quick-yielding and slow-yielding forms of investment.[1]

It is frequently asked why far more of the available investible resources are not applied so as to secure quick results in the form of additional production of the goods which workers consume. In this way the overriding bottleneck which limits investment could be more rapidly widened, and the growth of investment, as well as of consumption and employment, would be accelerated. In fact, it is usual to find that only a fraction of the total investment envisaged under a development plan is directed to agriculture. In the case of the Indian Second Five Year Plan, there was a last-minute decision of the National Development Council that 'it is imperative that the targets of agricultural production proposed in the Plan should be further improved upon'.[2]

On the other hand, the investment of resources in the build-up of, say, a steel industry, to be geared into a heavy machinery industry, and in the improvement of power and transport facilities, will ultimately, when the long periods of gestation have been completed, prove far more fruitful than the alternative quick-yielding investments – in terms of the consumption goods yielded. It may be well worth while making a sacrifice in the near future of some of the potential growth of consumption, and of employment, for the sake of much bigger gains in the more distant future.

This argument is a strong one and goes a long way. There is no clear-cut solution to the problem as to how far it should impose itself on the pattern of development. Essentially it is a question,

---

[1] The same sort of considerations are involved in dividing the available foreign exchange resources between the financing of imported equipment and the financing of imported consumption goods (and raw materials required to make them) and of loss of exportable surpluses resulting from the stepping-up of domestic consumption.

[2] Indian *Second Five Year Plan*, p. 3.

once again, of the rate at which the more distant future is discounted (the concept of discounting the future being interpreted in the widest possible sense). The difficulty is that one does not know what rates of discount are implicit in any particular plan.

It so happens that very often long gestation periods go with high durability of the plant and equipment (which to a considerable extent is in such cases in the nature of constructions rather than ordinary machinery). This means that the more distant future, over which 'the much bigger gains' might be available, may be strung out very far indeed.

And of course long gestation periods and high durability mean that the techniques in question are highly capital-using. This brings one back to the question at what point, in relation to the distant horizons which the elaborate build-ups are aimed at, reasonably full employment is likely to be achieved. Part of the point of the question is, of course, that the allocation of investible resources to these slow-yielding capital-intensive forms of investment itself holds up the process of absorbing surplus manpower.

Despite the difficulties involved in the making of the relevant decisions, it is natural to ask what would be the economic implications of putting back in time, say by ten years, a part of the section of a plan which involves the long-term build-up. It would involve postponement – not by ten years but by something approaching ten years – of a part of the ultimate benefits, which in any case will not be fully realized for many years to come. Might not the postponement seem worth suffering for the sake of a more rapid absorption of surplus manpower and a more rapid growth *in the near future* of consumption – as well as of investment?

Whether that is so or not, the case which I have tried to indicate for securing bigger sacrifices – either absolute though temporary or at the expense of rates of improvement of standards – from the rest of the community, for the sake of drawing people more rapidly out of unemployment and imperfect employment, is strengthened if the whole of the resultant additional investment could be conceived as taking quick-yielding shape.

Before leaving this topic I would mention three further doubts. The first one arises over the extent to which under development plans the growth of consumption of basic necessities may be sacrificed for the sake of growth of consumption of less essential goods and services.

This doubt gives rise to two separate questions. Is the benefit which development aims at insufficiently concentrated on the large majority of the community who are really poor? Secondly, is sufficient influence conceived as being exercised on the pattern of consumption of the poorer classes, in the form of discriminatory taxation and controls? It is natural enough with the growth of income that the demand for passenger travel, for the domestic use of electricity and for consumer capital goods should rapidly grow. But these particular demands involve high capital-output ratios and it would be well to contain them for a time.

My second doubt arises on the technique of planning. To secure internal consistency in a plan is not easy. But it is important (within limits). Is there, however, a danger that because a plan is internally consistent there will be a tendency to regard it as being necessarily a good plan?

My third doubt can also be expressed in the form of a question. Is there a danger that on the distant horizon, to which so much in these plans has to be aimed, it is a high rate of accumulation rather than a high rate of consumption which the build-up is designed to facilitate? Is there a danger of accumulation being regarded as an end in itself?

VI

Before I close I must include a sketchy elucidation of the implications of 'imperfect employment', as I have used the term, in my typical underdeveloped country. More important than total unemployment is underemployment, particularly in agriculture. But still more important is imperfect employment. This results from the overcrowding of workers into particular occupations, to such a degree that if some of them were diverted to other work the resulting loss of product would be small in relation to their own consumption. Imperfect employment, like underemployment, is particularly associated with agriculture, especially among peasant proprietors whose numbers are increasing at all rapidly. It is bound up with lack of alternative opportunities. But under a system in which each member of the family shares the fruit of the family's toil so long as he lives and works with them but ceases to receive his share if he leaves the family holding, the incentive to the individual to seek work elsewhere is unlikely to reflect the full economic benefit which the family, and society generally, would derive from his diversion to more productive work. The economic benefit is measured roughly by the excess of the wage in industry over the marginal product in agriculture, whereas the private incentive is measured roughly by the excess of the industrial wage over the agricultural average product. The agricultural marginal product under conditions of over-population tends to be very low indeed – it is sometimes described as zero or even negative.

The idea of imperfect employment can also be applied to those middle-man activities which yield a smaller social than private gain. Insofar as they are often conducted by uneconomically large family units, this then accentuates the imperfection. And some self-employment in service trades is also imperfect, in the same kind of sense.

In applying the foregoing analysis to a diversion of labour from agriculture to industry, allowance has to be made as a social cost for the loss of the marginal product in agriculture if it is at all appreciable, and to that extent the conclusions require qualification. The marginal product in the relevant sense should, however, be estimated after proper allowance has been made for the stimulating effect on agricultural efficiency of a withdrawal of surplus manpower – a factor which in itself will tend towards a low marginal product. Allowance also has to be made for the social cost involved in providing new dwellings and other services for immigrants into the towns.[1]

The standard of living among peasant proprietors tends for three separate reasons to benefit from a high rate of development; and where there is a landlord he will absorb some or most of this benefit. Firstly, there is the favourable effect of high and rising levels of income and expenditure on the terms on which food is exchanged for products of industry. Secondly, there is the favourable effect on agricultural efficiency of development in agriculture itself. And,

---

[1] There must often be a strong case for small-scale industrialization in the rural districts, as well as for constructional activity based on the village, so that the labourer can continue to live as part of a peasant family, draw a share of the agricultural product and work for correspondingly low industrial wages, and be available for work at harvest time on the family holding.

Professor Arthur Lewis, who has been quoted earlier in the text on the shortage of labour in Ghana, points out elsewhere that 'in the Gold Coast, although there is an acute shortage of male labour, any industry which offered good employment to women would be besieged with applications' ('Economic Development with Unlimited Supplies of Labour', p. 143) – surely a strong argument for dispersed industrialization.

thirdly, there is the effect of restraint, resulting from withdrawal of labour into the towns, on the number of people who have to share the produce of any particular area of land.

To some extent a rise in rural standards of living is properly regarded as highly desirable, even though it operates at the expense of the growth of industrial employment (and at the expense therefore of the alleviation of rural overpopulation). The important thing is that any such rise should be purposive and not accidental, and that it should be limited to the minimum which appears essential. This is especially important because of the acute conflict between a rise in the rural standard of living and a rise in the standard of living of an unemployed worker who is drawn into employment – both being expressed in considerable measure in an increase in consumption of food. It is important also because any rise which has to be allowed in the rural standard of living necessitates an equivalent rise in the standard of living in the towns required to attract labour from the villages.[1]

The obvious mechanism to employ to restrain the rise in the rural standard of living is the land tax. It is of outstanding importance that the hesitation to increase land taxes, or even to restore their incidence in real terms to what it was, should be overcome.[2] As is stated by the ECAFE Working Party, 'the need for channelling a part of the increase in agricultural incomes to the exchequer can hardly be exaggerated'.[3] In India 'the land revenue at present...amounts to only 1 per cent of the net product of agriculture'.[4] It remains to be seen whether anything will be done to increase it.

This of course raises in acute form the question of political feasibility which, in one form or another, is raised by nearly everything that I have said. The question to my mind is what is really meant by the 'democratic means and process' through which, according to the Indian Planning Commission, 'development...should be achieved'.[5]

---

[1] Cf. A. Lewis, 'Economic Development with Unlimited Supplies of Labour', p. 172.
[2] Cf. A. Lewis ibid., p. 168. On p. 174 of this article Professor Lewis mentions the early experience of Japan, which is referred to also on p. 50 of the ECAFE working paper.
[3] From the Report of the ECAFE Working Party, p. 9. Cf. Report of the Expert Group on the Economic Development of Southern Europe, p. 21.
[4] N. Kaldor, Indian Tax Reform, p. 4.
[5] Indian Second Five Year Plan, p. 24.

Sometimes it is almost as though they are trying to tell you that nothing should be done which would not secure a clear majority on a referendum. Witness the following from the Report of the ECAFE Working Party:

The problem of conflicts among objectives cannot be resolved by a bureaucratic decision in a democratic society. The people register their choice among different objectives...continuously in the market place, and at the ballot box and through various forums for the expression of public opinion. Where plans, programmes and budgets do not conform to popular decisions they are changed.[1]

Certainly the plans, programmes and budgets entailed in a bold development policy would on this basis receive inadequate public support, the minority who lack work being too small to carry the day. At the other end of the income scale the interests of an even smaller, though more vocal, minority do not seem to be overwhelmed through lack of voting power. 'If the gap between planned expenditure and resources is too great to be bridged otherwise than through such disastrous proposals, a better alternative is obviously to cut our plans down' was Mr C. Rajagopalachari's recent comment on the announcement of the new Indian taxes on wealth and expenditure.[2]

The fact is of course that it is not plans which are changed in accordance with popular decision but governments. No government can be expected to run a serious risk of being turned out as the result of introducing unpopular measures. Short of that, democratic governments are constantly putting through measures which would fail to secure a majority on a referendum. They do it partly through the instinct of self-preservation. Governments are judged not only by their failure to introduce unpopular measures but also by their failure to achieve results. If one is looking at all far ahead it is not timidity which appears to offer a safeguard against political upheaval.

[1] From the Report of the ECAFE Working Party, p. 3.
[2] *The Times*, London, 17 May 1957.

9

EXERCISES IN THE ANALYSIS
OF GROWTH*

The development in the last few years of theories of economic growth
has introduced new concepts and called on unfamiliar tools. In this
lecture I intend no more than to take out for an airing a few of the
concepts to which Mrs Robinson and others have introduced us and
to try out the edge of a few of the tools. I am not attempting to build
up a theory of growth and still less to arrive at any conclusions.

I will begin with the fundamental identity, based on treating income as divided between capitalists' incomes and wages. At any and
every moment of time there is a simple relationship between the
rate of growth in the value of the stock of capital and the ratio to that
value of the stock of capital of the current incomes of the capitalists.
This relationship involves the proportion of capitalists' incomes
which is saved and the proportion of wages which is saved. The only
other factor which enters into the relationship or identity is the ratio
of the value of the stock of capital to the value of output, but this
drops out if only a small proportion of wages is saved.[1]

* *Oxford Economic Papers*, June 1959.
[1] Let α be the proportion saved out of capitalists' incomes and β out of wages.
Then investment = saving

$$= \text{capitalists' saving} + \text{wage-earners' saving}$$
$$= \alpha \text{ (capitalists' incomes)} + \beta \text{ (wages)}$$
$$= \alpha \text{ (capitalists' incomes)} + \beta \text{ (total income}$$
$$- \text{capitalists' incomes)}$$
$$= (\alpha - \beta) \text{ (capitalists' incomes)} + \beta \text{ (value of output)}.$$

It follows that the rate of growth of the value of the stock of capital, which
is measured by

$$\frac{\text{investment}}{\text{value of stock of capital}},$$

is identically equal to

$$(\alpha - \beta) \frac{\text{capitalists' incomes}}{\text{value of stock of capital}}$$

$$+ \beta \frac{\text{value of output}}{\text{value of stock of capital}}.$$

What is necessary for this simple relationship to be generally valid is that *income* should be defined in a suitable manner, so that the excess of income over consumption is the same thing as the rate of change in the value of the stock of capital. This requires that the owner of a piece of capital equipment should include in his income any increase in its value which, after due deduction of depreciation, arises apart from any physical work conducted on it by way of improvement (and that he should deduct any fall in its value apart from depreciation). As a corollary, the relationship, if it is to be valid, requires that any such changes in the value of capial equipment are included in investment, which has to be defined as the rate of change in the value of capital and not in any sense as the value of the change in the amount of capital.

The same kind of relationship could be expressed in terms of alternative definitions of income provided that the rate of growth of the stock of capital was appropriately defined. For example, if we follow ordinary social accounting procedure, investment is measured by the cost of additions to the stock of capital and income does *not* include additions to the value of existing capital equipment which result, say, from a rising price level or from improving profit expectations. For the relationship to hold, the rate of growth would then have to be defined as the rate of expenditure on additions to the stock of capital (less depreciation, with the logical problems therein involved) divided by the value of the stock of capital.

The magnitude of the capitalists' savings coefficient depends on the definition of income which is adopted – unless capitalists do not consume at all, in which case the coefficient is always unity. And the natural choice of definition turns on the extent and manner in which increments in the value of capital influence capitalists' consumption.

This problem of definition is considerably eased if all values are measured in terms of consumption goods rather than money. This

The form of this relationship was established and used by Mr Kaldor in his 'Model of Economic Growth', *Economic Journal*, Dec. 1957, p. 611. It is used by Professor Champernowne in his 'Capital Accumulation and Full Employment', *Economic Journal*, June 1958, p. 218. As I have reproduced it here it must, however, be regarded for the present purely as an identity.

If $\alpha = 1$ and $\beta = 0$, the rate of growth becomes identically equal to the ratio of capitalists' incomes to the value of capital. This is the simplified form in which Mrs Robinson had presented the relationship in her *Accumulation of Capital* (1956), p. 76.

convention I will adopt, and when, for example, I speak of 'wage-rates' I shall mean 'real wage-rates'. The implications of an expectation of rising prices are not, however, by this device entirely eliminated and I shall have to return to the problem.

On whatever set of definitions the relationship is based, I have said nothing so far which imbues it with any causal force. It is purely an identity – a glorified version of the identity between savings and investment, which I claim to be a useful instrument for detecting error against those detractors who contemptuously dismiss it as a 'truism' or, more contemptible still, a 'tautology'. Our glorified version of the Keynesian identity would be as consistent, so far as anything emerges from what I have stated so far, with a system of ideas under which the rate of growth of capital was derived from the rate of profit as with a system under which the rate of profit is derived from the rate of growth. Also the identity is valid irrespective of any technical or other conditions – it does not require that the character of technical progress should conform to any particular pattern, and it is independent of the behaviour of the labour force and of employment and unemployment.

It is to be observed, however, that the relationship is not expressed in terms of the *rate of profit*. It is expressed in terms of the ratio of capitalists' incomes to the value of the stock of capital. It is the *current* incomes of capitalists which enter into the relationship. The rate of profit, on the other hand, if properly defined, is a matter of *expected* capitalists' incomes. At least this is what the rate of profit should signify if the term is used in the context of investment decisions, and in particular if it is regarded as having any correlation of a technical character with the stock of capital.

Let me now take one step forward and inquire what the position is if for some reason or other I can postulate that the rate of growth of capital is constant over a long period of time and that expectations are consistently such as, in the broad, to be realized, so that conditions of long-period equilibrium prevail. It follows from the relationship that if the proportion of wages saved is small, the ratio of capitalists' incomes to the value of capital is constant through time. Such a case is not only consistent with the assumption that capitalists' incomes are *expected* to grow at the same rate as the value of capital, but is highly congenial to the assumption that, in the broad, capitalists' expectations turn out to be justified. Then my postulate results in a rate of profit which is constant through time. And indeed it is only when the rate of profit is constant through time that it can be uniquely defined and unambiguously measured.

So far I have – for fun, as it were, without offering any justification – postulated a constant rate of growth of capital and I have shown that the same conditions which underlie the postulate, whatever they may be, will establish a rate of profit which is also constant. The only other *assumption* is that the two savings coefficients are constant and that for wage-earners the saving coefficient is small. Now I want to take another step forward and make a set of assumptions about technical progress. The assumptions are heroic. I do not make them because I believe in their validity in practice. The reason why I make them is that, for my own part, I desire to learn to walk before I try to run. First of all, I assume that the stage of technical knowledge can at any moment of time be represented by a production function which indicates the technical character of the new plant which it is decided to produce, and the character of its intended utilisation. Given the production function, the choice of technique depends on expectations over the prospective lifetime of the plant of the relationship between the price of the particular product and the cost of producing it. With a rate of profit which is constant through time there is a unique relationship between the rate of profit and the techniques which are being adopted at any moment of time, in the sense of higher rates of profit being associated with lower degrees of mechanisation.

In the second place, I assume that the state of technical knowledge at each moment of time, as depicted in the production function, and the development of technical knowledge, as depicted by the movement of the production function through time, are independent factors, and in particular do not depend on the rate of accumulation of capital. In the third place, I assume that the progress through time of technical development is neutral: this means that if the conditions are such as to entail a constant rate of profit the rate of growth of output per head will be the same at earlier stages in the process of production as at later stages; that this condition holds good for every rate of profit within the relevant range; and that this uniform growth of productivity proceeds at the same rate for all rates of profit within the relevant range. All this is entailed in assuming neutral technical progress.

With these assumptions I now want to combine the postulate of a constant rate of profit, entailing a constant rate of growth of the value of capital if conditions of long-period equilibrium are assumed, in which expectations are realised in the broad and in particular in which on the average equipment is used in the manner intended. The ratio of the value of capital to the value of output will then be constant through time. And the relative shares of capitalists' and wage-earners' incomes will remain constant.[1]

The magnitude of this constant capital–output ratio will depend on the technical conditions of production, whereas the relationship between the rate of profit and the rate of growth of capital depends only on the savings coefficients. For any given technique, the capital–output ratio depends on the relative prices of capital-goods and consumption-goods. This depends on the wage-rate and the rate of profit, in the sense that a higher wage-rate by itself results in a higher capital–output ratio and a lower rate of profit by itself in a lower ratio. Which effect is the stronger depends on the time pattern of the application of labour in the productive process.[2] The result of technical substitutibility between capital and labour is, taken by itself, that a lower rate of profit means a higher capital–output ratio – the greater the technical substitutibility (the wider the choice of technique at a given stage of technical development) the stronger this tendency will be.

Given the rate of profit, the wage-rate, which plays a part in determining the capital–output ratio, depends on the magnitude of the capital–output ratio and on the value of output per head. The fact that these various magnitudes depend on one another does not mean that the equation involved will not provide a solution. What it does mean is that the wage-rate, and the distribution of income, are related to the technical characteristics of the productive processes, as well as to the

[1] Since the ratio of the value of output to the value of capital is constant, the relationship which establishes consistency between a constant rate of growth of capital and a constant rate of profit no longer turns on β, the proportion saved out of wages, being small.

The relationship can also be expressed in terms of the share of capitalists' incomes in total income and the share of investment in output, as has been done by Mr Kaldor ('L'évolution capitaliste à la lumière de l'économie Keynésienne', *Économie Appliquée*, 1957, p. 268; also *Review of Economic studies*, no. 61 (1955), p. 95). If the rate of growth of the value of capital is constantand the capital–output ratio is constant, then the share of investment in output is constant.

[2] See I. M. D. Little, 'Classical Growth', *Oxford Economic Papers*, June 1957, pp. 158 and 175.

rate of growth and the saving coefficients – to which alone the rate of profit is related.[1] Even therefore when the rate of growth can be isolated as an independent factor – a matter which I shall have to deal with – it is only the rate of profit which can be imputed solely to it and to the savings coefficients. If we are interested in how wages and the distribution of income are determined, the technical conditions have to be brought in.

One statement that it is, however, possible to make about a state of constant growth with neutral technical progress is that the distribution of income remains constant through time.

A further such statement is that output per man employed, and the wage-rate, both grow at a rate equal to the rate of technical progress, irrespective of the rate of growth of capital. On the other hand, the aggregate of real wages grows with aggregate output at a rate equal to the rate of growth of capital.

The reconciliation lies in the behaviour of employment. This increases at a rate equal to the excess of the rate of growth of capital over the rate of technical progress. If the two are equal, employment remains constant. If the rate of technical progress exceeds the rate of growth of capital, employment diminishes.

I have said nothing so far about the labour force or, as I shall put it, population. The relation between the behaviour of employment and the behaviour of population determines the behaviour of unemployment.[2] I therefore make a further assumption. I assume that if population changes at all it grows (or diminishes) at a constant rate. And to match this assumption I assume also that the rate of technical progress is constant.

Then if the rate of growth of capital is equal to the rate of technical progress *plus* the rate of growth of population, the proportion of unemployment will remain constant. If at any stage there is full employment, there is full employment continuously.

I have now, as a result of a succession of postulates and assumptions, arrived at Mrs Robinson's Golden Age[3] of equilibrium growth with full employment. Her picturesque phrase provides, I think,

---

[1] If the wage-earners' savings coefficient is small.
[2] For the sake of simplicity, I assume that the unemployed subsist at the expense of the standard of living of those who are employed.
[3] Joan Robinson, *Accumulation of Capital*, p. 99.

a convenient method of identification, provided that the emotive undertones remain subdued. We must guard against any suggestion that the Golden Age is an ideal. Mrs Robinson herself points out that a higher rate of accumulation than seems to be called for to secure a Golden Age with given technical conditions is likely itself to alter the conditions, and in particular the rate of technical progress: 'the pressure of scarcity of labour, driving up wage-rates, would induce more inventions to be made, and hasten the diffusion of improvements already known'. In other words, Mrs Robinson is pointing out the unreality of the heroic assumptions, as I have described them, about technical progress. Moreover, we must be careful not to exclude, as a possibly more desirable alternative, a higher rate of growth of consumption, obtained at the expense of a temporarily lower current level of consumption, as a result of a higher rate of growth of capital and consequent progression to higher degrees of mechanisation. In other words, we have to consider Mr Little's *platinum age*[1] as a possibly more desirable alternative to Mrs Robinson's Golden Age.

A further reason for guarding against the implication that a Golden Age represents some kind of ideal is that any particular Golden Age is based on given thriftiness of capitalists and of wage-earners. A higher proportion of incomes saved, on the part of either or both, would mean that, given the state and growth of technical knowledge and given the growth of population, the Golden Age would have built into it a lower rate of profit, so as to secure the correct relationship with an unchanged rate of growth of capital (equal to the rate of technical progress *plus* the rate of growth of population).[2] This lower rate of profit would, at each moment of time, go with a higher degree of mechanisation than in the Golden Age adjusted to the lower level of thriftiness, and it would go with a larger total output, with a larger output of consumption goods, and with a higher wage-rate.

There is a practical reason why it is important to consider the implications of the degree of thriftiness. In the usual models of

---

[1] See I. M. D. Little, *Oxford Economic Papers*, 1957, p. 172.

[2] A cursory inspection of the relationship, as set out in my first footnote, might suggest that the capitalists' and wage-earners' savings coefficients, α and β, pull in opposite directions on the rate of profit called for by a given rate of growth. But this is illusory. The expression can be redeployed so that the factor $(\alpha - \beta)$ no longer occurs, and it should be borne in mind that the reciprocal of the capital–output ratio must exceed the rate of profit if wages are not to be negative.

economic growth, such as Mrs Robinson's Golden Age, the State is left out of the picture and in particular there is no room for saving by the State. Now, an economy might be developing as a Golden Age, but, thriftiness being low, the methods of production are often so primitive, as a result of scarcity of capital, that the word 'golden' is a mockery. The practical question which then arises is whether the economy would not be in a happier condition if the State were contributing to saving out of the proceeds of higher taxes. For the purpose of analysis one can regard such State saving as assimilated into the simpler model which disregards it. For in so far as it is financed by taxation of profits its effects are the same as those of a higher capitalists' savings coefficient; in so far as it is financed by indirect taxation, it is equivalent in its effects to those of higher savings coefficients for both capitalists and wage-earners, to the extent of their consumption of the taxed commodities.[1]

I must now emphasise that what is involved in this line of exercise is a comparison of the Golden Ages between which there exists a stated difference but which in other respects are subject to the same conditions. It is one thing to *correlate* two characteristics involved in such a comparison, such as the savings coefficients on the one hand and on the other hand the rate of profit and the degree of mechanisation – but it would be quite another thing, for which justification would have to be produced, to regard the one as causatively determining the other.

This brings me to the more fundamental question what process of causation might be held conceptually responsible for the establishment

---

[1] The beneficial influence on the wage-rate associated with a higher degree of thrift is the larger, the smaller is the effect (expressed algebraically) in causing the capital–output ratio to be higher. This effect is smaller

    (i) the smaller is the substitutibility of capital and labour;

    (ii) the smaller is the effect of a higher wage-rate, and the larger is the effect in the opposite direction of a lower rate of profit, on the prices of particular kinds of capital-goods in terms of consumption-goods.

If these factors operate with sufficient strength, higher thrift will benefit wages to such a degree that even though practised entirely by wage-earners, their standard of living is on the average actually higher, in each state of technical knowledge, despite the higher thrift.

It then follows equally, under such conditions, that indirect taxes devoted to State saving, even if confined to commodities consumed by wage-earners, will actually entail *higher* real wage-rates (and that taxation of wages, devoted to State saving, will entail wages which are higher by more than the amount of the taxes paid out of them).

and persistence of any particular Golden Age? The simplest case to conceive is that in which for a long time in the past the underlying conditions have operated in a constant and uniform manner and the Golden Age appropriate to them has in fact existed. A tranquil past breeds expectations based on past experience. The constant rate of profit is, as a matter of expectation, firmly based on experience. The structure of capital – and in particular the proportions in which specialised equipment is divided between what is designed for making consumption-goods, for making capital-goods for making consumption-goods, and for making capital-goods for making capital-goods – is such as to result in a flow of capital-goods the value of which grows at the same rate as the value of the total stock of capital. As Mrs Robinson puts it, entrepreneurs 'desire to accumulate at the same proportional rate as they have been doing over the past'.

This explanation is, however, too general. It justifies a state of equilibrium growth at *any* conceivable rate – what the rate happens to be being a matter of historical accident. It might be a rate less than the rate of technical progress, so as to result in steadily diminishing employment even though the population was constant or growing. And, as I have already indicated, the rate of growth may exceed the rate of technical progress, and employment may therefore be growing, but there may nevertheless be unemployment. It seems to me convenient to be able to describe such a state of equilibrium growth which has all the attributes of a Golden Age other than that of full employment. I suggest that it be called a Bastard Golden Age.

I now want to inquire whether there is any mechanism which can be said to determine the existence of a Golden Age proper, with a determined rate of growth, as opposed to a Bastard Golden Age with a rate of growth dependent on historical accident. What mechanism is there which is brought into operation at the point of full employment? Clearly we do not need to look beyond the familiar Keynesian rationalisation of the classical processes of thought. The decision to invest depends not only on the prospective profit but on a comparison of that profit with the cost of financing the investment or, if the finance is available from internal sources, with the yield which could be secured by using it on the financial and capital markets. In simple terms any Golden Age, whether bastard or legitimate, must have had built into it a rate of interest which matches the rate of profit, and which discourages capitalists from embarking on projects likely to yield less than the Golden Age rate of profit. This rate of interest is not to be conceived in any simple sense. It is simply a phrase used for convenience to sum up the state of finance. The risks of enterprise must be allowed for. The fact that in a Golden Age capitalists' expectations are realised *in the broad* does not exclude the risks involved in the vagaries of technical processes and of consumers' behaviour. For these reasons the risk-free rate of interest would even in a Golden Age lie below the rate of profit, with which yields on ordinary shares are more comparable since they involve the same kind of risks as physical investment. Imperfections of the financial and capital markets are also likely to be important factors limiting investment. To meet the requirements of a Golden Age it is only necessary to assume either that the number of capitalists grows at the Golden Age rate of growth or that the limits on the finance available to each expand on the average at the same rate of growth.

The possibility of a Bastard Golden Age turns on the absence of any progressive tendency towards the easing of the state of finance, and, more particularly, towards a lowering of rates of interest and of yields on ordinary shares. If, for example, money wage-rates tend to fall progressively under the pressure of unemployment or the quantity of money tends to rise faster than money wages or the monetary authority in the face of unemployment deliberately makes credit progressively cheaper, there will be such a progressive tendency and this will undermine the equilibrium of a Bastard Golden Age. In the absence of unemployment, on the other hand, there need be no such progressive easing of the state of finance. And with full employment any momentary tendency for investment to rise above the equilibrium rate will result in money wages being forced up under the pressure of unsatisfied demand for labour, until investment is pushed back to the Golden Age equilibrium rate. The rate of growth of a legitimate Golden Age, which grows in such a way as to maintain full employment, can thus be based on some idea of determinacy and not just historical accident.

Once the rate of growth is tethered in this way so that it can be inferred from the rate of technical progress and the rate of growth of population, it is possible to say that the rate of profit is *determined* by the rate of growth and by the savings coefficients.

Looked at in this way a statement that thrift has no influence on the rate of growth of capital is devoid of significance. If the rate of growth is determined in such a way as to secure full employment, it must match the growth of technical knowledge and population, and that is what it has to be equal to.

Thrift is important, however, because it determines the real wage-rate in a Golden Age, with given technical conditions at each stage and given rates of neutral technical progress and growth of population. In a certain sense growth is easier if at each stage the real wage-rate is higher – in the sense that a smaller sacrifice is called for from wage-earners. In this sense thrift is helpful to the process of growth.

This brings me to the 'inflation barrier'.[1] So far I have assumed that any real wage will be tolerated, no matter how low, and that only the approach to full employment will bring into operation a financial check resulting from the inflationary pressure on money wages of an unsatisfied demand for labour. It may be, however, that real wages which fail to reach a certain limit are unacceptable, in the sense that any attempt to enforce such real wages, even with the existence of unemployment, will bring into operation an inflationary movement of money wages such as will result in a check on investment through its effect on the state of finance. Or the real wage may lie below the subsistence level. The inflation barrier is the minimum real wage-rate which will be tolerated without provoking reactions inconsistent with a state of equilibrium growth. To that minimum real wage-rate there corresponds, given the technical and thriftiness conditions, a particular Bastard Golden Age, with a rate of growth just sufficiently low to secure this minimum real wage-rate for those employed.[2] In such a Bastard Golden Age, the rate of growth is limited by the operation of the inflation barrier. Thrift can now be regarded as an influence on the rate of growth. It is the real wage-rate which is independently determined and greater thriftiness means a higher rate of growth and a less rapid increase of unemployment.

[1] Joan Robinson, *Accumulation of Capital*, p. 48.
[2] To make equilibrium growth possible, it must be assumed either that there is no technical progress, so that the real wage-rate is constant, or that the minimum real wage-rate which constitutes the inflation barrier rises, as a matter of human progress and the development of ideas about minimum standards, at the same rate, purely by way of coincidence, as the rate of technical progress.

Professor Champernowne introduces the inflation barrier in terms purely of a minimum rate of growth of the minimum real wage-rate, the absolute level at any stage of development being apparently immaterial (*Economic Journal*, 1958, p. 224).

The inflation barrier may be in operation for a time even though the Golden Age real wage would be perfectly acceptable to the wage-earners. It may be that on account of the character of the development of the system back in history, unemployment still prevails and that the maximum possible rate of equilibrium growth is such as to bring the real wage-rate to the minimum and the inflation barrier into operation. Any higher rate of growth would bring inflationary forces into operation against itself; while any lower rate would be inconsistent with equilibrium because the state of finance would progressively ease, as a result of the existence of unemployment for which the inflation barrier was not responsible. Full equilibrium will therefore demand a Bastard Golden Age with a rate of growth greater than the legitimate Golden Age rate. Unemployment will progressively diminish until, with full employment in sight, there is no longer a valid basis for this Bastard Golden Age. The speed with which the position of full employment is attained will depend on the operation of the inflation barrier – the higher the minimum real wage-rate the lower the speed will be. It is shortage of capital which is the cause of such unemployment and the remedying of the shortage depends on the readiness of those who are in employment to make a temporary sacrifice on their real wage-rate.[1] And of course thrift here again operates as an influence on the rate of growth – the greater the savings propensities, the more rapidly will the shortage of capital be overcome and unemployment be eliminated.

I now want to say something about the relation between profits and investment. In ordinary short-period economics, we are in the habit of associating higher profits with greater investment. This association involves two entirely different meanings of the word 'profit' and two different processes of cause and effect. The word 'profit' is often loosely used to signify what I have called capitalists' current incomes. In that sense high profits are caused by high investment – purely as a current phenomenon. But if the emphasis is on 'rate of profit', then it is the expectation of capitalists' incomes which is the subject of

[1] It is realistic to conceive of the inflation barrier to operate, as I do here, in terms of a minimum real wage-rate. It would be more logical but less realistic, to conceive it to operate in terms of the standard of living of those employed, after allowance for the support of the unemployed, or, better still, of the average standard of living of all the potential wage-earners, including the unemployed.

the association with the rate of investment, and the causation is the other way round: high investment is caused by high profits. In dealing with problems of non-equilibrium growth, such as I am not attempting, the difference between the two concepts of profit, and between the two types of causation, should be kept firmly in mind. With equilibrium growth the future is like the present. But although the rate of profit is the same viewed in current terms as in terms of expectations, the nature of the causation is still important.

If two different Golden Ages are compared, with the same savings coefficients but different rates of growth, the higher rate of growth is associated with the higher rate of profit.[1] This higher rate of profit is to be attributed to the higher rate of growth of capital rather than the other way round.

Indeed, in all these cases of equilibrium growth – Bastard as well as legitimate Golden Ages – the rate of growth of capital is inferred from factors other than profits: from rates of technical progress and population growth, from the minimum real wage-rate which constitutes the inflation barrier, and from pure historical accident. The reason why the causation does not operate the other way round as well is that a state of equilibrium growth requires a state of finance which has been built into the equilibrium system, in such a way that the deterrent influence on investment of the difficulty and cost of financing investment, and of the attraction of alternative methods of laying out financial resources, just matches the stimulating influence of profit expectations. The rate of interest, and all that goes with it in the financial sphere, has accommodated itself to the rate of profit and neither the rate of profit nor the rate of interest can be regarded as independent influences on investment.

This leads to the question what happens if the appropriate rate of profit is too low to be matched by terms on which finance can be made available. There is in practice a minimum – a bottom-stop – below which it is difficult, or impossible, for the rate of interest to be forced down by monetary means.[2] Even if any particular minimum is likely to be broken down after long experience of consistently very low rates of interest, it is relevant that negative rates of interest are not conceivable and that the risk premium has to be added on to the rate of

---

[1] Once again wage-earners' thrift is taken to be small.
[2] See Keynes, *General Theory of Employment, Interest and Money* (1936), p. 309.

interest before the rate of profit is matched against it. If finance cannot become sufficiently easy to match the Golden Age rate of profit, and if other methods of stimulating investment are excluded, then the Golden Age is not possible.

Mr Kaldor has pointed out that an expectation of rising prices can in such a situation provide a basis for a Golden Age and save the economy from the decay which is the alternative. If we continue to calculate our values in terms of consumption-goods rather than money, we must represent such an expectation as a lowering of the 'real' rate of interest corresponding to any particular money rate of interest bottom-stop, leaving the Golden Age rate of profit and rate of growth unaffected. If, on the other hand, we prefer to think in terms of the money rate of interest, then the rate of profit and rate of growth must be evaluated in money rather than in real terms and they will both be greater by reason of the rising prices.

Or rather this will be so if income is defined so as to include the increase in the value of capital equipment resulting from the rise in prices. If, on the other hand, the normal social accounting definition of income is employed, it makes no difference to the evaluation of the rate of growth whether prices are rising or not. And it makes no difference to the ratio of capitalists' current incomes to the value of the stock of capital. But this ratio is not a rate of profit which can be set against the rate of interest. As the prospective change in the value of capital equipment is left out of the account, the return from a given amount of current investment measured in money of current purchasing power is an annuity, the elements of which are progressively greater, on account of the expected rise in prices, as they attach to more distant points of time in the future. By reason of the expectation of rising prices, the rate of profit in the relevant sense exceeds the ratio of capitalists' current incomes to the value of the stock of capital.

Profit expectations and the rate of interest are not, in ordinary short-period economics, the only influences on investment. Having decided that neither of them has any influence on the rate of long-period equilibrium growth, I go on to ask myself about the part played in a Golden Age by Keynes' 'animal spirits' – 'a spontaneous urge to action rather than inaction...If the animal spirits are dimmed... enterprise will fade and die.'[1]

[1] *Ibid.*, pp. 161–2.

High animal spirits can usefully be considered in four different aspects:

(i) They promote the growth of scientific knowledge. In this aspect they take a part in contributing to the rate of growth of the Golden Age.

(ii) They promote the exploitation of scientific knowledge, i.e. its conversion into technical knowledge. This is a more important way in which again they promote technical progress, and the growth of the Golden Age.

(iii) They promote an optimistic view of the future. In this aspect high animal spirits are incompatible with the conditions of a Golden Age, in which the prospect of the future is strictly determined by knowledge of the present and the past.

(iv) On the basis of given expectations, high animal spirits strengthen the urge to invest. In this aspect high animal spirits are in no sense incompatible with the conditions of a Golden Age. But they exert no influence on the rate of growth, their effect being rendered nugatory by reason of the terms on which finance is available. The stronger the animal spirits the higher has to be the rate rate of interest, and the tighter generally have to be financial conditions, while the rate of profit is unaffected.

In conclusion, I want to emphasise what I have *not* been doing in this paper. I have talked about Golden Ages. But I have only touched on the question whether a system which is in Golden Age equilibrium is likely to stay there. And I have not discussed at all the really important question whether a system which is not in Golden Age equilibrium will tend to move towards the Golden Age.

Equally, I have not discussed what would be entailed in a movement, if it could be contrived, out of one Golden Age into another, within some definite limited period of time – or out of a Bastard Golden Age into a legitimate Golden Age. For example, I indicated that, other things being the same, if two Golden Ages differed only in respect of thrift, the one with the higher thrift was the preferable one, and that it was possible that even though the extra thrift was entirely at the expense of the wage-earners, the actual standard of wage-earners' consumption might be higher as a result of it. But when one speaks of a Golden Age being preferable in that sort of sense, it means that it would be preferable to be in it. But to be in it involves *having* been in it for a long time past, and enjoying the legacy of the past in terms of the accumulated stock of capital and the degree of mechanisation. The desirability of a movement from the one Golden Age to the other, and the manner in which it might be smoothly negotiated, is one of the important and difficult problems of economic growth. What I have said in this paper is intended as no more than prolegomena to the solution of the real problems.

10

NOTES ON THE RATE OF INTEREST
AND THE GROWTH OF FIRMS

I

The rate of interest, as the term implies, is associated with fixed-interest securities – bonds, bills, bank advances. The role of the rate of interest in the economy is traditionally linked with the fixed-interest security as the basic vehicle for putting personal savings at the disposal of managements. The ordinary share has not conveniently fitted into the analysis and its function has until recently been given only a passing glance, without any systematic attempt to assimilate the return on ordinary shares to the general ideas inherent in the concept of the rate of interest. When businessmen have been questioned about the influence of the rate of interest on investment, the questions have been framed in terms of the rate payable on bonds or on bank advances, and not in terms of the prices of ordinary shares, as quoted on the Stock Exchange, in relation to dividends and earnings.

Robin Marris' recent work opens up a new field.[1] To provide a general setting for studies of this kind it seems worthwhile to outline, on the basis of the simplest possible assumptions and for the simplest possible cases, the relevant characteristics of an economy in which managements issue no bonds but only ordinary shares (a restricted niche for bank advances is inserted in the concluding Section of these Notes).

The basic simplifying assumption is that expectations, both of managements and shareholders, are entertained with complete conviction. The argument is confined to an economy developing in a state of tranquillity, with, on the average for the economy as a whole, a constant rate of growth of capital and in which the overall average rate of profit (in both senses defined below) is constant. These

---

[1] Robin Marris, *The Economic Theory of 'Managerial' Capitalism* (1964). See also R. Marris and A. J. B. Wood, eds. *The Corporate Economy* (1971), p. 23, where reference is made to an earlier draft of this paper.

assumptions are severe and highly unrealistic. In particular, it may seem paradoxical to discuss the Stock Exchange in terms of confident expectations, but the assumptions are designed to identify certain fundamental issues, which would be lost to view among all the complicated cross-currents of reality. Within the compass of these short Notes it is not feasible to explore the consequences of relaxing these assumptions. The object here is to clear the ground for further elaboration. The analysis is concerned with the interrelations of the growth of companies, their rates of profit and the general rate of interest, in so far as it is possible to do so, subject to these severe simplifying assumptions.

A further simplifying assumption which renders the treatment even more unreal is that there are no taxes, and at a later stage, when the economy as a whole is discussed, it will be assumed that there is no Government expenditure and no foreign trade.

These Notes follow the work of Joan Robinson, as elaborated by Robin Marris, in taking as the starting point the creative urge of managements – expressed by Keynes' 'animal spirits'. The management is regarded as identifying themselves with the company as such, and the interests of the shareholders exert only a limited influence on policy.[1]

The scope of these Notes is restricted to dealing with the rate of growth at which a company settles down in a position of tranquillity, with a constant rate of profit. This is an entirely artificial concept – far more artificial than that of an economy, or even of an individual industry, in a state of tranquillity. But consideration of what *would* be entailed in a sustained rate of growth of a company if its characteristics remained unchanged and it operated in an environment in which change was tranquil is a necessary prolegomenon to dealing with changing rates of growth of individual companies.[2]

The sustained rate of growth adopted by the management of an

---

[1] In practice – but this takes us at once outside the narrow scope of these Notes – such desire to promote the interests of the shareholders as may exist on the part of managements is likely to be fortified as a result of their being unduly optimistic about the prospects of their own companies and of each rentier having his own pet companies about the prospects of which he is often unduly optimistic.

[2] The development of the traditional economics of the firm took place the other way round – Marshall's trees in the forest led on to Pigou's equilibrium firm – but the reversal of the logical order did not assist the development of the subject.

individual company can be regarded as the outcome of contrary pressures, propulsive and retroactive. The propulsive factors take the form of the ambition and creative urge of the management, expressing itself through the physical development of the company to which they are committed, as well as to some extent the inducement of higher emoluments (the remuneration of the management is one of the few issues on which the shareholders are by convention deemed to be entitled to take an interest, and the remuneration per head that is acceptable grows with the size of the company). The retroactive factors are partly psychological. A higher rate of growth comes up against inertia and resistance to change: it means more onerous tasks for the management and longer hours of work (convention does not permit adequate compensation by way of higher remuneration for growing faster, as opposed to being larger). The retroactive factors are also economic in character in so far as a higher rate of growth entails higher costs[1] and so, with a given behaviour of the economy, a lower rate of profit for the individual firm,[2] which, as we shall see, is a deterrent against adopting a higher rate of growth though only to a limited extent, depending on the extent of the feeling of loyalty to the shareholders on the part of the management.[3]

The propulsive factors are weaker as the rate of growth is higher and the retroactive factors are stronger. The sustained rate of growth

[1] Marris indicates '*Managerial*' *Capitalism*, p. 111) the extent of our debt in this, and related, issues to Mrs Edith Penrose's *The Theory of the Growth of the Firm*, (1959).

It is convenient to slip in at this point the further assumption that there are no economies of scale as such. For a particular type of firm the technique of production is assumed to depend on its sustained rate of growth, but not on how much it has grown, although of course the passage of time as such yields the fruits of technical progress.

[2] No reader of these Notes who has survived so far needs to be warned of the pitfall of supposing that if all companies – as a result, say, of some difference in the psychological climate or in established convention, entailing higher animal spirits – were growing faster, the rate of profit would actually be lower. It would of course be higher (if the thriftiness conditions were the same). The rate of growth of each company means greater profitability for all the others. The microeconomic schedule indicated in the text relating the rate of profit of a company taken in isolation to its own individual rate of growth would now have been bodily shifted upward.

[3] This does not mean, however, that the microeconomic schedule showing how the rate of profit of each company treated in isolation would be lower if its own particular rate of growth were higher is not an influence in determining the rate of growth adopted for each company, and so in helping to determine the rate of growth of the economy.

adopted by the management can be regarded as a point of balance between the two sets of opposing pressures. The rate of growth will be represented by g.

Profit, represented by P, is net of depreciation. It can either be *current* – the quasi-rents less depreciation being currently earned – or *prospective* – the profits expected at various dates in the future. On the basis of confident expectations, *the rate of prospective profit*, represented by π, can be calculated either as the rate of discount at which the present value of the prospective quasi-rents to be yielded by a new physical asset is equal to its cost, or as the ratio to the cost of the asset of the prospective profit maintained perpetually constant through time by making good depreciation.[1] If this rate of profit is constant through time, the rate of profit realised on the investment is equal to the rate of prospective profit. It is then, and only then, that it is safe to use *simpliciter* the phrase *rate of profit*.

The value of an old physical asset is to be regarded as the present value of its expected future earnings capitalised at the rate of prospective profit on a new asset of the corresponding type.[2] It is then a matter of circular argument to state that this rate of profit is yielded by all assets of that particular type, whether new or old. The value of the assets of a company earning a rate of profit π will be represented by C.

The return received on a share over any particular period of time is made up of two parts, the dividends and the capital appreciation. The *rate of return* on a share is then equal to the current dividend yield, represented by y, *plus* the rate of appreciation, z, of the price, p, of the share, z being the same as $\dot{p}/p$.[3]

The assumption of indifference as between dividends and capital appreciation means that in a perfect capital market the rate of return on all shares will be equal. (It is the rate of *current* capital appreciation of the price of a share which is relevant, or the rate confidently

---

[1] Cf. Joan Robinson, *Collected Economic Papers*, vol 2 (1960), p. 221.
[2] Robin Marris describes this as book value. It is what the book value would be if depreciation had been correctly allowed for and if the price level were constant. In the real world of uncertainty, all these concepts are somewhat hazy.
[3] Cf. Marris, '*Managerial*' *Capitalism*, p. 21. The rate of appreciation in question is the rate of expected appreciation but unexpected appreciation cannot take place within the framework of the assumptions made for the purposes of these Notes.

expected over the immediate future.) The return on shares in general will be described as the rate of interest,[1] represented by i.[2]

Our concern is essentially with a monetary economy. Everything is reckoned in terms of money, and not of commodities. But we do not want to postulate that the conditions – namely influences on the behaviour of money wage-rates – are necessarily such as to result in stable prices. To simplify exposition, the discussion will be conducted *as though* commodity prices were constant. We do not assume that they are constant, but to avoid tedious reiteration we assume that the expected rate of change of prices, represented by h, is tacitly brought into the argument and into the identities and equations wherever it is called for.[3]

The individual owners of wealth, who in this article are shareholders, will be described as rentiers,[4] to indicate that their function is a purely passive one, as opposed to that of *managements*.

The determination of the retention ratio, represented by r, and the extent to which companies rely on new issues is not discussed in these Notes. It is only when the assumption of confident expectations is removed, and with it the idea of indifference between dividends and capital appreciation, that the determination of the retention ratio can be discussed. This is outside the scope of these Notes. Meanwhile we may suppose that one management may find it less troublesome to rely mainly, or even exclusively, on retentions and another may like to have frequent opportunities of offering their shares to a wider public and may rely mainly, or even exclusively, on external finance.

[1] Robin Marris calls this the *rate of discount*, k (*ibid.*).

[2] In the final Section of these Notes, i' is the money rate of interest, i being the commodity rate of interest, so that $i' = i + h$, where h is the rate of increase of the commodity price level.

[3] *Money* rates of interest, *money* rates of return and *money* rates of prospective profit differ from *commodity* rates of interest, *commodity* rates of return, and *commodity* rates of prospective profit by the expected rate of change of the price-level of commodities measured in terms of money. A capital asset which yields a constant profit measured in commodity terms yields a changing profit measured in money, so that the expected money rate of profit differs from the ratio of current profits to the value of the asset. If there is an expectation of changing prices, the expected rate of change, h, has to be added to the rate of interest, etc. whenever it appears in the analysis, based on the assumption of constant commodity prices – as also to the prospective rate of appreciation, z, of a share (but not, of course, of the current dividend yield, y).

[4] Cf. Joan Robinson, *Accumulation of Capital* (1956), p. 8.

According to where the retention ratio lies between zero and unity, the return on a share, which is equal to the rate of interest, is made up of a current dividend yield lying between π and zero and a rate of appreciation of the price of the share lying between zero and π. The company increases the number of its issued shares at a rate equal to the excess of its rate of growth over $r\pi$, which is the rate of appreciation of the price of the share. From the point of view of the rentier the shares of one company may yield a return consisting largely of dividends, and in another consisting largely of capital appreciation, but the rate of return will be the same.

II

We must now consider the relation between the value of a company from the point of view of its earning assets compared to the amount of rentier wealth that it represents.

The valuation ratio, v, is the ratio of the value of the shares of the company as assessed by the Stock Exchange to the value of the company's assets, C. If N is the number of the company's shares

$$v = \frac{Np}{C}$$

It follows that

$$\dot{v}C + v\dot{C} = N\dot{p} + \dot{N}p \tag{1}$$

$$g = \frac{\dot{C}}{C}$$

Equation (1) then becomes

$$\dot{v} + vg = v\left(\frac{\dot{p}}{p} + \frac{\dot{N}}{N}\right)$$

Under conditions of tranquil growth the valuation ratio will settle down to a level which remains constant through time. With $\dot{v}$ equal to zero, we now have

$$g = \frac{\dot{p}}{p} + \frac{\dot{N}}{N} \tag{2}$$

The investment of the company is paid for partly by retained profits and partly by the proceeds of new issues. It follows, r being the retention ratio and π the rate of profit, that

$$g = r\pi + \frac{p}{C}\dot{N}$$

213

It follows that

$$g = r\pi + v\frac{\dot{N}}{N} \tag{3}$$

On the basis of the assumption of indifference, the return on the shares is equal to the current dividend yield *plus* the rate of appreciation of the price, p. And it is equal to the rate of interest, i.

Hence

$$i = \frac{(1-r)\,\pi C}{Np} + \frac{\dot{p}}{p}$$

It follows that

$$i = \frac{1}{v}(1-r)\,\pi + \frac{\dot{p}}{p} \tag{4}$$

From (2), (3) and (4), it follows that[1]

$$v = \frac{\pi - g}{i - g} \tag{5}$$

This demonstrates that if the rate of profit is constant, it is possible for a company to grow with the aid, partly or wholly, of external finance with a valuation ratio for its shares which remains constant at a level which differs from unity. The rate of interest, if it differs from the rate of profit, requires that the shares of the company are quoted by the market at a price different from the value of the underlying assets.

When the rate of profit, π, for a particular company is equal to the rate of interest, i, the valuation ratio, v, is unity. The value of the shares is equal to the replacement cost of the capital assets which underlie them. The income of the rentiers is equal to the current profits of the company, the one being the value of the shares multiplied by the rate of interest and the other the value of the company's assets multiplied by the rate of profit. The income, regarded as a rate of return on the value of the shares, is equal to the current earnings yield. It is made up of two parts: the current dividend yield and the rate of appreciation of the price of the share. The two parts added together make up the rate of interest, which in this case is equal to the rate of profit.

[1] I.e.

$$i = \frac{\pi - r\pi}{v} + \frac{\dot{p}}{p}$$

by substitution from (2) and (3)

$$i = \frac{\pi - g + v(\dot{N}/N)}{v} + g - \frac{\dot{N}}{N}$$

$$\therefore\ i = \frac{\pi - g}{v} + g$$

The identity of the capital appreciation with the retention ratio multiplied by the rate of profit seems obvious enough for a company which finances its growth entirely out of retained profits. But the identity remains valid if the growth of the company is financed partly by issuing new shares. There is no 'dilution' of the equity, and no curtailment of the appreciation of the price of the share. The point is that so long as external finance is contributing to growth, the extra growth of the assets results in an addition to the growth of profits which just provides the additional earnings for the newly issued shares.

Next, consider the implications of a rate of profit below the rate of interest.

The demonstration that $v = (\pi - g)/(i - g)$ applies to any individual company which is growing at a constant rate, is securing a constant rate of profit and the return on the shares of which is constant. It is, however, important to emphasise the dependence of the proof on the assumption of indifference on the part of rentiers between dividends and capital appreciation.

It is sometimes convenient to write

$$v = \frac{\pi}{i} \frac{(1 - g/\pi)}{(1 - g/i)} \tag{5a}$$

The following illustrative table of magnitudes may be helpful. The rate of profit, π, is taken as 10% throughout.

Rate of interest (i)	Rate of growth (g) (percentage rates)	Valuation ratio (v)
10	Anything	1
12	0	$\frac{5}{6}$
12	4	$\frac{3}{4}$
12	8	$\frac{1}{2}$
12	9	$\frac{1}{3}$
20	0	$\frac{1}{2}$
20	4	$\frac{3}{8}$
20	8	$\frac{1}{6}$
20	9	$\frac{1}{11}$

For some purposes it is convenient to use the discount on the value of the underlying assets represented by the price of the shares.

$$\mathrm{I} - v = \frac{i - \pi}{i - g} \qquad (5b)$$

Or
$$\mathrm{I} - v = \frac{\mathrm{I} - (\pi/i)}{\mathrm{I} - (g/i)} \qquad (5c)$$

The discount is lowest, and equal to $\mathrm{I} - (\pi/i)$, when there is no growth, i.e. when $g = 0$. It then simply represents the result of valuing profits at a discount rate, i, which is higher than the rate of profit, π. With a positive rate of growth the discount widens, and as the rate of growth, g, approaches the rate of profit, π, the discount approaches unity, and the valuation ratio zero.

The reason why growth as such – the rate of profit of the firm and the ruling rate of interest being taken as given – lowers the valuation ratio is that it entails acquiring capital assets which cost more than the value indirectly placed on them by the Stock Exchange, and the larger the scale on which this operation is conducted the greater is the damage to the shares in the company.[1]

The character of the damage which growth may be said to impose on the shareholders is revealed most clearly by enquiring into the income of a company's shareholders. They receive, in the form of dividends and capital appreciation, the going rate of interest on the aggregate market value of the company's shares, i.e. their income from the company is iNp. This is of course saying no more than that the price of the shares is such as to make it so.

But since $Np = vC$,
$$iNp = i\frac{\pi - g}{i - g} C$$

or
$$\pi\frac{\mathrm{I} - (g/\pi)}{\mathrm{I} - (g/i)} C \qquad (6)$$

[1] This explains why the valuation ratio, i.e. the price of the shares, approaches zero as the rate of growth approaches the rate of profit. In the limiting case in which $g = \pi$, the whole of the profit is absorbed in this way. There is no finite issue of shares which will be sufficient to finance that part of the growth which is not financed out of retained profits. Dilution occurs to an infinite degree: $\dot{N}/N$ is infinite. The price of the shares is zero. (It falls at an infinite rate, so as almost to counterbalance the infinite current dividend yield.)

The loss of income, being the excess of πC over what the shareholders receive, is

$$g\frac{1-(\pi/i)}{1-(g/i)}C \qquad (6a)$$

or $$g(1-v)\,C \qquad (6b)$$

So long as the company's growth rate is zero the shareholders receive as income the whole of the profit, just as they do when the rate of interest is equal to the rate of profit. It is the capital value of their shareholdings, not their income, which is then adversely affected by an excess of the rate of interest over the rate of profit. But if in addition the company's growth rate is positive, the shareholders do not receive as income the whole of the profits, as the capital value of their shareholdings is still more adversely affected. With higher and higher growth rates, income approaches zero as the growth rate approaches the rate of profit.

No shareholder who has bought shares since the company assumed its present pattern of growth has suffered any absolute loss by so doing. His income from his shares has constituted a full rate of interest on what he paid for them. And no shareholder who owned shares in the company at some date in the past has suffered any absolute loss by retaining them. He too has received the rate of interest on what they were worth at that time. The loss which, on the part of both classes of shareholders equally, is suffered by reason of growth is deprivation of a potential gain. If at any time the company ceased to grow the income of those who were shareholders at that time would rise by $g\,(1-v)\,C$ to πC, v being the valuation ratio before the growth ceased. And the value of their shares would rise in the same proportion, the old valuation ratio being

$$\frac{\pi-g}{i-g}$$

and the new one $$\pi/i$$

The only people who suffer an absolute loss in the course of the company's history are those who were responsible originally for financing it.

It has been shown that the financing policy of the management, for any given growth rate, has no effect (on our present assumptions) on the valuation ratio, or indeed on the Stock Exchange valuation of the company's assets at each stage of its development. On our present

assumptions, strictly interpreted, managements are indifferent between profit retention and new issues and there is no question of one
body of shareholders, say 'old' shareholders, benefiting at the
expense of another body of shareholders, say 'new' shareholders.[1]

The character of the relationship between the rate of growth of
a company taken in isolation and the income of its shareholders and
the value of their shares means that, in so far as the management have
any feeling of loyalty towards the shareholders, the rate of growth will
be pushed below the level which would be established if the rate of
interest were equal to the rate of profit. The extent of such restraint
on growth depends of course on the degree of loyalty to the shareholders and on the size of the gap between the rate of interest and the
rate of profit.

However, a more powerful factor restraining growth than loyalty
to the shareholders is likely to be the fear of a 'take-over'.[2] Here it
must be remembered that a 'take-over' which is designed as a means
of cheaply acquiring physical assets, and which will destroy the
management as an entity, would in any case be a serious threat merely
by reason of the rate of profit being significantly below the rate of
interest – even if the rate of growth were zero. Illustrative figures
worked out above for valuation ratios show that over a wide range of
the relevant magnitudes the addition to the risk of a 'take-over'
caused by the fact of growth is considerable.

A 'take-over' may not be attempted with the object of satisfying
the urge to grow of the management of the 'taking-over' company – it
may not be designed as a means of giving way to their animal spirits.
It may be intended to keep the threatened company as a going con-

---

[1] But the financing policy of the management does affect the number of
shares, and their price, at each stage of the company's development. It
might therefore be held to affect the composition of the shareholding body.
It is perhaps not too inconsistent with the assumption of indifference on
the part of rentiers between dividends and capital appreciation to suppose
that there is some tendency for a company's shareholders to devote their
savings to building up their interest in the company in so far as their
income takes the form of capital appreciation, but to buy shares in other
companies in so far as it takes the form of dividends. If therefore the
management believe that the loss of a potential gain, established by growth,
might one day be remedied, partially or wholly, as a result of growth
slackening or declining, and if their loyalty is stronger to the older than to
the more recent shareholders, they will be inclined towards profit retention
as opposed to new issues.

[2] See Marris, '*Managerial' Capitalism, passim.*

cern but to secure the benefit of stopping its growth – as a purely financial operation. The management of the threatened company may expect to be kept in being as an entity. But their animal spirits would be thwarted – growth would be forbidden. The risk of this kind of 'take-over' is negligible when the rate of growth is low, and therefore depends even more significantly on the rate of growth itself. The management is prompted to indulge in less growth than they would have liked so as to reduce the risk of being compelled to eschew it altogether.

We now consider the implications of a rate of profit which is above the rate of interest. The algebraical conclusions of the preceding argument apply.

It is sufficiently obvious how the argument requires to be re-written when the sign of the algebraic difference between the rate of interest and the rate of profit is reversed, and there is no need to spell it out at any length. The valuation ratio remains, as in equations (5) and (5 a)

$$v = \frac{\pi - g}{i - g}, \quad \text{or} \quad v = \frac{\pi (1 - g/\pi)}{i (1 - g/i)}$$

But it is now greater than unity. With g equal to zero, it is equal to π/i and it increases indefinitely with positive values of g as g becomes greater. The rate of growth, g, has now to be less than the rate of interest, i, rather than the rate of profit, π, for it to be possible for a company to continue with a constant rate of growth and constant valuation ratio. As g approaches i, v approaches infinity.[1] An illustrative table is again supplied (p. 220) on the basis throughout of the rate of profit, π, being 10%.

Instead of a discount on the value of the underlying assets, there is a premium

$$v - 1 = \frac{\pi - i}{i - g} \tag{7}$$

Or

$$v - 1 = \frac{(\pi/i) - 1}{1 - (g/i)} \tag{7a}$$

Growth now entails the acquisition of capital assets which cost less

---

[1] It is easy to see why v approaches infinity as g approaches i. For the present value discounted at a rate of discount i of an annuity increasing at the same rate i is infinite.

For values of g between i and π, v is negative; v becomes positive again for values of g that exceed π. But these algebraical results have no economic significance.

than the market value placed on them indirectly by the Stock Exchange. The larger the scale on which this operation is conducted the greater the benefit to the shares in the company, the price of which approaches infinity as the rate of growth, g, approaches the rate of interest.

Rate of interest (i)	Rate of growth (g) (percentage rates)	Valuation ratio (v)
10	Anything	1
8	0	$1\frac{1}{4}$
8	4	$1\frac{1}{2}$
8	7	3
5	0	2
5	2	$2\frac{2}{3}$
5	4	6
5	$4\frac{1}{2}$	11

The current dividend yield is

$$\frac{1}{v}\,\pi(1-r),$$

but with the rate of profit above the rate of interest, the dividend yield is now bound to be below the rate of interest, and the price of the shares is now bound to appreciate, the more so of course the greater the retention ratio.

In general, the shareholders receive an excess of income over profit, in consequence of growth, equal to

$$g(v-1)\,C$$

Those who originally launched a company made an absolute gain.

Apart from those who originally launched the company, there has been no absolute gain to any shareholder at any stage if the rate of growth has been constant. But if at any time the rate of growth was increased, the incomes of those who were shareholders at that time would rise and the value of their shares would rise in the same proportion.

In the foregoing discussion the formula for the valuation ratio has been taken to extremes but it is obvious that the proposition that the valuation ratio, v, will assume a value which is constant through time if

$$v = \frac{\pi - g}{i - g}$$

makes sense only if g is considerably less than π or i, whichever is the smaller. If i is the smaller, as g approaches it the value of v approaches infinity. If π is the smaller, as g approaches it, v approaches zero. It is obviously absurd for expectations to be entertained that v is going to be either very high or very low. In short our whole set of assumptions about confident expectations becomes untenable unless g is considerably lower than both π and i.

III

We now consider the relation of the rate of profit of a particular company to the general rate of profit throughout the economy. This opens up a number of questions. The first concerns the accommodation of the composition of output to the changing composition of demand in an expanding economy. This Section is devoted to the differentiation between companies which arises from differences in the character of their products. In other respects we shall continue to abstract from differences between companies.

Companies are not rigidly confined to a particular range of products, but in general it may be supposed that for any one company there is a certain range of products with which it has become associated and which it is easiest, in a technical sense, to expand. Such a range of products corresponds to the rough and ready notion of an 'industry' – 'a group of firms engaged in production of commodities alike in their methods of manufacture'.[1] The average income elasticities of demand for the different ranges of products of different industries vary considerably among themselves.[2] A relatively high income elasticity of demand means that for the range of products in question the growth of demand will maintain a relatively high rate of profit. The upward pressure of demand means higher profit margins

[1] Joan Robinson, 'Imperfect Competition Revisited', *Collected Economic Papers*, vol. 2 (1960), p. 222. Joan Robinson is here drawing a distinction between the idea of an 'industry' and that of a 'market', which presents a 'demand for a group of commodities which are close substitutes for each other'.

[2] Income elasticity of demand attaches to the markets in which the products of an industry are sold rather than to the products of any particular industry. But for simplicity of expression it will be treated in the text as attaching to the products.

to an extent depending on the degree of responsiveness of the long-period supply of these products to the relative rate of profit.

A hierarchy of rates of profit is thus established corresponding to the hierarchy of income elasticities of demand for the range of products of different industries. The ruling rate of interest may lie somewhere within the hierarchy of rates of profit or, possibly, completely outside it at one end or the other. In any case, corresponding to the hierarchy of rates of profit and of income elasticities of demand, there is a hierarchy of differences (measured algebraically) between each rate of profit and the ruling rate of interest. This results in differential rates of growth of the various industries based on the mechanism described in the two preceding Sections. The rate of growth of the economy as a whole, and therefore of each of its parts, depends on where the ruling rate of interest lies in relation to the hierarchy of rates of profit, and therefore in relation to the over-all rate of profit.[1]

So long as prices of the products of different industries are changing relatively to one another progressively through time, their relative growth depends on price elasticities as well as on income elasticities of demand. For the purpose of these Notes, restricted in scope to cases of tranquillity, it is assumed that the average income elasticities of demand for the different ranges of products of the different industries are each constant through time, and that each industry has settled down with a rate of profit, corresponding to its position in the hierarchy, that is constant. There is a certain awkwardness in discussing movements of this kind subject to the assumption of tranquillity. However, it may be supposed that the economy passes through long phases within which the differential rates of profit may be expected to persist, each at its own constant rate, for an indefinite future. Transition from one phase to another requires a more complicated type of analysis.

In such a state of tranquillity, the rate of growth of each industry is equal to the rate of growth of the economy as a whole multiplied by the average income elasticity of demand for the industry's range of products.[2] The industry's rate of profit has to be such that, taken in

[1] And, in its turn, the over-all rate of profit, and the level at which the hierarchy is established, depends on the rate of growth of the economy and therefore on where the ruling rate of interest lies in relation to the rate of profit.

[2] Apart from deviations of the rate of technical progress from the over-all average.

relation to the ruling rate of interest, it engenders this rate of growth, and the rate of growth of the economy as a whole is aggregated from the rates of growth of its various parts.

The process here described, in which the rate of growth of each company is accommodated to the income elasticity of demand for the range of products with which it is associated by the operation of differential rates of profit, is assisted by three subsidiary processes. The bigger the contribution made by these subsidiary processes, the smaller will be the dispersion of rates of profit.

First of all, there is the influence of new entries, which tends to limit the degree of profit differentiation. The extent to which it does so depends on the total contribution to growth which would be made by newly established companies if there was a uniform rate of profit and a rate of interest equal to it; the position of the rate of interest in relation to the hierarchy of rates of profit; and the extent to which the obstacles to the establishment of new companies are on the one hand general in character, or are on the other hand specific in the sense that for a particular group which is launching a new company entry into some industries is more difficult than into others, so that it is not simply a matter of choosing the highest available rate of profit.

Secondly, differential profit rates instigate a progressive process of diversification. Companies associated with lower income elasticities of demand, and therefore lower rates of profit, progressively push out into markets offering higher rates of profit. But diversification, like growth of the simpler type, is a process which comes up against obstacles – partly economic (the most important, of course, being sales resistance, which can be overcome only at the expense of profit margins) and partly psychological. The resistance offered by these obstacles increases as the speed of the process grows. In this way equilibrium rates of diversification can be considered as being established.

Thirdly, the fear of a 'take-over' also helps to slow down growth in those parts of the economy where income elasticities of demand are relatively low if the rate of interest lies substantially above the rates of profit ruling in those parts of the economy. This fear operates with extra force if the rate of interest lies in the middle of the hierarchy of rates or profit; for this means that the relatively high income elasticities of demand form the basis of valuation ratios well above unity, and that the management of a company at this end of the hierarchy have a strong inducement to buy a company at the other end, financing the purchase by issuing their own shares. Growth of those high-profit companies whose managements are tempted by such an opportunity is stimulated, so as to establish an even higher valuation ratio. In so far as such a 'take-over' is effected, diversification occurs in the opposite direction to that already considered. It is, however, a passive process, as opposed to the active process discussed previously. When a company associated with a range of products for which the income elasticity of demand is relatively high enters a low income elasticity field by acquiring the assets of a company engaged in it, it does not contribute to growth in it, and may actually slow it down.

A second question on which some light is thrown by the analysis of this Section is the implication for growth of imperfection of competition in commodity markets. We are still abstracting from differences between companies in respect of their attitudes to growth. Let us take a company which is typical in this sense, but the demand for the product of which is growing at a considerably lower rate than the rate of growth of the economy. For a time this company may have been progressively cutting its prices and increasing its selling expenses. Its sales will then be growing faster than the demand for its product, in spite of retaliation from its competitors. A point will, however, be reached at which its rate of profit will in this way have been pushed down to a level, in relation to the ruling rate of interest, such that the management do not wish to push their sales faster than the autonomous growth of their market. Here again accommodation is secured by differential profit rates. Rates of growth – either of the economy as a whole or of any of its parts – are not affected by imperfection of competition. A fine profit margin, and heavy advertising expenses, make a company's sales bigger than they would otherwise be at any particular point of time, but to achieve a higher rate of sustained growth of sales would require a *progressively* finer profit margin, and advertising expenses which increased *progressively* as a proportion of sales revenue. Each company's rate of profit is such as to cause the management to want to expand their output of the product sold in their company's own individual market at the rate at which that market is autonomously growing. The greater the degree of imperfection of competition, the larger is the part played by advertising expenses and the higher is the price of the product, *ceteris paribus*, in relation to production costs. This is the manner in which the average degree of imperfection of competition prevailing in the economy influences the real wage-rate.

The degree of dispersion of rates of profit required to accommodate any particular dispersion of income elasticities of demand depends on the elasticities of response of individual rates of growth with respect to the size of the gaps between individual rates of profit and the ruling rate of interest. In general, these elasticities will be greater the closer is the rate of interest to the average rate of profit and the higher are the rates of growth in question.

IV

The differences between companies which underlie the preceding Section are differences in the income elasticities of demand for the ranges of products with which they have become associated. In all other respects, apart from age and therefore size, the companies and their managements have continued to be treated as though they were all alike. In its unreality this assumption matches the assumption that companies have settled down in a state of tranquillity. Discussion of a state of tranquillity involves the assumption that autonomous changes affecting the distribution of demand between companies – whether progressive changes through time of income elasticities of demand or changes of a less systematic or more random type – occur very slowly. The extent to which random changes undermine the assumption of tranquillity depends on the degree of imperfection of competition generally prevailing. If competition were generally fairly perfect, it would take a long time for any particular change to be digested; for a deviation in the course of a particular demand would then call for a relatively large long-term change in supply to meet it and would generate only a relatively small change in the long-term inducement – the relative rate of profit. With a high degree of imperfection of competition digestion is rapid, and there is more justification for a discussion based on the assumption of tranquillity.

When we come to differences between companies other than differences in income elasticities of demand, the device of basing the discussion on the assumption of tranquillity, and abstracting from the processes involved in changes in relative shares of markets, leads to results which are so bizarre, and so far removed from reality, that it does not seem worth while discussing them. Perhaps the most important differences between companies to be brought into the analysis are differences in the magnitude of the propulsive factors, associated with differences in the efficiency of management – the managements which are subject to the stronger autonomous urge to grow, by way of animal spirits, being also the more efficient. But when one is making a comparison of different companies in the same industry, there is no sense in imbuing them, on any permanent basis, with differences of efficiency and of the buoyancy of the animal spirits of their managements. Relative shares of the industry's output ebb and flow as first one company and then another comes to the fore, and it would be going far to assume even for the purposes of argument a position of tranquillity based on permanent differences in the characteristics of the companies.[1]

V

We now apply this analysis to the relations of the rate of interest, the rate of growth and the rate of profit in the economy as a whole. First, as we have seen, a lower rate of interest tends to lead to a higher rate of growth of established firms. We must also consider the foundation of new companies. The establishment of a new company involves a discontinuity – an economic size must be deemed to be achieved at the outset. The contribution to the growth of the economy made by the establishment of new companies can again be regarded as turning on a balance between propulsive and retroactive factors, depending on the relation of 'animal spirits' to the objective prospects.

[1] These words are written in the context of these Notes. For the purposes of a full-scale study it would be profitable to investigate the results of making assumptions which, in their departure from reality, are even more extreme than those made here, and which lead to even more bizarre conclusions. For example, on the basis of tranquillity, differences between companies which are confined to differences in efficiency (without any associated differences in the operation of the retroactive factors) mean that the relatively low-cost companies have cut their prices to a corresponding degree. Their shares of the markets are correspondingly greater, but their rate of profit is the same as for high-cost companies, and all grow at the same rate. Differences confined to differences in the strength of animal spirits mean that the more ambitious managements have secured correspondingly higher shares of the markets, but at the expense of rates of profit, which are relatively low just to the extent required to offset their high animal spirits, so that the growth of these companies conforms to the general rate.

We have already seen that for a company whose rate of profit is less than the rate of interest, at some time in the past a loss has been suffered. On the other hand, when the prospective rate of profit is above the rate of interest a capital gain accrues to the promoters at the moment when a company of economic size is launched. This of course stimulates the creation of new companies. Thus we may suppose that the lower the rate of interest, the more readily will new companies be set up.

We must now consider the relation of saving to investment in the economy as a whole. We define rentier income to include both dividends received and the capital appreciation due to retentions.[1] The excess of rentiers' income, thus defined, over their consumption will be defined as rentiers' *saving*. A simple relationship can be established for the economy as a whole, transactions between firms being netted out.

As the net value of output is made up of investment and total consumption, it follows that:

Profits = investment *plus* the excess of total consumption over
the wages bill.

Profits are made up of distributed profits, or dividends, and retained profits. Retained profits pay for that part of investment which is not financed externally by the issue of new shares. It is assumed that wage-earners do not save. It then follows that:

Finance raised externally = dividends *minus* rentiers'
consumption.

There is no reason why dividends should not exceed rentiers' consumption. External finance is then negative. This means that companies are buying their own shares and cancelling them. This may take place directly or through a series of intermediaries, some companies buying other companies' shares.

The assumption that shareholders entertain their expectations with complete confidence means that they must be assumed to be indifferent as between dividends and capital appreciation. The assumption of indifference between dividends and capital appreciation also means that any relationship between a rentier's consumption and his

---

[1] On the basis of this definition of rentiers' income and saving, retained profits are not separately added in arriving at national income and national saving: corporate saving does not exist as an ingredient of national saving, which is made up of rentiers' subscriptions for newly issued shares and of the capital appreciation of their shareholdings enjoyed by them.

income is independent of the division of his income between dividends and capital appreciation.

We must now consider the determination of the general rate of interest.

The economy discussed in these Notes is essentially a monetary economy. The rate of interest and the rates of profit are the *money* rate of interest and *money* rates of profit, and money is used throughout as the unit for measuring values. It is not sufficient that money should be a unit of account, i.e. that wages should be fixed in money terms and all prices, incomes, etc., measured in terms of money. To complete the system allowance must be made for the holding of money balances. And by completion of the system in this way it will be possible to bring in the determination of the rate of interest, in the wide sense in which the term is being used in these Notes. In this final Section the behaviour of the price level is explicitly brought into the discussion.

A simple banking system is assumed. It is supposed that deposits with the banks constitute the only form of money. The ratio of the stock of money to the national income measured in money terms determines the rate of interest, i.e. the prices of shares in relation to the money incomes received by shareholders, the elasticity of the long-run liquidity preference schedule depending on the responsiveness of the transactions motive to the rate of interest.[1]

It would be possible to describe a system in which the banks held shares, and through their holdings of shares determined both the stock of money and the price-level of shares that carried with it the rate of interest which the stock of money involved.

We prefer, however, to assume that the banks' assets, apart from the buildings, etc. required for their operation, consist entirely of short-term money advances. It will be supposed that the banks provide temporary finance for the whole of the excess of each company's

---

[1] When an economy has settled down in a state of tranquillity, the confidently expected rate of interest is the actual current rate and there is no room for the long-run operation of the precautionary and speculative motives. For low rates of interest the dependence of the transactions motive on the rate of interest is low. This does not, however, mean that the rate of interest is liable to large fluctuations as a result of random short-run aberrations in the operation of monetary forces. On the contrary, the mere possibility of such aberrations means a strong short-run operation of the speculative and precautionary motives. The elasticity of the short-run liquidity preference schedule is under the conditions here visualised very high, not low.

investment over its retained profits in addition to the finance which firms require to enable them to hold working balances. Each company issues new shares at discrete intervals and not continuously. The banks operate by deciding at what intervals of time companies shall pay off their overdrafts by making new issues of shares. The charge payable to the banks on their short-term advances is sufficiently low to induce each company to make its new issues at as long intervals as the banks will allow. When a new issue is made it is supposed, for the sake of simplicity, that the banks do not require more than that it should pay off the whole of the existing overdraft. Thus companies do not hold money balances (except working balances).

The strictness of monetary control is indicated by the length of the intervals between new issues. The shorter the interval the smaller, *ceteris paribus*, are the amount of bank advances and the stock of money, and the higher is the rate of interest.

A state of tranquillity requires that the rate of interest is constant. This necessitates that the stock of money increases at the rate at which, in terms of money, the economy is growing. This behaviour of the stock of money is secured if the interval insisted on by the banks between successive new issues by each individual company is left constant. For bank advances are then a constant proportion of the rate of investment, which increases at the same rate as the value of the economy's capital assets.[1] Part of the investment of the economy as a whole is financed by the increase of bank advances, this being balanced by the personal saving which is devoted to building up money balances as opposed to holdings of shares.

If the rate of interest maintained in this way by the banks is i' in money terms and h is the rate of increase of the commodity price-level, the commodity rate of interest $(i' - h)$ is the i of the preceding Sections (in which the system was discussed as though the price-level was constant).

The behaviour of the price-level depends on the behaviour of money-wages. The price-level rises if money-wages rise faster than productivity. g cannot be greater than the natural rate of growth but the closer it is pushed up against the natural rate the more rapidly money-wages will rise with scarcity of manpower, and the greater will

---

[1] The matter is more complicated if technical progress is not neutral, so that the economy's income increases at a rate different from its capital assets.

be h, the rate of increase of the price-level, and the rate of increase of bank advances and the stock of money.

The behaviour of money-wages depends partly on the degree of shortage of manpower. To a much lesser extent it depends on the degree of any surplus of manpower over what can be employed. It is conceivable that sustained growth at a rate equal to the natural rate would be established with a constant proportion of surplus manpower. The commodity rate of interest, i, required for such a state of tranquillity is independent of the proportion of surplus manpower but the money rate of interest $(i+h)$ depends on the rate of increase of money-wages. It *may* be possible, with a sufficiently high proportion of surplus manpower, to achieve a constant price-level with money-wages rising no faster than productivity. In any case considerable skill must be imagined on the part of the banking system to get the economy settled down at a growth rate equal to the natural rate with a substantial though constant proportion of surplus manpower.

If, with surplus manpower, the commodity rate of interest is lower than the rate which corresponds to growth at the natural rate, the proportion of surplus manpower is falling. At some stage the banks will have to start changing their policy (unless they are prepared for shortage of manpower to operate in a physical sense so as to limit the rate of growth and for the high rate of increase of the price-level that goes with it). They will have to reduce the intervals allowed between successive issues of capital, thus reducing the ratio of the stock of money to money income until the commodity rate of interest – a sufficiently long interval of time being allowed for the system to move into another state of tranquillity – corresponds to growth at the natural rate.

We are here relying on the view, developed in these Notes, that the size of the gap between the rate of interest, regarded as the rate of return on ordinary shares, and rates of profit is a material factor in determining the rate of growth of companies on which their managements decide. Underlying this is of course the dependence of the size of this gap on the pattern of valuation ratios, as established in equation (5).

No matter how low the commodity rate of interest is brought down towards zero, the rate of growth may still remain below the natural rate. But it is the money rate of interest, i'', not the commodity rate, i, that cannot fall to – still less below – zero. Now $i = i'-h$, where h is the rate of increase of the price-level. If $h > i'$, i is negative and the greater h the greater the arithmetical value of i. To such circumstances one can apply Nicholas Kaldor's statement that 'a slow and steady rate of inflation proves a most powerful aid to the attainment of a steady rate of economic progress', and that 'in a weakly growing economy, price stability will mean stagnation unless the propensity to consume is raised...'.[1]

In practice, of course, the authorities *should* operate on the propensity to consume through fiscal policy rather than confine themselves to monetary policy and operate it either so as to fail to secure adequate growth or so as deliberately to cause inflation. Indeed for various reasons fiscal policy should play an even more important part than monetary policy in securing a harmonious behaviour of an economic system.

But fiscal policy is outside the scope of these Notes. Monetary policy, taken by itself, is subject to the possible limitations resulting from irresponsiveness of the rate of growth to lower rates of interest when the rate of interest is already low. Nevertheless, the considerations advanced in these Notes are partly intended to support the view that there may be some degree of reality in the idea of a full employment mechanism, but that it is important to explain what form the mechanism takes.

Basic to the analysis of these Notes, and to any demonstration of the stability of the system, is the concept of an economic system as an organic structure, consisting of companies the managements of which have personalities and propensities. The limited elasticity relating the rate of growth of any individual company to the difference between its rate of profit and the rate of interest provides the clue to much that

[1] Nicholas Kaldor, 'Economic Growth and the Problem of Inflation', *Economica*, November 1959, pp. 289, 290. Although Professor Kaldor did not express himself in quite the same terms, it is clear that, in this context at any rate, he attributed some importance to the rate of interest. His inflation is required to make a positive money rate of interest compatible with a negative commodity rate of interest. Actually Kaldor was here concerned about the gap between the rate of profit, which includes an allowance for risk, and the risk-free rate of interest on loans. It is the risk-free money rate of interest that cannot be brought down to zero, and if allowance were made for risk in these Notes, the money rate of interest, redefined as the return on ordinary shares, could not be lowered below a finite positive rate, depending on the degree of risk. If h were small the maximum rate of growth which could be secured by monetary policy might be very limited.

is puzzling if an attempt is made to generalise in long-period form the analysis of the determination of investment contained in Keynes' *General Theory*.

Acceptance of the view that the behaviour of the system is not insensitive to the rate of interest carries with it the implication that serious disturbance is liable to be caused by the state of the balance of payments on income account and the international mobility of capital funds. What is apt to happen is that in a country like Britain the rate of interest, instead of being set at a low level so that the flagging spirits of her businessmen are stimulated, is set nearer to the level called for in order to restrain the buoyancy of the businessmen, of, say, Germany. The disharmony is aggravated if, as a result of the higher rate of technical progress in Germany, the balance of payments on income account is favourable for Germany and unfavourable for Britain.

These disharmonies again underline the inadequacy of a model in which no place is provided for fiscal policy.

INDEX

Expectations
  and rate of interest, 73–8, 81–3, 91–2
  capitalists', of profit, 194, 201, 204, 206, 211
  certain, assumed, 208
  of rising prices, 205, 212
Exports
  effect on of increase in investment, 25
  effect on of reduction in imports, 19n
  effects of slump in, 62–3
  effects of stimulating, 64
  elasticities of, 43–7, 56

Fellner, W., 86
Firms
  demand for products of, 221–4
  growth of, 208–32
  ordinary shares, 79, 208
  profit, rate of, 208–32; and general rate of profit, 221–5
  retention ratio, 212–13
  'takeovers', 218–19, 223–4
  valuation ratio, 213–21
Fiscal policy, see Budgetary policy and Taxation
'flight from the pound', 27
Foreign exchanges
  effect on, of increase in investment 25–7
  shortage of in underdeveloped countries, 173, 175; see also Balance of payments and Exchange rates
Foreign investment, and public works, 23, 25
Foreign lending, sensitivity to rate of interest, 25
Free market equilibrium, see Equilibrium, classical
Free trade, 36, 42–3, 50–1, 55
  classical theory of, 49
Frisch, Ragnar, 56n

Gaitskell, Hugh (Chancellor of Exchequer 1950–1), 67, 69
GATT (General Agreement on Tariffs and Trade), 135
Germany, and British interest rates, 232
Ghana/Gold Coast, 154, 189n
Gold Standard, 3
Golden Ages, 197–9, 201–2, 204–5
  and causation, 199–201
  assumption of, 209
  Bastard Golden Age, 200–3

Government borrowing
  for purpose of building roads, 2–3, 18
  from banking system, 30–1
  from public in an underdeveloped country, 164
Government expenditure on road building, 1, 8, 21, 23–6
Government investment, and prices, 5–8; see also Public works
Government policy, see Budgetary Policy, Development Plans and Monetary policy, also Great Britain, policy
Graham, Frank, 43n, 48n
Great Britain
  balance of payments of, 134, 232
  capital development in postwar, 64, 68, 70
  inflation in, 134, 139
  policy, and balance of payments, 70, 99, 129; and full employment, 97–102; and money wages, 100, 103, 142–4; and unemployment, 2n, 67–8, 97–8; monetary, 60, 67–70
Greek Economic Development Programme, 160, 162, 164
Growth
  and balance between consumption and investment, 107–8, 126
  and employment, 197, 200, 201
  and rate of profit, 194
  fundamental identity, 192–4
  in the United States, and dollar shortage, 52–4
  of firms, 208–32
  of productivity, see Productivity; see also Accumulation and Development

Haberler, G., 35, 37n, 38n, 40n, 43n, 48n, 52–4, 55n, 58
Hansen, A. H., 95–6
Harris, Seymour, 35n, 37n, 52n
Harrod, R., 38n, 64, 68, 72
  Life of Keynes, 110, 119, 121
Hawtrey, R. G., 81n
Henderson, A. M., 50n, 51n, 58n
Henderson, H. D., 47n, 48n, 53n
Hicks, J. R., 72, 73n, 78, 96
  theory of interest rates, criticism of, 73–8

Imports
  and dollar shortage, 36–7, 41
  effect on exports of reduction in, 19n